La Cucina

Traditional Italian Cooking

PRION

This edition first published in Great Britain 1998 by PRION, 32-34 Gordon House Road, London NW5 1LP

Copyright © Prion Books 1998
Original recipes copyright © La Cucina Italiana

All rights reserved. No part of this book may be reproduced, stored in a retrieval system, or transmitted in any form or by any means, electronic, mechanical, photocopying, recording or otherwise, without the written permission of the publisher.

A catalogue record for this book can be obtained by the British Library.

ISBN 1-85375 268 1

Cover design by Bob Eames
Printed and Bound in Great Britain by Creative Print and Design, Wales

La Cucina Italiana

Traditional Italian Cooking

Contents

Soups	1
Pastas, Risottos and Gnocchi	27
Fish	91
Meat	143
Vegetables & Salads	205
Snacks	233
Desserts	251

SOUPS

Italian soups can be light meals in themselves, including pasta, rice, eggs, meat, fish and vegetables, or they can be less substantial versions served as an alternative to the pasta course. Two of the best-known types of soup featured here are fish soups, a speciality of the Adriatic coast, and variations on minestrone, the rich vegetable soup with dried beans or pasta.

Zuppa di pesce, ricca

Rich Fish Soup

3 kg/6½ lb mixed fish (scorpion fish, gurnard, mullet, John Dory and skate)	3 garlic cloves, crushed
	6 anchovy fillets
	1 small piece red chilli pepper
450 g/1 lb squid and small octopus	2 bunches of parsley
	6 basil leaves
450 g/1 lb prawns and king prawns/shrimp	450 g/1 lb ripe tomatoes, chopped and seeded
600 ml/1 pint/2½ cups dry white wine	12 mussels
	6 razor-shell clams
salt	oregano
olive oil	6 slices toast

SERVES 6
PREP/COOKING: 2 HRS

Gut and wash the fish thoroughly, cut off the heads and fillet the larger ones. Cut the others into similar-sized pieces, wash again and leave to drain. Clean the squid and octopus, removing the heads, the hard beaks and the viscera, then wash several times in plenty of water. Wash the prawns.

Heat the wine, 1 litre/1¾ pints/1 quart of water and the fish heads and bones in a large pan. Salt lightly and simmer over very low heat for about 1 hour.

Meanwhile, brown the garlic in 100 ml/4 fl oz/½ cup of olive oil in a small saucepan, and mash the anchovies in the oil. Add the prawns, salt lightly, pepper and then brown for about 10 minutes, turning them often. Pour the mixture into the pan containing the fish heads, add the piece of chilli pepper and continue to cook over very low heat.

Wash the parsley and basil and chop them finely. Heat about 100 ml/4 fl oz/½ cup of oil in a very large saucepan. As soon as it is hot add the puréed tomatoes, salt lightly and cook until the sauce is thick. Place the squid and octopus in the pan and, after about 20 minutes, add the fish. Cover and cook over high heat without stirring.

Strain the prepared stock through a fine cloth, discarding the heads; if you wish you can keep the prawns and add the shelled meat to the soup. Pour the stock into the pan containing the fish and cook for another 10 minutes. Five minutes before removing the soup from the heat, add the washed mussels and clams, the chopped parsley and basil and a pinch of oregano. Serve with toast.

Zuppa di Pesce, in Forno

Baked Fish Soup

4 1/2 lb/2 kg mixed fish (red mullet, skate, shark, John Dory, gurnard and hake)	2 garlic cloves
	1 lb ripe tomatoes
	olive oil
5–6 sprigs of parsley	salt and pepper
1 medium onion	150 ml/5 fl oz/2/3 cups dry white wine
2 bay leaves	
1 celery heart and leaves	4 slices bread

SERVES 4
PREPARATION AND COOKING TIME: ABOUT 1 1/2 HRS

Gut and wash the fish; leave the smaller ones whole and cut the others into pieces, removing as many of the bones as possible and cutting off the heads. Place the heads in a saucepan with the bones and scraps, cover them with water, salt lightly, add a sprig of parsley, a quarter of the onion cut in slices and a bay leaf. Put the saucepan on the heat and allow the stock to simmer for about 30 minutes, covered.

Preheat the oven to 200°C/400°F/gas 6. In an ovenproof dish with a lid, place the rest of the sliced onion, the celery heart, the rest of the finely chopped parsley sprigs, a whole garlic clove, a bay leaf and the chopped and puréed tomatoes. Arrange the fish on the vegetables, pour in 100 ml/4 fl oz/1/2 cups of olive oil, salt and pepper lightly and add the wine and the fish stock strained through a cloth. Cover the dish and bake for about 30 minutes.

Toast the bread in the oven; when golden brown rub the slices with the remaining garlic clove and place them in four soup plates. Pour over the soup, sprinkle each portion with a few finely chopped celery leaves and a few drops of olive oil, then serve.

ZUPPA DI MOLLUSCHI

Shellfish Soup

2 kg/4½ lb mixed shellfish (mussels, clams, razor-shell clams and Venus clams)
8 slices bread
olive oil
3 garlic cloves
a small piece red chilli pepper
2 tbspoons tomato sauce
750 ml/1½ pints/3 cups good fish stock
a few celery leaves

SERVES 4
PREP/COOKING: 40 MINS + 2 HRS SOAKING

Scrape the shells of the shellfish, holding them under cold running water, place them all in a large bowl, cover with cold water and leave undisturbed for about 2 hours. Then leave to drain for a while to remove any sand.

Fry the slices of bread on both sides in 100 ml/4 fl oz/½ cup of oil; while still hot brush them with a large halved garlic clove and arrange them in four soup bowls. Fry the remaining large lightly crushed garlic cloves and the chilli pepper in oil until browned, then discard them. Place the shellfish in the pan, cover and keep on the heat until all the shells have opened. Remove them from the pan one by one, detaching one half-shell and placing the other one containing the mussel or clam in a clean saucepan.

Strain through a fine cloth the liquid which the shellfish gave out during cooking and add it to the saucepan. Add 2 tablespoons of ready-made tomato sauce blended with the hot fish stock, shake the saucepan slightly and keep it on the heat for a few moments, then pour the soup over the bread slices. Sprinkle each portion with chopped celery leaves and a few drops of olive oil. Serve immediately.

MINESTRA DI RISO, PATATE E FUNGHI

Rice, Potato and Mushroom Soup

25 g/1 oz dried cep mushroom caps
1 1/2 litres/3 pints/1 1/2 quarts light stock
1 medium onion
1 garlic clove
1 celery stalk
50 g/2 oz/4 tbspoons

butter
olive oil
400 g/14 oz potatoes
100 g/4 oz/1/2 cup rice
25 g/1 oz/1/4 cup grated Parmesan cheese
ground nutmeg
a little chopped parsley

SERVES 4–6
PREP/COOKING: 2 HRS INCL. SOAKING

Soak the dried mushrooms in warm water for about 1 hour. Drain them well and slice thinly. Heat the stock. Finely chop the onion with the garlic and celery. Place the mixture in a saucepan, add half the butter and 2 tablespoons of olive oil, then sauté without browning, stirring occasionally.

Peel the potatoes, wash, and cut them into cubes of about 2 cm/3/4 inch. Add them to the lightly fried mixture together with the mushroom slices and leave for a few moments, then pour in the hot stock. Stir and slowly bring to the boil, then reduce the heat, cover the pan and simmer for 15 minutes.

Mash a few of the potato cubes, pressing them with a wooden spoon against the sides of the pan, then add the rice to the boiling soup, stirring with a wooden spoon. Cook over a rather high heat until the rice is *al dente*. Remove the pan from the heat and stir in the rest of the butter, cut into small pieces with the Parmesan cheese and the ground nutmeg. If you like, sprinkle the soup with chopped parsley.

Pavese di Tapioca

Tapioca and Egg Soup

75 g/3 oz/6 tbspoons butter
8 slices white bread,
  1 day old
1 litre/1 3/4 pints/1 quart
  good meat stock

100 g/4 oz tapioca
4 eggs
25 g/1 oz/1/4 cup grated
  Parmesan cheese
a little chopped parsley

SERVES 4
PREP/COOKING: 30 MINS

In each of two separate frying pans melt 25 g/1 oz/2 tablespoons of butter. Fry the bread slices until they are golden brown, then place them in four soup plates. Keep them warm in the oven. Heat the stock in a saucepan and gradually bring to the boil. As soon as it starts boiling, sprinkle in the tapioca and whisk. Simmer gently for about 10 minutes, stirring occasionally.

Meanwhile heat the rest of the butter in the second frying pan. When it has melted, break the eggs into the pan and fry over low heat so that the white cooks but does not harden. Cut the eggs out with a 10 cm/4 inch pastry cutter and place them on top of the bread. Sprinkle the Parmesan cheese over the eggs and pour in the boiling tapioca soup. Garnish with a little parsley and serve.

Zuppa contadina all'uovo

Farmhouse Egg Soup

2 stock cubes
100 g/4 oz butter
4 slices white bread

4 very fresh eggs
50 g/2 oz/1½ cup grated Parmesan cheese

SERVES 4
PREP/COOKING: 20 MINS

Heat about 1 litre/1¾ pints/1 quart of water in a saucepan, dissolve the stock cubes and bring to the boil. Melt half the butter in a large frying pan and fry the bread, lightly browning on both sides. Place on a baking tray or plate and keep hot.

As soon as the stock begins to boil, reheat the frying pan in which the bread was fried and melt the remaining butter. When it is bubbling hot, break in the eggs, which have been kept at room temperature until this point, very carefully so as not to break the yolks, and fry. Do not let the whites become brown and dry. Cook until the yolks are done on the outside but still almost raw inside.

Place a slice of fried bread in each soup plate and sprinkle with a tablespoon of grated Parmesan cheese. Remove the eggs from the frying pan, draining off as much fat as possible. Place an egg on each square of fried bread and, using a ladle, pour in the soup very carefully at the side of the plate so as not to break the egg.

ZUPPA DI VALPELLINE

Valpelline Soup

50 g/2 oz/4 tbspoons cooking fat
about 450 g/1 lb cabbage
bread
150 g/5 oz rindless Fontina cheese
juices from a roast
50 g/2 oz/4 tbspoons butter
100 g/4 oz raw ham
about 1 litre/1 ¾ pints/ 1 quart good stock

SERVES 4
PREP/COOKING: 2 HRS

Preheat the oven to 170°C/325°F/gas 3. Heat the blade of a sharp knife and finely chop the fat on a chopping board. Melt it in a large frying pan over low heat. Trim the cabbage, removing the outer leaves and the thick ribs. Wash the rest, drain well and fry in the fat until tender and slightly browned.

Meanwhile slice the bread and toast, either in the oven or under the grill. Cut the Fontina cheese into very thin slices. Place a slice of toast in each of four soup bowls and pour over a little of the juices from the roast. Make a layer of cabbage and sprinkle with freshly ground pepper, then a layer of raw ham followed by Fontina. Cover with another layer of bread and continue alternating the ingredients until they are all used up. Finish with a layer of Fontina and add slivers of butter.

Put enough stock into each bowl to cover the layers of bread. Place in the oven for about 1 hour until the surface is golden brown. Serve piping hot straight from the oven.

ZUPPA DI VERZA E FONTINA

Cabbage and Cheese Soup

2–3 slices bacon
50 g/2 oz/4 tbspoons butter
cabbage heart, ribs removed

2 litres/4 pints/2 quarts meat stock
small French loaf
175 g/6 oz Fontina cheese

SERVES 4–6
PREP/COOKING: 1 HR

Pound the bacon and fry it gently in half the butter. Add the cabbage and sauté it slowly, then add 250 ml/8 fl oz/1 cup of the stock, put a lid on and leave it on a moderate heat for about 40 minutes or until tender.

Preheat the oven to 190°C/375°F/gas 5. Cut the bread into slices about 2 cm/¾ inch thick, melt the rest of the butter and let the bread soak it up, then toast the slices in the oven. Increase the oven temperature to 200°C/400°F/gas 6.

Slice the Fontina thinly. In a wide soup tureen arrange layers of toast, cabbage and cheese, finishing with the cheese. Bring the remaining stock to the boil and pour it over the other ingredients. Cook for 15 minutes in the oven, then serve.

MINESTRONE DI VERDURE CON SEMOLINO

Minestrone with Semolina

½ small onion
1 large garlic clove
2 slices bacon, diced
25 g/1 oz/2 tbspoons butter
olive oil
400 g/14 oz frozen mixed vegetables
1 tbspoon tomato paste
2 litres/4 pints/2 quarts boiling water
2 stock cubes
1½ tbspoons semolina
grated Parmesan cheese
black pepper

SERVES 4
PREP/COOKING: 1 HR

Finely chop the onion and garlic and fry gently in a saucepan with the bacon, butter and 2 tablespoons of olive oil until transparent. Add the mixed vegetables, cover the pan and cook for a few minutes over low heat.

Stir in the tomato paste and pour on the boiling water. Season with the crumbled stock cubes, cover the pan and cook for 30 minutes. Slowly add the semolina, stirring constantly. Cook for a further 10 minutes and serve with grated Parmesan cheese, black pepper and olive oil.

ZUPPA DI CASTAGNE E FUNGHI

Chestnut and Mushroom Soup

1 medium onion
4–5 tbspoons olive oil
40 g/1 1/2 oz/3 tbspoons butter
2 small cep mushrooms, trimmed
2 tbspoons Marsala wine

10 chestnuts, boiled and puréed
1 1/4 litres/2 pints/1 1/4 quarts good meat stock
2 teaspoons cornflour
100 ml/4 fl oz/1/2 cup whipping cream
4 thick slices white bread

SERVES 4
PREP/COOKING: 1 HR

Chop the onion and process in a blender with 2–3 tablespoons of the oil. Put the purée in a saucepan over low heat. Add 25 g/1 oz/2 tablespoons butter, cut into small pieces. Fry without letting the onion brown.

Wash the mushrooms and cut into small pieces. Add to the onion and fry for a few minutes, stirring all the time. Pour in the Marsala and, when it has evaporated, add the chestnuts. After 4–5 minutes, gradually add the boiling stock and mix with a small whisk. Bring to the boil, stirring occasionally. Lower the heat and simmer gently.

Put the cornflour in a bowl with the cream and mix until it has completely dissolved. After 20 minutes, add this to the soup. Bring the soup back to the boil and continue simmering for another 5 minutes. Cut the bread into small squares and fry in the rest of the butter and olive oil. When the soup is ready, taste and adjust the seasoning. Serve with the hot croûtons.

PASSATELLI AL LIMONE

Parmesan Strands in Lemon-flavoured Broth

juice and grated zest of 1 lemon	200 g/7 oz/1 3/4 cups grated Parmesan cheese
1 1/2 litres/2 1/2 pints/1 1/2 quarts chicken broth, degreased	salt
	nutmeg
	fresh parsley
100 g/4 oz/2 cups breadcrumbs	fresh chervil
	4 eggs

SERVES 5–6
PREP/COOKING: 40 MINS

Add 1 tablespoon lemon juice to the cold chicken broth, then bring to the boil.

Meanwhile, prepare the 'passatelli'. In a bowl, combine the breadcrumbs, Parmesan cheese, a pinch of salt, a grating of nutmeg, the lemon zest and 1 tablespoon parsley chopped with a few chervil leaves. Bind the mixture with the eggs and amalgamate thoroughly (it must be completely homogenous). Pass the mixture through the largest holes of a potato ricer to make large strands about 5mm/1/4 inch wide and 4 cm/1 1/2 inches long. Tip these into the boiling broth and, as soon as they rise to the surface, turn off the heat.

Divide the lemon-flavoured soup and 'passatelli' between six soup bowls or plates. Garnish each bowl with a few parsley or chervil leaves, and serve immediately, while it is piping hot.

CREMA DI CRIOFI

Cream of Artichoke Soup

4 globe artichokes
juice of ½ lemon
100 g/4 oz leek
25 g/1 oz onion
olive oil
white flour
300 ml/1 ½ pints/1 ¼ cups milk

1 ½ litres/2 ½ pints/1 ½ quarts hot vegetable stock
1 bay leaf
salt
100 ml/¼ fl oz/½ cup whipping cream

SERVES 6
PREP/COOKING: 1 HR 20 MINS

Trim the artichokes: cut off the spiny leaf tips and discard the hardest outer leaves and the fibrous parts of the base; halve the artichokes lengthwise and remove the hairy chokes, then cut the rest into thin slivers and toss them into a bowl filled with water acidulated with the lemon juice.

Trim and chop together the leek and onion, then sweat them in 4 tablespoons olive oil. Thoroughly drain the artichoke slivers, add them to the softened vegetables and brown over very high heat for 2–3 minutes. Sprinkle with 2 tablespoons flour, stir in the milk, taking care that no lumps form, then add the hot stock. Stir in the bay leaf, adjust the seasoning with salt, cover and cook for about 1 hour over medium heat.

When the soup is ready, transfer everything to a vegetable mouli fitted with a medium disc and purée the soup back into the original saucepan. Return the pan to the heat, stir and bind the soup with the cream. As soon as the soup comes back to the boil, pour it into individual bowls and serve with hot croûtons.

CREMA DI CECI GRATINATA

Cream of Chick Pea Soup Au Gratin

300 g/10 oz dried chick peas
1 medium onion
fresh sage
2 garlic cloves
50 ml/2 fl oz/¼ cup
olive oil
fresh rosemary
8 slices white bread
100 g/4 oz Emmental cheese

SERVES 8
PREP/COOKING: 1½ HRS + SOAKING THE CHICK PEAS

Soak the chick peas for 12 hours. To prepare the soup, drain off the soaking water and place the chick peas in a saucepan with 2 litres/4 pints/2 quarts cold water. Add the onion, halved, and 3 sage leaves. Place the pan on the heat and bring to the boil, then cover and cook the chick peas over medium heat for about 1¼ hours. When the chick peas are tender, transfer them with their cooking liquid to a blender. Blend on maximum speed for 2 minutes to obtain a cream (given the quantity of chick peas and liquid, it is best to do this in two batches). Lightly crush the garlic cloves, leaving them whole, and heat them with the oil and a sprig of rosemary. Strain the oil and add it to the soup, to give it a good flavour. Season with salt and pepper.

Divide the soup between eight ovenproof bowls or soup plates. Using a pastry cutter, cut out eight rounds of bread and toast them in the oven. Place one on each bowl, grate the Emmental and sprinkle it over the toast rounds. Place the soup bowls in a very hot oven or, better still, under the grill, until the cheese melts and forms a golden crust. Serve straight from the oven, piping hot.

MINESTRA DI ZUCCA

Pumpkin Soup

75 g/3 oz onion
olive oil
1 x 600 g/1 1/4 lb slice of yellow pumpkin
2 1/2 litres/4 1/2 pints/2 1/2 quarts hot vegetable stock
175 g/6 oz dried egg pasta
salt
40 g/1 oz/3 tbspoons butter
3 tbspoons grated Parmesan cheese
1 tbspoon chopped parsley

SERVES 6
PREP/COOKING: 1 1/4 HRS

Chop the onion, place in a large saucepan and sweat with 2 tablespoons oil.

Meanwhile, discard the pumpkin skin and seeds, dice the flesh and add it to the softened onion. Brown the diced pumpkin, stirring frequently with a wooden spoon, then pour the hot stock into the saucepan. Cover and cook the soup over medium heat for about 50 minutes.

When the soup is ready, add the pasta, stir, salt to taste and cook the pasta for about 5 minutes. Take the pan off the heat and whisk in the butter, Parmesan cheese and parsley. Pour into a soup tureen and serve.

Crema di lattuga e fagiolini

Cream of Lettuce and French Bean Soup

> 100 g/4 oz butter
> 50 g/2 oz/1½ cup rice flour
> 1½ litres/3 pints/1½ quarts meat stock
> 2 heads of lettuce, washed and separated into leaves
> 100 g/4 oz French beans
> salt and pepper
> 2 egg yolks
> grated Parmesan cheese
> 150 ml/5 fl oz/⅔ cup whipping cream
> croûtons

SERVES 6
PREP/COOKING: 1½ HRS

Melt half the butter in a large saucepan and stir in the rice flour. Gradually stir in the boiling stock and bring to the boil, stirring constantly. Add the lettuce leaves, cover the pan and cook over moderate heat for about 1 hour, stirring frequently.

Meanwhile, top and tail the beans and cook them in salted boiling water for about 8 minutes or until just tender. Drain the beans thoroughly and chop them coarsely. Mix the egg yolks, the remaining butter, melted, and a tablespoon of grated Parmesan cheese in a bowl, and stir in the cream.

Sieve the lettuce soup into a clean saucepan, season with pepper and stir in the cooked and chopped French beans. Bring to the boil and gradually blend in the egg and cream mixture, stirring constantly with a whisk. Serve the soup while piping hot with hot croûtons and grated Parmesan cheese.

ZUPPETTE DI GAMBERI IN CROSTA

Prawn Soup under a Pastry Crust

300 g/10 oz uncooked prawns/shrimp, in the shell
50 g/2 oz shallots
50 g/2 oz leeks
2 tbspoons olive oil
1 bay leaf
salt and pepper
brandy
dry white wine
350 ml/12 fl oz/1 1/2 cups cold water

25 g/1 oz/2 tbspoons, softened butter
20 g/3 oz/3/4 cup flour
150 ml/5 fl oz/2/3 cup whipping cream

FOR THE CRUST:
200 g/7 oz frozen puff pastry, thawed
1 egg

SERVES 2
PREP/COOKING: 1 HR 15 MINS

Thoroughly wash the prawns under cold running water. Finely chop the shallots and leek and sweat in a saucepan with the olive oil and bay leaf until tender. Add the prawns, season to taste and cook for 2–3 minutes until they turn pink. Pour on a small glass of brandy and flame it, or, if you prefer, evaporate the liquid over very fierce heat. Sprinkle a little white wine over the prawns, then pour over the cold water and boil for about 20 minutes.

Meanwhile, preheat the oven to 180°C/350°F/ gas 4.

Take the soup off the heat and take out the prawns. Remove the heads and shells and set aside the flesh. Return the soup to the heat and add the prawn heads and shells. Mash together the softened butter and flour, mix into the soup and cook for another 10 minutes. Pass the soup through a vegetable mouli, using the finest disc, or a fine-mesh sieve. Cut up the prawn flesh and add this to the soup, together with the whipping cream. Cook for another 10 minutes, until the soup thickens to the consistency of double cream. Divide the mixture between two ovenproof soup bowls.

Roll out the thawed pastry to a thin rectangle. Cut out two circles slightly larger than the diameter of the two ovenproof soup bowls. Brush the edges with a little beaten egg, then cover the filled bowls with the pastry circles, pressing the edges lightly against the sides of the bowls. Brush the lids with a little egg, then bake in the oven for about 20 minutes. Serve the soup straight from the oven.

Zuppetta di Spada e Peperoni

Swordfish and Sweet Pepper Soup

2 light stock cubes
1 medium onion
3 tbspoons olive oil
1 garlic clove
1 each small red and yellow pepper
fresh basil leaves
350 g/12 oz swordfish steaks, diced
salt and pepper

SERVES 6
PREP/COOKING: 30 MINS

Bring about 1 litre/1¾ pints/1 quart water to the boil with the stock cubes. Chop the onion and sweat in a saucepan with the olive oil and garlic. Peel and dice the peppers and add them to the onions, together with 3 or 4 basil leaves.

After about 10 minutes, add the diced swordfish. Increase the heat to high and cook for 2 minutes, then pour on the boiling stock. Remove the basil leaves, lower the heat and simmer for 5 more minutes.

Taste the soup, correct the seasoning and remove the pan from the heat. Leave to rest for 2–3 minutes before serving. If you like, place a round of toasted French bread or a few croûtons in the bottom of each serving bowl before ladling on the soup.

Zuppa di farro all'antica

Classic Spelt Soup

250 g/8 oz spelt
50 g/2 oz/1 med. stalk celery
150 g/5 oz/2 med. onion
75 g/3 oz/1 med. carrot
olive oil
150 g/5 oz smoked pancetta

250 g/8 oz beef
1 1/2 litres/2 1/2 pints/1 1/4 quarts hot vegetable stock
350 g/12 oz potatoes
salt and pepper
chopped parsley

SERVES 6
PREP/COOKING: 1 HR + SOAKING THE SPELT

Soak the spelt in cold water for about 2 hours. When you are ready to make the soup, peel the celery, onion and carrot, chop them and soften in 4 tablespoons oil. Add the finely chopped pancetta and the beef, cut into small, thin slices. Brown over high heat, then add the spelt, hot stock and potatoes, cut into small pieces. Adjust the seasoning with salt and pepper, then reduce the heat, cover and cook the spelt soup for about 50 minutes.

Sprinkle with parsley and serve, accompanied by triangles of white bread toasted in the oven, if desired.

MINESTRONE AL PESTO

Minestrone with Pesto

1 small onion
1 1/2 garlic cloves
butter
olive oil
450 g/1 lb frozen mixed vegetables
1 1/2 litres/3 pints/1 1/2 quarts boiling water

3 stock cubes
1 large potato
15 fresh basil leaves
1 tbspoon pine nuts
25 g/1 oz/1/4 cup grated Parmesan cheese
pinch of salt
a little chopped parsley

SERVES 4
PREP/COOKING: 1 HR

Finely chop the onion and 1 garlic clove, then soften in a pan in a large knob of melted butter and 2 tablespoons of oil; make sure they don't brown. Add the frozen vegetables and fry for a few moments, stirring with a wooden spoon. Pour in the boiling water and crumble in the stock cubes. Peel the potato, chop into 2–3 pieces and add to the *minestrone*; cook covered over medium heat for about 45 minutes, stirring two or three times as it simmers.

Meanwhile, place the basil leaves, half a large garlic clove, the pine nuts, a tablespoon of Parmesan cheese and a pinch of salt in a mortar. Pound with a wooden pestle, adding, in a trickle, 5 tablespoons of olive oil, until you have obtained a smooth *pesto*.

Remove the pieces of potato from the soup with a slotted spoon, mash them and return them to the pan. Add the *pesto*, stir, pour the minestrone into four soup bowls and sprinkle with chopped parsley. Serve with more Parmesan cheese.

'Maritata' di orzo e acetosa

Barley and Sorrel Soup

2 shallots, peeled
olive oil
250 g/8 oz/1 1/3 cups pearl barley
1 1/2 litres/3 pints/1 1/2 quarts hot vegetable stock
1 egg
2 tbspoons grated Parmesan cheese
1 tbspoon dried breadcrumbs
salt
2 slices white bread, made into crumbs
12 sorrel leaves

SERVES 6
PREP/COOKING: 1 HR

Chop the shallots and sweat in a large saucepan with the oil. Add the barley and toast it over high heat, then pour in the hot stock. Cover, lower the heat and cook the soup for about 40 minutes.

Meanwhile, in a bowl, mix the egg with the Parmesan cheese, dried breadcrumbs, a pinch of salt and the fresh breadcrumbs. When the soup is ready, wash and chop the sorrel leaves and put them into the soup. Tip in all the egg mixture at once. Stir (it will form into shreds) and cook for 1 minute from when the soup comes back to the boil. Then take the pan off the heat and serve the soup immediately, piping hot.

MINESTRONE RAPIDO CON I DITALONI

Quick Minestrone

1 small onion
1 garlic clove
olive oil
½ celery heart
3 small carrots
1 med. courgette/zucchini
1 small turnip
2 small potatoes
100 g/4 oz/1 cup peas
175 g/6 oz tinned kidney beans
100 g/4 oz peeled, puréed tomatoes
1½ litres/3 pints/1½ quarts vegetable stock
100 g/4 oz fluted pasta
freshly ground pepper
25 g/1 oz/¼ cup grated Parmesan cheese

SERVES 4–6
PREP/COOKING: 1¼ HRS

Finely chop the onion with the garlic and fry in 4 tablespoons of olive oil in a large saucepan, taking care not to let the vegetables brown.

Meanwhile clean and dice the celery, carrots, courgette, turnip and potatoes into 2 cm/¾ inch cubes. Add to the onion and leave for a few moments. Add the peas, the beans with their liquid and the tomatoes. Stir with a wooden spoon and simmer for about 10 minutes.

Boil the stock and pour into the mixture. Stir, cover and simmer for about 45 minutes over moderate heat. Add the pasta and stir. Simmer until the pasta is cooked *al dente* and remove from the heat. Add a little freshly ground pepper, 3 tablespoons of olive oil and the grated Parmesan cheese. Serve at once.

ZUPPA D'ORZO CON VERDURE

Pearl Barley and Vegetable Soup

75 g/3 oz/1 med. onion
25 g/1 oz pancetta, thinly sliced
olive oil
1 bay leaf
350 g/12 oz savoy cabbage
150 g/5 oz fresh spinach, trimmed
2 1/2 litres/4 1/2 pints/2 1/2 quarts hot vegetable stock
175 g/6 oz/1 cup pearl barley
salt
3 tbspoons grated Parmesan cheese

SERVES 6
PREP/COOKING: 1 1/4 HRS

Finely chop the onion and pancetta, place in a large saucepan and sweat with 3 tablespoons oil and the bay leaf. Meanwhile, trim the cabbage, wash the leaves thoroughly under running water and drain well. Shred the cabbage leaves and spinach, and add them to the saucepan. Leave the vegetables to soften for several minutes, then pour in the hot stock, cover and cook over medium heat for about 15 minutes.

Add the barley, stir, taste and add salt if necessary. Cover the pan again and cook for a further 40 minutes or so. Take the pan off the heat and whisk the Parmesan cheese into the soup. Pour into a soup tureen and serve.

PASTA, RISOTTOS & GNOCCHI

The *primo piatto*, as it is called in Italy, is the most Italian part of the meal, consisting as it does of pasta, rice always the short-grain variety grown in the northern part of the country), or gnocchi, small balls or parcels made from grains or potatoes and usually served with a sauce. Here we offer a whole selection of traditional and new classics to continue the meal in style.

RAVIOLI DI PESCE

Fish Ravioli

FOR THE PASTA
200 g/7 oz/1 ¾ cups flour
2 eggs
1 tbspoon olive oil
salt

FOR THE FILLING
3 slices white bread
50 ml/2 fl oz/¼ cup
   whipping cream
1 shallot
olive oil
50 g/2 oz/½ med. leek,
   trimmed and sliced
200 g/7 oz sole fillets

200 g/7 oz raw
   prawns/shrimp, peeled
salt and pepper
dry white wine

FOR THE SAUCE
2 shallots
250 ml/8 fl oz/1 cup dry
   white wine
200 ml/7 fl oz/1 cup
   whipping cream
chopped fresh herbs
   (parsley, thyme,
   marjoram)

SERVES 6–8
PREP/COOKING: 2 HRS

Sift the flour on to a work surface and make a well. Break in the eggs and mix them into the flour, together with the olive oil and a pinch of salt. Begin mixing with a fork, then use your hands to make a firm but elastic dough. Wrap it in cling film and refrigerate for about 30 minutes.

To prepare the filling, soften the bread in the cream. Chop the shallot and sweat it and the leek in 2 tablespoons oil. Add the fish and prawns. Season with salt and pepper, and moisten with about one-third of a glass of wine. Evaporate the liquid over high heat. Purée the mixture in a food processor and transfer to a bowl. Add the bread without squeezing it out. Mix to make a smooth paste.

Roll out the dough into two thin sheets. Put little heaps of the filling on half the dough, spacing them about 5 cm/2 inches apart. Cover with the other sheet of dough and press down around each heap of filling with your fingers to seal completely. Cut round each heap to make square ravioli. Re-roll the trimmings and continue to make more ravioli until all the ingredients are used up; you should have about 54 ravioli. Cook until *al dente* in plenty of boiling salted water; they are ready when they rise to the surface of the water.

While they are cooking, make the sauce. Chop the shallots, add the wine and reduce by three-quarters, then add the cream, ravioli and a pinch of chopped mixed herbs. Toss the pasta over high heat to flavour with the sauce, and serve.

TAGLIATELLE DI CASTAGNE

Chestnut Tagliatelle

FOR THE TAGLIATELLE
300 g/10 oz/2½ cups flour
200 g/7 oz/1¾ cups chestnut flour
4 eggs
salt

FOR THE SAUCE
2 shallots
100 g/4 oz/2 small carrot
40 g/1½ oz/3 tbspoons butter
175 g/6 oz calves' liver
250 ml/8 fl oz/1 cup whipping cream salt
½ teaspoon truffle paste

SERVES 10–12
PREP/COOKING: 1 HR

To prepare the tagliatelle (you can do this a day in advance), mix the two flours and sift them on to a work surface. Make a well and put the eggs and a pinch of salt in the middle. Mix with a fork, adding a few drops of water if the dough seems too dry, then work with your hands to make a smooth dough, firm but elastic. Wrap in cling film and leave to rest in the refrigerator for about 30 minutes.

Roll out the dough into thin sheets. Leave to dry, but take care not to let it dry out too much. If you are using a pasta maker, use the appropriate blade to cut it into tagliatelle, if not, carefully cut the thin sheets into long strips. Just before serving, cook the tagliatelle *al dente* in plenty of boiling salted water.

Meanwhile, prepare the sauce. Chop the shallots and peel and finely dice the carrot. Sweat the vegetables in the butter. Finely dice the liver and add it and the cream to the pan. Season with salt and the truffle paste, then put the tagliatelle into the sauce and sauté over high heat to flavour the pasta. Drain and transfer the tagliatelle to a serving dish and serve immediately.

Lasagne al ragù di cinghiale

Lasagne with Wild Boar Sauce

FOR THE PASTA
150 g/5 oz/1 1/4 cups flour
40 g/1 1/2 oz cooked spinach, drained and squeezed dry
1 egg
salt
oil

FOR THE BÉCHAMEL SAUCE
50 g/2 oz/1/2 cup white flour
50 g/2 oz/4 tbspoons butter
1 litre/1 3/4 pints/1 quart hot milk
salt
nutmeg

FOR THE SAUCE AND FINISHING THE DISH
450 g/1 lb wild boar fillet
400 ml/14 fl oz/1 3/4 cups robust red wine
250 g/8 oz/2 large carrots, chopped
150 g/5 oz/2 medium onions, chopped
1 celery stalk, chopped
2 bay leaves
1 teaspoon peppercorns
olive oil
salt and pepper
white flour
1 tbspoon tomato purée
100 g/4 oz/1 cup grated Parmesan cheese
butter for glazing

SERVES 6
PREP/COOKING: 3 HRS + MARINATING

Cut the wild boar fillet into pieces and marinate overnight in the wine, vegetables, bay leaves and peppercorns. Next day, strain off the marinade, reserving separately the wine, vegetables and meat. Remove and discard the peppercorns.

Brown the vegetables from the marinade in 3 tablespoons olive oil, then add the meat and brown well. Season with salt and pepper, and sprinkle on a heaped tablespoon of flour. Add the wine from the marinade and immediately afterwards, stir in the tomato purée. Cover the pan and cook over medium heat for about 2 hours. (This sauce can be prepared a day in advance.)

Now prepare the pasta. Put the flour on a work surface and make a well. Put in the spinach and break in an egg, mixing them into the flour with a pinch of salt and a tablespoon of olive oil. Begin by mixing with a fork, then use your hands to make a firm but elastic dough. Wrap it in cling film and place in the refrigerator for about 30 minutes. Roll out the dough through a pasta machine into lasagne sheets and spread out to dry on a tea towel.

While the pasta is drying, make the béchamel. Make a paste with the flour and butter, then gradually whisk in the hot milk. Season with salt and nutmeg and cook for 5 minutes, stirring constantly.

Preheat the oven to 240°C/475°F/gas 9. Chop the wild boar with its cooking liquid in a food processor. Pour a ladleful of béchamel into an ovenproof dish, then fill the dish with alternating layers of pasta, meat, béchamel and Parmesan cheese, until all the ingredients are used up. Dot the surface with flakes of butter and bake the lasagne for about 25 minutes.

Pasta con zucchini

Pasta with Courgettes

450 g/1 lb courgettes/
  zucchini
1 med. onion
a little parsley
1 large garlic clove
olive oil

½ vegetable stock cube
salt and pepper
350 g/12 oz fresh pasta
  a little grated Parmesan
  cheese

SERVES 3–4
PREP/COOKING: 45 MINS

Clean the courgettes and trim them. Wash and dry well, and cut into rounds about 5 mm/¼ inch thick. Finely chop the onion, parsley and garlic and fry in 5 tablespoons of olive oil without browning. Then add the courgettes and crumble in the stock cube with a little freshly ground pepper. Cover with boiling water and stir well.

Cover the pan and cook over moderate heat for about 10 minutes, until the courgettes are tender and the liquid has been absorbed. Season to taste.

Cook the pasta until *al dente* in plenty of salted boiling water, drain and stir in 2 tablespoons of olive oil. Mix in the sauce and serve at once with the Parmesan cheese.

Agnolotti con sugo di porcini

Agnolotti with Cep Mushroom Sauce

---

2 cabbage leaves
2 small onions
50 g/2 oz/4 tbspoons butter
olive oil
50 g/2 oz sausagemeat
175 g/6 oz cooked beef
100 g/4 oz roast pork
50 g/2 oz/1/2 cup grated
   Parmesan cheese
salt and pepper
nutmeg
5 small eggs

350 g/12 oz/3 cups flour
250 g/8 oz cep mushrooms
1 garlic clove
2–3 sprigs fresh parsley
4 tbspoons Marsala wine
1/2 beef or chicken stock
   cube
ground thyme
300 ml/1/2 pint/1 1/4 cups
   milk
3 tbspoons whipping
   cream

SERVES 4–5
PREP/COOKING TIME: 2 HRS

Wash the cabbage leaves thoroughly, then cook in boiling salted water for about 15 minutes.

Drain, and when the cabbage has cooled, squeeze out all the moisture. Finely slice 1 onion and fry in 25 g/1 oz/2 tablespoons butter and 1 tablespoon of olive oil. Add the cabbage leaves and crumble the sausagemeat before adding that too. Cook for about 10 minutes, then mince finely with the beef and the pork. Collect the mixture in a bowl and add 4 tablespoons of grated Parmesan cheese, a little salt, pepper and grated nutmeg. Bind with 2 small eggs to a smooth consistency. Taste and adjust the seasoning if necessary.

To prepare the pasta put the flour on a work surface and make a well. Break in the remaining eggs and mix them into the flour together with a pinch of salt and a tablespoon of olive oil. Begin by mixing with a fork, then use your hands to make a firm but elastic dough. Wrap it in cling film and store in the refrigerator for about 30 minutes. Roll out the dough into thin sheets, a little at a time, keeping the rest beneath an upturned earthenware dish. Cut out rounds about 5 cm/2 inches in diameter. Place a little of the stuffing on one half of each round, then fold over to make semicircular agnolotti, pressing down the edges well to seal in the filling. Cover with a clean tea-towel and leave in a cool place.

Trim the mushrooms, wash rapidly under running water and drain carefully. Finely chop the remaining onion together with the garlic clove and a handful of parsley and fry in the remaining butter and 2 tablespoons of olive oil, taking care not to brown them. Finely slice the mushrooms and add to the other ingredients. Cook for 3–4 minutes over fairly high heat, stirring with a wooden spoon. Pour in the Marsala and crumble in the stock cube. Add a pinch of thyme, stir and, when two–thirds of the Marsala has evaporated, pour in the boiling milk. Dissolve the cornflour in the cold cream and stir that in too. Mix thoroughly and simmer for a further few minutes until the sauce has thickened.

Cook the *agnolotti* until *al dente* in plenty of salted boiling water and when they are cooked, after a few minutes, remove with a slotted spoon. Pour over the sauce and remaining Parmesan cheese. Mix carefully and serve.

Salsa peverada per tagliatelle

Tagliatelle with Spicy Liver Sauce

100 g/4 oz chicken livers
100 g/4 oz calves' liver
1 chopped onion
4–5 sprigs fresh parsley
100 g/4 oz smoked bacon
50 g/2 oz capers
zest of 1/2 lemon
olive oil

6 anchovy fillets
2 garlic cloves
100 ml/4 fl oz/1/2 cup
  red wine
freshly ground pepper
450 g/1 lb tagliatelle

SERVES 4
PREP/COOKING: 20 MINS

Mince or chop the livers and reserve them. Chop the onion, parsley, bacon, capers and lemon zest and mix together.

Heat 3 tablespoons of olive oil in a pan and add the chopped anchovies and garlic. When the garlic is golden, remove and discard it. Add the chopped onion and bacon mixture to the pan and as soon as it is browned, pour in the red wine and add the livers. Cook over high heat for 5 minutes and season with freshly ground black pepper.

Cook the pasta until *al dente* in plenty of salted boiling water, drain and serve with the sauce.

SUGO ROSA PER FETTUCINE

Fettucine with Pink Sauce

1 sprig fresh rosemary
1 large garlic clove
150 ml/5 fl oz/²/₃ cup meat gravy, skimmed
150 ml /5 fl oz/²/₃ cup single cream
1 tbspoon tomato ketchup
brandy
1 x 400 g/14 oz tin of tomatoes
400 g/14 oz fettucine
salt
25 g/1 oz/¹/₄ cup grated Parmesan cheese
25 g/1 oz/¹/₄ cup grated Gruyère cheese
fresh parsley
ground paprika

SERVES 4
PREP/COOKING: 25 MINS

Chop the rosemary leaves finely with the garlic. Place them in a pan large enough to hold all the pasta, add the gravy and cream and simmer for 5 minutes, stirring frequently. Add the ketchup, a dash of brandy and the tomatoes, finely chopped. Simmer for about 10 minutes.

Cook the pasta in plenty of salted, boiling water until *al dente*, drain and tip it into the sauce. Bind with the two cheeses and sprinkle with chopped parsley and a pinch of paprika.

Fusilli con asparagi

Fusilli with Asparagus Sauce

butter	¼ vegetable stock cube
5–6 green asparagus tips, boiled and cooled	grated nutmeg
	100 g/4 oz fusilli
flour	salt and pepper
100 ml/4 fl oz/½ cup hot milk	2 tbspoons whipping cream

SERVES 1
PREP/COOKING: 30 MINS

Melt 25 g/1 oz/2 tablespoons butter in a small saucepan, add the asparagus tips and sauté gently, making sure that they do not brown. Sprinkle with a little sifted flour, stir and, after a few moments, pour in the hot milk in a trickle. Crumble in the stock cube and add a pinch of nutmeg. Stirring constantly, bring the sauce to the boil, then remove it from the heat and purée it.

Cook the pasta until *al dente* in plenty of salted boiling water. Meanwhile place the asparagus mixture on a very low heat in the saucepan and reheat gently. Stirring constantly, mix in the cream. Adjust the seasoning to taste.

Drain the pasta, but not too thoroughly, pour over the creamy asparagus sauce and garnish, if you like, with more asparagus tips tossed in a little butter. Serve at once.

Paglia e fieno con ragú pasquale

Noodles with Bolognese Sauce

1 medium onion	100 ml/4 fl oz/1/2 cup dry
1 garlic clove	white wine
1/2 sprig rosemary	25 g/1 oz/1/4 cup flour
1 small bunch of parsley	350 g/12 oz tomatoes
1 celery stalk	1 chicken stock cube
2 small carrots	salt and freshly ground
olive oil	black pepper
100 g/4 oz beef	450 g/1 lb green and white
100 g/4 oz lamb	tagliatelle
100 g/4 oz sausagemeat	25 g/1 oz/1/4 cup grated
2 slices bacon	Parmesan cheese

SERVES 6
PREP/COOKING: 2 HRS

Finely chop the onion with the garlic clove, the rosemary leaves and parsley. Dice the celery and carrots. Put these into a saucepan with 25 g/1 oz/2 tablespoons of butter and 3 tablespoons of oil. Soften but do not allow to brown.

Meanwhile, mince the beef, lamb and sausagemeat and dice the bacon. Add to the vegetables in the pan, stir and brown slightly. Pour in the white wine and allow to evaporate almost completely. Then sprinkle in a level tablespoon of flour, stirring thoroughly to prevent any lumps from forming.

Purée the tomatoes and add them immediately after the flour, together with 600 ml/1 pint/2 1/2 cups of cold water, the crumbled stock cube and some freshly ground black pepper. Stir and bring to the boil, turn the heat down to simmer, cover the pan and cook for about 1 1/2 hours. Stir occasionally and dilute with a little boiling water if necessary.

Cook the pasta until *al dente* in salted boiling water. Drain and mix in 2 tablespoons of olive oil, then serve with the sauce and the cheese.

Rigatoni al granchio

Rigatoni with Crab Meat

1 small shallot	1 tbspoon tomato paste
1 small piece celery heart	2–3 tbspoons
butter	concentrated fish stock
olive oil	salt and white pepper
50 g/2 oz crabmeat	100 g/4 oz large fluted
2 tbspoons sparkling white wine	rigatoni

SERVES 1
PREP/COOKING: 30 MINS

Finely chop the shallot and the celery heart and sauté, without browning, in 25 g/1 oz/2 tablespoons of butter and a teaspoon of olive oil. Meanwhile, drain the crabmeat, removing any cartilage, and shred finely before adding to the pan. Cook for a few minutes, stirring.

Next, moisten the crabmeat with a sprinkling of sparkling wine and let it evaporate almost completely, keeping the heat low and stirring often. Add the tomato paste and fish stock. Stir once more and leave the sauce to simmer for 5–7 minutes. If it dries out too much, moisten with another tablespoon of fish stock. Season with salt and white pepper.

Cook the pasta until *al dente* in plenty of salted boiling water. Drain, remove to a warmed plate and pour the hot crab sauce over it. Garnish, if you like, with celery leaves. Serve at once.

Fusilli 'Marechiaro'

Seafood Fusilli

600 g/1 1/4 lb firm, ripe
  tomatoes
1 med. onion
1 garlic clove
1 small green pepper
olive oil
100 g/4 oz cooked mussels
6 fresh basil leaves
salt and pepper
a little sugar
600 g/1 1/4 lb fusilli
1 sprig fresh parsley

SERVES 6
PREP/COOKING: 1 HR

Purée the tomatoes. Finely chop the onion, garlic and pepper and sauté the mixture gently in olive oil, taking care not to let it brown. Add the puréed tomatoes and the basil leaves. Salt lightly, then add the pepper and a good pinch of sugar. Stir and simmer for 30 minutes over a moderate heat with the lid half on the pan. Add the mussels about 6 minutes before the end of cooking time.

Cook the pasta until *al dente* in plenty of salted boiling water. Drain, and add the prepared sauce plus 3 tablespoons of olive oil and a little more pepper. Stir carefully, turn into a heated tureen, sprinkle with chopped parsley and serve.

CANNELLONI RIPIENI IN BIANCO

Canelloni in Cream Sauce

salt and pepper
1 small onion
1 carrot
1 celery stalk
1 bay leaf
half a chicken, weighing about 600 g/1 1/4 lb
4 chicken livers
1 stale bread roll
100 g/4 oz ham
150 g/5 oz butter
about 3 tbspoons Marsala wine
8 tbspoons grated Parmesan cheese
6 eggs
400 g/14 oz/3 1/2 cups flour
olive oil
200 ml/7 fl oz/1 cup single cream

SERVES 10
PREP/COOKING: 3 1/2 HRS

Bring about 1 litre/1 3/4 pints/1 quart of water to the boil in a saucepan and add a little salt, half the onion, the carrot, celery, bay leaf and chicken. Cover the pan and cook over moderate heat for about 1 hour.

Trim and wash the livers. Crumble the roll and soften it with some of the cooking liquid from the chicken. Finely chop the fat of the ham and the remaining half onion.

Place the chopped onion and ham fat in a small frying pan with a large knob of butter, and cook over very low heat for a few minutes. Add the chicken livers and cook for a further 10 minutes, occasionally pouring on a little Marsala. Remove from the heat.

Remove the chicken with a slotted spoon and allow it to cool slightly. Strain the stock. Bone the chicken and mince the meat finely in a food processor with the chicken livers and ham. Place the mixture in a bowl and stir in 4 tablespoons of grated Parmesan cheese, the drained bread and 3 of the eggs. Season to taste.

Prepare the pasta: put the flour on a work surface and make a well in the centre. Break in 3 eggs and add a tablespoon of olive oil. Begin by mixing with a fork, then use your hands to make a firm but elastic dough. Wrap it in cling film and place in the refrigerator for about 30 minutes. Roll out thinly.

Heat plenty of water in a large saucepan. Coat the rolled-out dough in flour, roll it up and cut it into pieces about 10 cm/4 inches wide. Unroll the strips and cut them into 10 cm/4 inch lengths. Once the water has come to the boil, add salt and a tablespoon of olive oil. Put the squares of pasta in the water, one at a time. As soon as the water comes back to the boil, drain the pasta and spread it out on a tea-towel to dry.

Place some of the prepared filling on each square of pasta and then roll them up and put them on a greased baking tray.

Preheat the oven to 200°C/400°F/gas 6. Melt 50 g/2 oz/4 tablespoons of butter in a saucepan and blend in 50 g/2 oz/$1/2$ cup of flour to form a smooth *roux*. Pour in 600 ml/1 pint/$2 1/2$ cups of the strained chicken stock, stirring constantly. Bring to the boil, blend in the cream and then season to taste.

Cover the cannelloni with the prepared sauce and dot with about 50 g/2 oz/4 tablespoons of butter, cut into small pieces. Sprinkle with the rest of the grated Parmesan cheese and bake in the oven for about 15 minutes.

Serve hot.

Linguine alle Vongole

Linguine with Clams

1 garlic clove
olive oil
1 small onion, finely chopped
250 g/8 oz frozen clams

350 g/12 oz clam sauce
1 vegetable stock cube
350 g/12 oz linguine

SERVES 4
PREP/COOKING: 20 MINS

Sauté the garlic cloves in 4 tablespoons of olive oil. Discard the garlic and add the finely chopped onion to the pan. Fry gently. Add the clams to the pan and allow to defrost over low heat. Stir in the clam sauce, and crumbled stock cube, and simmer over moderate heat.

Cook the pasta until *al dente* in plenty of salted boiling water, drain and pour into a warmed tureen. Dress with the prepared sauce and serve immediately.

FARFALLE AI GAMBERONI

Farfalle with Scampi

salt and pepper
400 g/4 oz farfalle
8 raw scampi tails
1 shallot
olive oil
white wine
40 g/1 1/2 oz/3 tbspoons butter
chopped parsley

SERVES 4
PREP/COOKING: 40 MINS

Bring a large pan of salted water to the boil and cook the pasta until *al dente*. Drain.

Shell the scampi tails, removing the black thread-like intestines. Chop the shallot and soften in 2 tablespoons olive oil. Add the scampi tails and brown them, then moisten with half a glass of wine. As soon as it has evaporated, add the butter and farfalle. Stir vigorously to flavour them, and season with salt and pepper and a bunch of chopped parsley.

TAGLIOLINI ALLE VERDURE

Tagliolini with Asparagus

FOR THE PASTA
200 g/7 oz/1 ¾ cups
　flour
2 eggs
salt
1 tbspoon olive oil

FOR THE SAUCE
350 g/12 oz asparagus

150 g/5 oz button
　mushrooms
1 shallot
olive oil
250 ml/8 fl oz/1 cup
　whipping cream
salt and pepper
chopped parsley

SERVES 4
PREP/COOKING: 40 MINS + RESTING THE PASTA

To prepare the pasta, sift the flour on to a work surface and make a well in the centre. Break in the eggs, then add a pinch of salt and the oil. Begin by mixing with a fork, then use your hands to make a firm but elastic dough. Wrap in cling film and leave to rest in the refrigerator for 30 minutes.

Meanwhile, make the sauce. Trim the asparagus and scrape the stalks, then cook them in two fingers of salted water until tender but still crisp. Drain and cut into short lengths, leaving the tips whole. Trim, wash and drain the mushrooms. Roll out the dough into very thin sheets, then (if you have a pasta machine) pass it through the appropriate cutter to make tagliolini; if you haven't, cut the sheets into long thin shreds. Cook in plenty of boiling salted water until *al dente*, then drain.

To finish the sauce, peel and chop the shallot and slice the mushrooms. Soften them in 2 tablespoons of oil, together with the asparagus lengths. Brown well, then add the cream and tagliolini. Toss well to flavour the pasta, season with salt, pepper and a pinch of chopped parsley. Serve, topped with the asparagus tips.

TORTELLONI CON CACIOTTINA E PATATE

Tortelloni with Goat's Cheese and Potatoes

FOR THE PASTA
200 g/7 oz/1 3/4 cups flour
2 eggs
salt
1 tbspoon olive oil
1/2 tbspoon chopped parsley

FOR THE FILLING
400 g/14 oz spinach beet
300 g/10 oz unpeeled boiled potatoes
1 egg

salt
20 g/3/4 oz/3 tbspoons grated Parmesan cheese
250 g/8 oz fresh goat's cheese

FOR THE SAUCE
1 shallot
25 g/1 oz/2 tbspoons butter
fresh thyme

SERVES 6
PREP/COOKING TIME: 1 1/2 HRS

To prepare the pasta, sift the flour on to a work surface and make a well. Put the eggs, a pinch of salt, the oil and parsley in the centre. Begin by mixing with a fork then use your hands to make a firm but elastic dough. Wrap in cling film and leave to rest in the refrigerator for at least 30 minutes.

Meanwhile, make the filling. Wash the spinach beet in several changes of water, then cook it in just the water clinging to the leaves. Drain, squeeze dry and chop coarsely. Peel the potatoes and mash them through a potato ricer set over a bowl. Add the egg, a pinch of salt, the chopped spinach beet, Parmesan cheese and sieved goat's cheese. Mix well to make a smooth paste.

Roll out the dough into thin sheets. Brush with cold water, then arrange little heaps of filling about 6 cm/2 1/2 inches apart in a single row on each sheet of pasta. Fold the other half of the pasta over the filling to cover it. Press down around the filling with your hands, then cut out around each heap to make securely closed 5 cm/2 inch squares (tortelloni). Cook the tortelloni in plenty of boiling salted water until *al dente*, then drain.

Peel and chop the shallot and soften in the butter. Add the tortelloni and sauté over high heat to flavour them. Season with a generous pinch of fresh thyme, transfer to a serving dish and serve immediately while still piping hot.

Penne 'due torri'

Penne with Mortadella and Cream

50 g/2 oz mortadella sausage
50 g/2 oz ham
1 small onion, thinly sliced
1 garlic crushed clove
butter
olive oil
100 ml/4 fl oz/½ cup dry white wine
1 teaspoon cornflour

600 ml/1 pint/2½ cups light chicken or vegetable stock
350 g/12 oz penne
100 ml/4 fl oz/½ cup single cream
2 tbspoons grated Parmesan cheese
2 tbspoons chopped fresh parsley

SERVES 4
PREP/COOKING: 40 MINS

Cut the mortadella and ham into 5 mm/¼ inch cubes. Gently fry the onion and garlic in 25 g/1 oz/2 tablespoons of butter and 2 tablespoons of olive oil until transparent. Add the cubes of mortadella and ham and cook for a few minutes. Pour on the wine and allow it to evaporate almost completely. Dissolve the cornflour in 3 tablespoons of cold water and add it to the pan, together with the boiling stock. Stir and simmer gently until the liquid has reduced by two-thirds to form a creamy sauce.

Cook the pasta until *al dente* in plenty of boiling salted water, drain and stir it into the prepared sauce. Blend in the cream. Remove the pan from the heat and stir in the grated Parmesan cheese and chopped parsley. Serve at once.

'SEDANI' AL TONNO E PEPERONE

Pasta with Tuna and Peppers

1 small onion
olive oil
2 small red peppers
100 g/4 oz tinned tuna
350 g/12 oz short
  macaroni
200 ml/7 fl oz/scant 1 cup
  tomato sauce

1 vegetable stock cube
1 sprig fresh parsley
a little grated Pecorino
  cheese

SERVES 4
PREP/COOKING: 25 MINS

Finely chop the onion and fry gently in 3 tablespoons of olive oil until transparent. Meanwhile wash the peppers and cut in half, discarding the stalks and seeds. Cut into short, thick strips and add them to the onion and cook for a few minutes. Drain the tuna, break it into pieces with a fork and add it to the pan.

Cook the pasta until *al dente* in plenty of boiling salted water and drain. Add the tomato sauce and the crumbled stock cube to the tuna mixture and cook for a few minutes over low heat.

Pour the pasta into a tureen and dress with the prepared sauce. Top with chopped parsley and serve immediately with the grated Pecorino cheese.

Farfalle con pollo e gamberetti

Farfalle with Chicken and Prawn Sauce

½ small onion
butter
small chicken breast
few shelled prawns/shrimp
1 tbspoon brandy
2 tbspoons dry white wine
100 ml/4 fl oz/1½ cup cold chicken stock

½ teaspoon cornflour
4 tbspoons single cream
salt and pepper
100 g/4 oz farfalle

SERVES 1
PREP/COOKING: 40 MINS

Finely chop the onion and soften it gently, without browning, in 25 g/1 oz/2 tbspoons butter. Meanwhile, finely mince the trimmed chicken breast and prawns. Add them to the onion and let them cook over low heat, stirring frequently with a wooden spoon. Moisten with the brandy and, when it has evaporated almost entirely, pour in the white wine.

When the wine has been absorbed, pour in the chicken stock, in which you have dissolved the cornflour, and the cream. Stir and simmer gently over very low heat for a few minutes, then liquidise in a blender to obtain a smooth and creamy sauce. Season with pepper, adjust the salt to taste and keep it warm.

Cook the pasta in plenty of boiling salted water until *al dente*. Drain and pour over the chicken and prawn sauce and serve at once.

ORECCHIETTE CON POMODORO E SALSICCIA

Orecchiette with Tomato and Sausage Ragoût

- 1 small onion
- 1 celery stalk
- 1 small carrot
- 50 g/2 oz bacon
- 75 g/3 oz/4 tbspoons butter
- 1 garlic clove
- 1 sprig basil
- 3–4 sprigs parsley
- 100 g/4 oz skinned and mashed sausages
- 100 ml/4 fl oz/1½ cup dry white wine
- flour
- 450 g/1 lb ripe tomatoes
- salt and pepper
- 400 g/14 oz orecchiette pasta
- olive oil
- 4 tbspoons grated mild Pecorino cheese

SERVES 4–5
PREP/COOKING: 2 HRS

Finely chop the onion, celery and carrot and fry with the diced bacon in the butter until they are soft but not browned. Add the garlic clove (to be removed and thrown away later) the sprig of basil and the parsley, tied in a small bunch. Add the sausages, mashed with a fork. Moisten with the wine and let it evaporate almost completely, then sprinkle with a teaspoon of flour. Skin and purée the tomatoes then add them to the pan. Stir, season lightly and cook over very low heat for about 1½ hours, moistening with a small amount of hot water or stock when the sauce becomes too thick.

About 10–20 minutes before the ragoût is ready (check cooking instructions on packet), cook the pasta until *al dente* in plenty of boiling salted water. Drain the orecchiette and mix immediately with 3 tablespoons of olive oil. Add the ragoût, discarding the garlic and the small bunch of seasoning herbs. Sprinkle with the Pecorino cheese, mix once more and serve at once.

Sugo al Mascarpone per Tagliolini

Tagliolini with Mascarpone Sauce

100 g/4 oz prosciutto
150 g/5 oz Mascarpone cheese
350 g/12 oz tagliolini or other thin pasta

25 g/1 oz/¼ cup grated Parmesan cheese
25 g/1 oz/¼ cup grated Gruyère cheese

SERVES 4
PREP/COOKING: 15 MINS

Cut the ham into fine strips. Warm the Mascarpone in a wide saucepan with the ham over a low heat, stirring with a wooden spoon.

Cook the pasta until *al dente*, in plenty of boiling salted water, drain and tip into the sauce. Add the grated cheeses, stir and serve at once.

FETTUCCINE RICCIA AI FUNGHI

Fettucine with Mushrooms

1 thick slice onion	1/2 teaspoon cornflour
few fresh sprigs parsley	milk
1 garlic clove	100 g/4 oz fettucine
butter	salt
1 cep mushroom	a little chopped parsley
1 tbspoon Marsala wine	
1/4 vegetable stock cube	

SERVES 1
PREP/COOKING: 30 MINS

Finely chop the onion, parsley sprigs and the garlic clove. Fry them in 25 g/1 oz/2 tablespoons butter, until soft but do not allow to brown. Meanwhile, scrape the dirt from the mushroom stalk and wash or wipe the cap. Slice thinly and add the slices to the onion mixture. Sauté for a few minutes, stirring gently.

Next, moisten with the Marsala and season with the stock cube. Dissolve the cornflour in 2 tablespoons of cold milk and add it to the slices of mushroom, stirring gently. Leave the sauce on a very low heat for 4–5 minutes.

Cook the pasta until *al dente* in plenty of boiling salted water. Drain and pour over the mushroom sauce, to which you have added, at the very last moment, a little chopped parsley.

Pasta e lenticche

Pasta with Lentils

250 g/8 oz/1 1/2 cups dried
    lentils
150 g/5 oz potatoes
2 sage leaves
1 large garlic clove
a little parsley
100 g/4 oz peeled
    tomatoes

olive oil
2 vegetable stock cubes
250 g/8 oz pasta shells
3 tbspoons grated
    Parmesan cheese
chopped parsley

SERVES 6
PREP/COOKING: 2 HRS

Pick over the lentils to make sure there are no impurities or grit. Wash under warm running water and place in a saucepan. Peel and dice the potatoes and put these in too. Chop the sage, garlic and parsley and add to the pan. Purée the tomatoes and add these together with 3 tablespoons of olive oil. Stir and pour in 2 litres/3 1/2 pints/2 quarts of cold water and bring to the boil. Turn the heat down to the minimum as soon as the mixture starts to boil, crumble in the stock cubes, cover and simmer for about 2 hours, stirring from time to time.

When the cooking is completed, purée a ladleful of the mixture and return the purée to the pan. Stir in and bring back to the boil, then add the pasta. Stir and cook until the pasta is *al dente*. Remove from the heat, add a little freshly ground pepper, 3 tablespoons of olive oil and the Parmesan cheese. Serve, sprinkling each portion with a little chopped parsley to garnish.

TORTELLONI DI ZUCCHINI

Tortelloni with Courgettes

450 g/1 lb courgettes/
  zucchini
100 g/4 oz button
  mushrooms
olive oil
garlic
100 g/4 oz/1 cup grated
  Parmesan cheese
5 eggs

a little marjoram
325 g/11 oz/3 cups
  flour
nutmeg
salt and pepper
350 g/12 oz tomatoes
50 g/2 oz/4 tbspoons
  butter
fresh basil

SERVES 6
PREP/COOKING: 2 HRS

Clean and dice the courgettes and mushrooms. Heat 150 ml/5 fl oz/$2/3$ cup olive oil in a large frying pan and add a garlic clove (to be removed before blending). Add the mushrooms and courgettes and cook for 10 minutes, then remove from the heat and allow to cool. Blend the mixture in a food processor then stir in the Parmesan cheese, 2 egg yolks, a sprinkle of marjoram, a level tablespoon of flour, a sprinkle of nutmeg and salt and pepper to taste.

To prepare the pasta, sift the flour on to a work surface and make a well. Break in the three remaining eggs and mix them into the flour, together with a pinch of salt. Begin by mixing with a fork, then use your hands to make a firm but elastic dough. Wrap it in cling film and place in the refrigerator for about 30 minutes.

Roll out the dough into thin sheets and cut into 5 cm/2 inch strips; now cut the strips into 5 cm/2 inch squares. Put a teaspoon of courgette mixture on to the centre of one half of each square, then fold over to make a triangle, sealing the edges firmly with your fingertips.

To make the sauce, peel and dice the tomatoes. Melt the butter in a large frying pan, add the tomatoes, salt to taste and seven chopped basil leaves and cook the sauce for about 5 minutes or until all the ingredients are thoroughly combined and hot.

Meanwhile, cook the tortelloni in a large pan of boiling salted water until *al dente*. Drain (remove from the pan with a slotted spoon) and add to the sauce. Cook together for a few minutes, then transfer to a serving bowl and serve while still hot.

FUSILLI CALAMARI

Fusilli with Squid

12 small squid (about 450 g/1 lb)
a small bunch of fresh parsley
1 garlic clove
3 slices white bread
40 g/1 1/2 oz/1/4 cup grated Parmesan cheese

olive oil
salt and pepper
2 med. onions
200 ml/7 fl oz/scant 1 cup dry white wine
450 g/1 lb fusilli

SERVES 6
PREP/COOKING: 1 HR

Preheat the oven to 375°F/190°C/gas 5. Clean the squid; separate the heads from the body sacs and remove the cartilage and intestines from the sacs. Wash the sacs, taking care not to tear them. Chop a good bunch of parsley with the squid heads and garlic and place in a bowl. Add the bread, finely crumbled, the Parmesan, a tablespoon of olive oil and salt and pepper to taste. Mix this stuffing thoroughly, then fill the squid with it, closing the openings with wooden cocktail sticks or thread.

Slice the onions very thinly. Heat 4 tablespoons of oil in a flameproof baking dish, then put in the onions and sweat until transparent. Immediately add the squid and cook over high heat for several minutes, then pour in the white wine and a little water and season. Cover the dish with foil, transfer to the oven and cook for about 40 minutes.

When the squid are ready, cook the fusilli until they are *al dente* in plenty of boiling salted water. Take the squid out of the baking dish and remove the cocktail sticks. Drain the pasta and tip it into the dish with the sauce.

Transfer to a serving dish, toss the squid into the pasta, sprinkle with chopped parsley if you wish, and serve.

Ravioli di pesce con panna e basilico

Fish Ravioli with Cream and Basil

FOR THE PASTA
200 g/7 oz/1 ¾ cups
    flour
2 eggs
tbspoon olive oil
salt

FOR THE FILLING
300 g/10 oz sole fillets
100 g/4 oz uncooked
    prawns/shrimp, shelled

2 egg yolks
3 tbspoons cream
a bunch of fresh parsley,
    finely chopped
salt and pepper

FOR THE SAUCE
a bunch of fresh basil
3 tbspoons butter
250 ml/8 fl oz/1 cup
    whipping cream

SERVES 4–6
PREP/COOKING: 1 ½ HRS

Sift the flour on to a work surface and make a well. Break in the eggs and mix them into the flour with a pinch of salt and the oil. Begin mixing with a fork, then use your hands to make a firm but elastic dough. Wrap it in cling film and refrigerate for 30 minutes.

Meanwhile, prepare the filling. Mince the sole fillets and prawns and place in a bowl. Add the egg yolks, cream, parsley, a few grindings of pepper and a small pinch of salt.

Roll out the dough into thin sheets, about 5 mm/¼ inch thick and about 60 cm/24 inches square. Spoon little heaps of the stuffing on to the lower half of each sheet, spacing them at regular intervals. Fold over the top half of each pasta sheet to cover the filling, pressing well to seal. Using a fluted pasta cutter or sharp knife, cut out individual ravioli about 5 cm/2 inches square.

Cook the ravioli in plenty of boiling salted water until they are *al dente*. Chop the basil leaves and sweat in a shallow pan with the butter. Add the cream and bring to the boil. Drain the ravioli, pour on the sauce, mix and serve at once.

TROFIE AL SUGO DI MARE

Spiral Pasta with Seafood Sauce

400 g/14 oz scampi/ langostinos
100 g/4 oz king prawns/jumbo shrimp
1 large onion, peeled
a small bunch of fresh parsley
olive oil
150 ml/5 fl oz/$^2/_3$ cup dry white wine
150 g/5 oz/$^2/_3$ cup tomato passata (sieved tomatoes)
2 shallots
50 g/2 oz/4 tbspoons butter
450 g/1 lb spiral pasta
salt

SERVES 6
PREP/COOKING: 1 HR

Carefully wash the scampi and prawns, then shell them, reserving the shells. Using poultry shears, cut up the shells into tiny pieces. Slice the onion very thinly and finely chop half the parsley. Put 3 tablespoons of olive oil in a saucepan, add the onion, parsley and crustacean shells and colour over high heat for 3–4 minutes, stirring continuously with a wooden spoon. Pour in half the white wine, let it evaporate, then add the tomato passata and 600 ml/1 pint/2$^1/_2$ cups cold water. Mix again, bring to the boil, lower the heat and simmer gently for 40 minutes. Check the sauce from time to time, and if it starts to dry out, add another glass of water. When the sauce is ready, tip it into a sieve, and press down hard on the shells.

Finely chop the shallots and sweat in a shallow pan with a tablespoon of oil; add the prawns and scampi and colour lightly, stirring with a wooden spoon, then add the remaining wine and evaporate it. Season the strained sauce with salt and mix it with the shellfish, bring to the boil and cook for 5 minutes. Pour the mixture into a blender and liquidise on full power for 1 or 2 minutes.

Meanwhile, cook the pasta in plenty of boiling salted water until it is *al dente*. One minute before draining it, melt the butter in a shallow pan, add the remaining finely chopped parsley and soften it, then pour in the blended sauce and finally the drained pasta. Mix well so that the sauce goes right into the spirals and serve immediately.

CONCHIGLIE MARINARE

Pasta Shells "Sailor-Style"

250 g/8 oz king prawns/ jumbo shrimp
250 g/8 oz huss/shark steak
olive oil
2 garlic cloves, lightly crushed
salt and pepper

a small bunch of fresh parsley, chopped
100 ml/4 fl oz dry/$^1/_2$ cup white wine
200 g/7 oz/scant 1 cup tomato passata
450 g/1 lb pasta shells (conchiglie)

SERVES 6
PREP/COOKING: 40 MINS

Remove and discard the prawn shells. Cut the huss into 1 cm/$^1/_2$ inch slices.

In a large frying pan, heat 4 tablespoons of olive oil, add the lightly crushed garlic and cook until well coloured. Remove the garlic and put the prawns and huss slices into the pan. Season and, over high heat, let the fish absorb the flavours for a few minutes. Add a tablespoon of chopped parsley, pour in the wine and allow it to evaporate.

As soon as the wine has evaporated from the sauce, add the tomato passata and half a glass of water, mix and simmer over low heat for 15 minutes.

Meanwhile, cook the pasta in plenty of boiling salted water until it is *al dente*. Drain and add it to the pan with the sauce. Toss well and transfer to a serving dish.

TORTELLI DI BROCCOLETTI AL BURRO FUSO

Tortelli with Broccoli and Butter Sauce

FOR THE PASTA
250 g/8 oz/2 cups
   flour
1 tbspoon tomato purée
1 tbspoon olive oil
salt
2 eggs

FOR THE FILLING
800 g/1 3/4 lb broccoli
20 g/3/4 oz/1 1/2 tbspoons
   butter

2 shallots, chopped
4 slices white bread soaked
   in milk
100 g/4 oz/1 cup grated
   Parmesan cheese
salt and pepper
nutmeg

FOR THE SAUCE
75 g/3 oz butter
grated Parmesan cheese

SERVES 6
PREP/COOKING: 1 1/4 HRS

First prepare the pasta. Put the flour on to a work surface and make a well. Put the tomato purée, oil, a pinch of salt and the eggs in the middle. Begin by mixing with a fork, then use your hands to make a firm but elastic dough. Wrap the dough in cling film and place in the refrigerator for about 30 minutes.

Meanwhile, prepare the filling. Carefully trim the broccoli, dividing it into florets and cutting off the hardest and most fibrous parts of the stalks. Cook in plenty of boiling salted water.

Brown the butter and flavour it with the chopped shallots. As soon as the broccoli is cooked, drain it and toss it immediately in the butter. Place in a food processor with the squeezed-out bread and mix to a paste. Transfer to a bowl, mix in the Parmesan cheese and season with a pinch of salt and pepper and a little nutmeg.

Roll out the dough into thin sheets. Pile the filling in small heaps, 6 cm/2 1/4 inches apart, on half the sheets. Cover with the other pasta sheets, then press down all round and cut out the tortelli with a fluted

5 cm/2 inch pastry cutter. Cook the tortelli in plenty of boiling salted water until *al dente* and dress them with the butter, heated until nutty brown. Sprinkle the cooked tortelli generously with Parmesan cheese.

Tagliatelle alla Marinara

Tagliatelle with Seafood Sauce

200 g/7 oz/1 ¾ cups
  flour
2 eggs
olive oil
salt

FOR THE SAUCE
1 med. onion
olive oil
275 g/9 oz whiting fillets,
  cut into bite-sized pieces

100 g/4 oz peeled
  prawns/shrimp
50 ml/2 fl oz/¼ cup
  white wine
1 tbspoon tomato purée
1 x 400 g/14 oz tin
  chopped tomatoes
salt and pepper
1 tbspoon finely chopped
  parsley

SERVES 4
PREP/COOKING: 1 ¼ HRS

First prepare the pasta. Sift the flour on to a work surface and make a well. Break in the eggs and mix them into the flour with a tablespoon of olive oil and a pinch of salt. Begin by mixing with a fork, then use your hands to make a firm, but elastic dough. Wrap it in cling film and place in the refrigerator for 30 minutes.

Meanwhile, finely chop the onion, then sweat it gently in a saucepan with 2 tablespoons of oil. As soon as the onion is soft, add the whiting fillets and the prawns. Seal the fish on both sides for a couple of minutes, then sprinkle with white wine. When the wine has evaporated, add the tomato purée and the chopped tomatoes. Season to taste, then cover the pan and simmer for about 35 minutes.

Roll out the dough into thin sheets, then cut into thin strips. Cook in plenty of boiling salted water until *al dente*. Drain and place in a serving dish. Pour over all the sauce, sprinkle with chopped parsley and serve at once.

AGLIO, OLIO E PEPERONCINO PER FUSILLI BUNGHI BUCATI

Garlic, Oil and Hot Pepper Sauce for Macaroni

6 garlic cloves
2 hot chilli peppers
450 g/1 lb macaroni
175 ml/6 fl oz/¾ cup good olive oil

50 g/2 oz/½ cup grated Parmesan cheese
50 g/2 oz/½ cup grated Pecorino cheese

SERVES 6
PREP/COOKING: 35 MINS

Chop the garlic and chilli peppers coarsely and liquidise them with 100 ml/4 fl oz/½ cup of cold water. Add this to a panful of salted hot water, bring to the boil and simmer for 15 minutes, then strain the liquid into a second pan. Boil the pasta in this and, when it is cooked *al dente*, drain it and add the olive oil and the two cheeses, stirring well.

Lumaconi ai quattro

Pasta Shells with Four Cheeses

50 g/2 oz Parmesan cheese
25 g/1 oz Sbrinz cheese
25 g/1 oz Emmental cheese
25 g/1 oz Fontina cheese
20 g/¾ oz/1 ½ tbspoons butter

50 ml/2 fl oz/¼ cup milk (not skimmed)
nutmeg
1 egg yolk
100 g/4 oz pasta shells
a little chopped parsley for garnish

SERVES 1
PREP/COOKING: 30 MINS

Grate the Parmesan and Sbrinz cheeses and cut the Emmental and Fontina cheeses into small cubes; mix all the cheeses together well.

In a saucepan melt the butter without browning. Remove the saucepan from the heat and add the four cheeses, stirring vigorously with a small wooden spoon. Place the saucepan again over a very low heat and, stirring constantly, melt the cheeses slightly. Add the warm milk in a trickle, mixing constantly until thoroughly smooth and blended, then season it with a grinding of nutmeg. Take off the heat, and add a fresh egg yolk. Keep the sauce warm, stirring often.

Cook the pasta in plenty of boiling salted water until *al dente*. Drain, pour the cheese 'fondue' over it and sprinkle with a pinch of finely chopped parsley. Serve at once before the cheese mixture becomes firm.

TORTELLONI VERDI ALL'ANATRA

Green Tortelloni with Duck

FOR THE PASTA
250 g/8 oz/2 cups flour
2 eggs
25 g/1 oz spinach, cooked,
    squeezed dry and finely
    chopped
salt

FOR THE FILLING
2 duck legs, boned
150 g/5 oz pork fillet
olive oil
2 shallots, chopped

1 bay leaf
nutmeg
dry white wine
50 g/2 oz prosciutto
50 g/2 oz/1½ cup grated
    Parmesan cheese
salt and pepper

FOR THE SAUCE
100 g/4 oz butter
40 g/1½ oz/⅓ cup grated
    Parmesan cheese

SERVES 6
PREP/COOKING: 1¾ HRS

To prepare the pasta, sift the flour on to a work surface and make a well. Break in the eggs and mix them into the flour with the finely chopped spinach and a pinch of salt. Begin by mixing with a fork, then use your hands to make a firm but elastic dough. Wrap in cling film and place in the refrigerator for 30 minutes.

Meanwhile, cut the duck meat and pork into bite-sized pieces and brown in 4 tablespoons oil, together with the chopped shallots, bay leaf and a grating of nutmeg. When the meat is browned, sprinkle on half a glass of wine and, when this has evaporated, add a small ladleful of hot water. Reduce the heat, cover and cook the meat for about 35 minutes. Remove from the pan and chop it finely in a food processor with the cooking liquid and ham. Transfer to a bowl. Mix the filling with the Parmesan cheese and season with salt, pepper and nutmeg.

Roll out the pasta into very thin sheets and cut into 5 cm/2 inch squares. Put a teaspoon of filling in the middle of each square, then fold the pasta into a triangle, sealing the edges well and forming it into a ring. When all the tortelloni are ready, cook them in plenty of boiling salted water until *al dente*.

Toss in melted butter, sprinkle with grated Parmesan cheese and serve immediately, piping hot.

TAGLIATELLE CON VONGOLE E ZUCCHINE

Tagliatelle with Clams and Courgettes

400 g/14 oz clams
1 garlic clove
olive oil
350 g/12 oz tagliatelle

salt
250 g/8 oz courgettes/
zucchini
fresh basil
fresh sage

SERVES 4
PREP/COOKING: 20 MINS

Rinse the clams in several changes of water, then leave them to soak in fresh water for at least 2 hours to remove all traces of sand. Split the garlic clove and lightly crush it, using the flat edge of a knife. Place in a large shallow pan with 1 tablespoon of olive oil, heat, then add the clams. Trim the courgettes and cut them into rounds.

In another shallow pan, heat 3 tablespoons of olive oil, flavour with a few basil and sage leaves, then add the courgettes. Season and sauté over very high heat. Transfer the open clams still in their shells from the other pan (discard any that are not open) and strain over all their cooking juices.

Leave to simmer while you cook the tagliatelle in plenty of boiling salted water until it is *al dente* then drain it. Pour the pasta into the sauce, shake the pan vigorously to disperse the flavour, then transfer to a serving dish and serve at once.

PENNE AI FRUTTI DI MARE

Penne with Shellfish

450 g/1 lb cockles
400 g/14 oz queen scallops
400 g/14 oz mussels
olive oil
1 garlic clove
1 shallot
1/2 leek
40 g/1 oz/3 tbspoons butter
salt and pepper

1 tbspoon chopped fresh
herbs (parsley, sage,
thyme, rosemary,
marjoram)
4 tbspoons dry white wine
400 g/14 oz penne

SERVES 4
PREP/COOKING: 1 HR

Scrub the shellfish and wash in cold water to remove all traces of sand or beard. Discard any scallops or mussels that are open. Heat 2 tablespoons of oil with the garlic in a saucepan, then add each type of shellfish separately and cook them until they open. (Discard any that do not open.) Set aside. Strain the mussel cooking juice and reserve it.

Meanwhile, chop the shallot and leek and sweat in the butter for 2 minutes. Add the shellfish and season with a pinch each of salt and pepper and the chopped herbs. Sprinkle over the white wine and evaporate it over high heat, then add half a glass of the mussel juice. Reduce by about half.

Cook the pasta until *al dente* in plenty of boiling salted water. Drain it, then add immediately to the sauce and, still over high heat, toss the pasta to flavour it well. Transfer to a serving dish and serve immediately.

CROCCHETTE DI RISO CON SPINACI E FONTINA

Rice Croquettes with Spinach and Cheese

---

450 g/1 lb fresh spinach
50 g/2 oz/1 small onion
olive oil
400 g/14 oz/1 ¾ cups arborio rice
75 ml/3 fl oz/⅓ cup dry white wine
1 litre/1 ¾ pints/1 quart hot vegetable stock

50 g/2 oz/4 tbspoons butter
40 g/1 ½ oz/⅓ cup grated Parmesan cheese
salt
100 g/4 oz Fontina cheese, finely diced
white flour
3 eggs, beaten
breadcrumbs

SERVES 6
PREP/COOKING: 1 HR 20 MINS

Trim the spinach and wash in several changes of water to eliminate any dirt. Cook briefly in just the water clinging to the leaves after washing. Drain, squeeze thoroughly and chop coarsely.

Chop the onion and soften in 3 tablespoons olive oil. Add the rice, toast it over high heat, then sprinkle on the wine. As soon as this has evaporated, start adding the hot stock, a little at a time, until the risotto is cooked (about 20–25 minutes). Take the pan off the heat and beat in the chopped spinach, butter, Parmesan cheese and a pinch of salt. Leave until cold, then stir in the diced Fontina.

Divide the risotto into 12 equal parts and form each one into a long croquette. Roll the croquettes first in a little flour, then in the beaten eggs and finally in the breadcrumbs. Coat the croquettes twice. Fry in deep hot oil, drain on a double thickness of kitchen paper, and serve, decorating the plate as you wish.

RISOTTO SAPORITO

Risotto with Trout

1 shallot
olive oil
300 g/10 oz/1 1/2 cups Italian rice, such as arborio
75 ml/3 fl oz/1/3 cup dry Martini
900 ml/1 1/2 pints/3 3/4 cups hot vegetable or fish stock
150 g/5 oz trout fillet
50 ml/2 fl oz/1/4 cup single cream
salt
1 tbspoon chopped fresh herbs (parsley, sage, rosemary, marjoram)

SERVES 4
PREP/COOKING: 30 MINS

Peel and chop the shallot and sweat it in a saucepan with 2 tablespoons of olive oil. Add the rice and toast it over high heat, then sprinkle on the Martini. As soon as it has evaporated, start adding the hot stock, a little at a time.

Remove any bones or skin from the trout and cut the fish into small pieces. Add these to the half-cooked rice. Finish cooking the rice until it is *al dente*, but still moist (about 20–25 minutes), then remove from the heat and stir in the cream to give it a rich texture. Season with salt and the chopped herbs.

Cover the pan and leave the risotto to cool for 2–3 minutes. Transfer it to a serving dish and decorate as you wish.

Risotto con le quaglie

Risotto with Quails

4 quails, cleaned and
  prepared
olive oil
50 g/2 oz/1 stalk of celery,
1 carrot, 1 onion
1 teaspoon tomato purée
chopped fresh herbs
  (parsley, sage, rosemary)
1.2 litres/2 pints/1 1/4 cups
  hot chicken stock

salt and pepper
1 small onion (for the
  risotto)
300 g/10 oz/1 1/2 cups
  arborio rice
dry white wine
20 g/3 oz/6 tbspoons
  butter
1 tbspoon grated
  Parmesan cheese

SERVES 4
PREP/COOKING: 1 HR

Brown the quails in 3 tablespoons oil. Meanwhile, finely dice the celery, carrot and onion. As soon as the quails are well browned, add the vegetables and soften over low heat, then add the tomato purée, a pinch of herbs and half the stock. Season with salt and pepper, cover and braise over medium heat for about 30 minutes.

When you are ready to cook the risotto, finely chop the small onion and soften in 3 tablespoons oil. Add the rice, toast it over high heat, then sprinkle with half a glass of wine. As soon as this has evaporated, lower the heat and continue to cook, adding the sauce from the quails and the hot stock, a little at a time. Stop cooking when the rice is still *al dente* and slightly soupy (about 20 minutes). Season with salt and beat in the butter and a spoonful of Parmesan. Cover and leave the risotto to rest for a few minutes before serving it with the quails.

Risotto alla marinara

Seafood Risotto

FOR THE RISOTTO
1 medium onion, chopped
olive oil
300 g/10 oz/1 1/4 cups Italian rice, such as arborio
generous 600 ml/1 pint/ 2 1/2 cups light fish or vegetable stock, more if necessary
butter for the mould

FOR THE GARNISH
400 g/14 oz mussels
olive oil
2 garlic cloves
250 g/8 oz small squid
150 g/5 oz uncooked prawns/shrimp
oregano
1 tomato, peeled and chopped

SERVES 6
PREP/COOKING: 1 HR

Soften the onion in 3 tablespoons of olive oil. Add the rice, toast it over high heat, then sprinkle on a little stock. As soon as this has evaporated, start adding the rest of the stock, a little at a time, until the risotto is just cooked (about 20 minutes). Preheat oven to 200°C/400°F/gas 6.

Meanwhile, scrub the mussels, removing the beards and any that are open. Put them in a saucepan with 2 tablespoons of olive oil and a lightly crushed clove of garlic. Set over high heat and, as soon as they open, take them out of their shells and strain and reserve the cooking juices. Discard any that do not open. Clean the squid, removing the cartilage and eyes. Then separate the tentacles and bodies and cut into pieces. Shell the prawns and chop them.

Heat 3 tablespoons of olive oil and half a chopped garlic clove in a saucepan, add a grinding of pepper, oregano to taste and the squid tentacles and bodies. Add the tomato and, when the sauce is almost boiling, add the prawns and mussels. Thin the sauce with the mussel juices, season with salt and boil for 3 minutes. Pour the sauce over the prepared risotto.

Butter a fish-shaped (or any other suitable shape) mould and fill with the seafood risotto. Stand the 'fish' in a bain-marie and cook in the preheated oven for about 20 minutes. Leave to stand for a moment before unmoulding on to a serving dish. Decorate as you wish, and serve immediately.

ZUPPETTA DI COZZE AL RISO

Mussel Stew with Rice

olive oil
250 g/8 oz/1 cup arborio rice
about 450 ml/¾ pint/ 2 cups light vegetable or fish stock
a small bunch of fresh parsley
½ garlic clove, crushed
about 800 g/1 ¾ lb mussels

250 g/8 oz chopped tomato pulp
1 medium onion, chopped
salt
oregano
50 ml/2 fl oz/¼ cup dry white wine

SERVES 4
PREP/COOKING: 40 MINS

Preheat the oven to 200°C/400°F/gas 6. Heat 2 tablespoons of olive oil in a saucepan, add it to the rice and toast it over high heat. Sprinkle over a little of the stock then, as soon as it has evaporated, start adding the rest of the stock, a little at a time, until the risotto is just cooked (about 20 minutes). Transfer to a large bowl. Wash, drain and finely chop the parsley leaves. Season the rice with a trickle of olive oil, chopped parsley and the crushed garlic.

Wash the mussels and scrub to remove the beards and impurities. Discard any that are open. Using a sharp knife, open them raw, leaving the mussel in place and the two halves of the shell still joined. Place a spoonful of the prepared rice in each shell, close and tie with kitchen thread so the mussels do not open during cooking.

In a baking dish, make a bed of tomato pulp. Scatter over the chopped onion and a pinch of salt and oregano. Arrange the mussels on this bed, sprinkle over the white wine and a trickle of olive oil, then cook in the preheated oven for about 20 minutes. Serve the mussels piping hot.

TIMBALLO DI RISO AI CARCIOFI

Rice and Artichoke Timbale

1 small onion, finely chopped
1 sprig fresh sage
1 garlic clove, finely chopped
50 g/2 oz/4 tbspoons butter
olive oil for frying
1 slice bacon, cut into thin strips
100 g/4 oz boned breast of chicken, cubed
flour
1 tbspoon brandy
4 tbspoons dry white wine
150 ml/5 fl oz/²/₃ cup milk
¼ chicken stock cube, crumbled
a pinch of grated nutmeg
1 sprig fresh parsley, chopped
2 fresh artichokes
800 ml/1 ½ pints/3¾ cups good meat stock
1 tbspoon dry sherry
350 g/12 oz/1 ½ cups rice
1 pinch saffron

SERVES 4
PREP/COOKING: 1 ¼ HRS

Fry a third of the onion, a sage leaf and half the garlic gently in 25g/1oz/half of the butter and a tablespoon of olive oil. Coat the chicken cubes in flour and fry the bacon and chicken gently for a few minutes, then add the brandy and wine. As soon as the wine has evaporated, pour on the boiling milk, blended with the stock cube and the nutmeg. Stir, cover and allow to reduce slowly.

Fry another third of the onion, the remaining garlic and the parsley gently in 3 tablespoons of oil. Top and tail the artichokes and remove the tough outer leaves. Add them to the pan. Cook for a few minutes and then add half the boiling stock and the sherry. Stir, cover and cook over low heat for 15 minutes or until the artichokes are tender. Drain them, retaining the stock. Preheat the oven to 200°C/400°F/gas 6.

Heat the remaining stock with the stock from the artichokes. Sauté the rest of the onion in the remaining butter in a deep ovenproof pan. Add the rice and cook for a few minutes. Add the saffron, then the stock, stir and bring back to the boil. Cover with foil and bake for 15 minutes or until the rice has absorbed the stock. Remove from the oven and use three quarters of the rice to line a 800 ml/1 1/2 pint/1 quart oiled baking mould. Add the chicken mixture and cover with the remaining rice. Cook in the oven a further 5 minutes. Unmould on to a warmed dish and garnish with the artichokes. Serve at once.

RISO AL POMODORO CON FUNGHI

Rice with Tomatoes and Mushrooms

350 g/12 oz mushrooms (preferably ceps)
25 g/1 oz butter
3 tbspoons olive oil
1 garlic clove, crushed
2–3 sprigs fresh parsley
pepper
350 g/12 oz/1 1/2 cups rice
250 ml/8 fl oz/1 cup tomato sauce
grated Parmesan cheese

SERVES 4
PREP/COOKING: 1 HR 10 MINS

Clean the mushrooms carefully, scraping any earth from the stalks and wiping the caps. Rinse quickly, dry carefully and then slice them. Melt the butter with the oil and the garlic. Add the mushrooms and cook for about 10 minutes, then add some pepper and the parsley.

Cook the rice in plenty of boiling water until just tender. Drain, turn on to a heated deep serving dish and combine with the boiling tomato sauce. Add the mushrooms, which should also be hot.

Serve immediately, with grated Parmesan cheese.

Risotto alla rusticana

Peasant Risotto

6 leaves savoy cabbage
3–4 shallots
50 g/2 oz/4 tbspoons butter
olive oil
350 g/12 oz/1 1/2 cups
  arborio rice
3 tbspoons dry white wine
1 litre/1 3/4 pints/1 quart
vegetable stock

50 g/2 oz Italian sausage
75 g/3 oz tinned chick peas
75 g/3 oz tinned borlotti
  beans
salt
50 g/2 oz/1 1/2 cup grated
  Parmesan cheese

SERVES 4
PREP/COOKING: 40 MINS

Remove the central rib from the cabbage leaves, wash the leaves and cook in boiling salted water for about 10 minutes. Remove them from the water with a slotted spoon and lay them on a sloping plate to drain. Meanwhile heat the stock.

Chop the shallots and soften half of the butter and a tablespoon of oil. Add the rice, toast it over high heat, then sprinkle on the wine. As soon as this has evaporated, add the hot stock a little at a time.

When the rice is half-cooked, mix in the coarsely chopped cabbage leaves, the skinned sliced sausage, and the drained chick peas and beans, a third of them pureéd. Taste and add salt if necessary. Once the rice is cooked but still a little firm, remove the pan from the heat and mix in the remaining butter, softened and cut into pieces. Stir in the grated Parmesan cheese and then serve.

Gnocchi sardi in salsa d'uova

Gnocchi with Egg Sauce

2 eggs	450 g/1 1/4 lb small
100 g/4 oz cooked ham	dumplings (gnocchi)
100 g/4 oz mushrooms	2 tbspoons vinegar
50 g/2 oz capers	salt and pepper
12 green olives, pitted.	50 ml/2 fl oz/1/4 cup
5 dill pickles/gherkins, finely sliced	olive oil
	75 g/3 oz cheese

SERVES 8
PREP/COOKING: 30 MINS

Hard-boil the eggs and cool them under running water. Cut the ham into tiny cubes, discarding any fat. Place the mushrooms, capers, olives and dill pickles in a large salad bowl.

Cook the gnocchi in plenty of boiling salted water until *al dente*, drain well and spread on a tray to cool. Shell the eggs then finely crumble the yolks into a bowl. Moisten with the vinegar and season with a little salt and pepper. Gradually blend in the olive oil.

Place the gnocchi and the diced ham in the salad bowl with the other ingredients. Dress with the prepared sauce and stir well. Dice the cheese and stir it into the salad. Serve at once.

Gnocchi alla Bava

Gnocchi with Cheese Sauce

700 g/1 1/2 lb potatoes
100 g/4 oz/1 cup flour
2 egg yolks
salt and pepper
nutmeg

50 g/2 oz Parmesan cheese
(in a block)
50 g/2 oz/4 tbspoons
butter
50 ml/2 fl oz/1/4 cup
single cream

SERVES 4
PREP/COOKING: 30 MINS

Boil the potatoes in salted water, drain, peel and mash them. Add the flour, 1 egg yolk, a little salt and some grated nutmeg. Knead together and divide the dough into small balls. Give the dough balls an interesting texture by rolling them on the back of a cheese grater.

Remove the rind from the cheese and dice it. Put it in a pan with the melted butter and the cream. Place over low heat and stir with a wooden spoon until the cheese has melted. Add the other egg yolk and a generous grinding of pepper, and stir briskly.

Cook the gnocchi in plenty of boiling salted water until *al dente* and they rise to the surface. Drain. Pour the cheese sauce over the boiled gnocchi and serve them at once.

TIMBALLO DI GNOCCHI AGLI SPINACI

Timbale of Spinach-Flavoured Gnocchi

FOR THE GNOCCHI
1 kg/2 1/4 lb potatoes
300 g/10 oz/2 1/2 cups flour, plus extra for dusting
1 egg
100 g/4 oz spinach, cooked, squeezed dry and finely chopped
salt
2 tbspoons grated Parmesan cheese

FOR THE SAUCE
200 g/7 oz cep mushrooms
olive oil
1 garlic clove, chopped
chopped parsley
salt and pepper
75 g/3 oz tinned chopped tomatoes

FOR THE BECHAMEL
40 g/1 1/2 oz/3 tbspoons butter
40 g/1 1/2 oz/6 tbspoons flour
500 ml/18 fl oz/2 1/4 cups hot milk
salt

FOR THE TIMBALE
250 g/8 oz/2 cups flour, plus extra for dusting
100 g/4 oz butter, plus extra for greasing
salt
4 tbspoons grated Parmesan cheese

SERVES 6
PREP/COOKING: 1 1/4 HRS

Peel and boil the potatoes, then press them through a potato ricer, letting the pulp fall on to a floured work surface. Add the flour and egg, then the chopped spinach, salt and Parmesan cheese. Combine into a dough, then divide the dough into cylinders and cut into small pieces ('gnocchi'). Cook in salted water, drain well and refresh.

To prepare the timbale, quickly make a dough with the flour, butter, a pinch of salt and 75 ml/3 fl oz/⅓ cup water. Leave to rest in the refrigerator for 30 minutes. Preheat the oven to 190°C/375°F/gas 5. On a well-floured surface, pull the dough into a 24 cm/10 inch diameter circle and use it to line a buttered and floured round mould. Line the dough with baking parchment and fill with baking beans, to prevent it from puffing up as it cooks. Bake in the oven for 25 minutes, then remove the parchment and beans and bake for a further 5 minutes.

To make the sauce, slice the ceps, then stew them in 3 tablespoons oil with the garlic and a pinch of chopped parsley. Season with salt and pepper and add the tomatoes. Cook for 5 minutes until the ingredients are combined and heated through. Finally, prepare the béchamel. Melt the butter in a saucepan, remove from the heat and stir in the flour to make a smooth paste. Pour in the hot milk and a pinch of salt, return to the heat and, stirring constantly, cook for 2–3 minutes or until the sauce thickens. Remove from the heat.

Fill the timbale with alternating layers of gnocchi, tomato sauce and béchamel. Top with 4 tablespoons Parmesan cheese, dot with butter and bake at 240°C/475°F/gas 9 for 10 minutes. Remove from the oven and carefully remove the timbale from the mould on to a serving dish. Serve at once.

Gnocchetti di pesce

Fish Gnocchi

1 small onion, finely chopped
olive oil
1 garlic clove, whole
1 bay leaf
600 g/1 1/4 lb whiting fillets, cut into pieces
50 ml/2 fl oz/1/4 cup dry white wine
a small bunch of fresh parsley
nutmeg

FOR THE SAUCE
1 shallot, finely chopped
olive oil
fresh sage and rosemary
1 anchovy fillet
350 g/12 oz/1 1/2 cups tomato passata
250 ml/8 fl oz/1 cup whipping cream

FOR THE GNOCCHI
1 kg/2 lb potatoes
250 g/8 oz/2 cups flour, plus extra for dusting
2 eggs

SERVES 8
PREP/COOKING: 1 HR 10 MINS

Soften the onion in a shallow pan with 3 tablespoons of olive oil, the garlic and bay leaf. Add the fish to the pan. Pour in the wine, season and cook over high heat until tender.

Make the gnocchi. Cook the potatoes in salted water for about 20 minutes or until tender. Peel and push through a potato ricer or sieve on to a lightly floured work surface.

Remove the garlic clove and bay leaf from the fish, break up the fish with a fork and add it to the potatoes, together with the finely chopped parsley leaves. Season with salt, pepper and a grating of nutmeg. Add the flour and eggs, and mix to a smooth dough.

Divide the dough into several pieces and roll them along the work surface into long cylinders. Cut each cylinder into short pieces and press them against the back of a fork to create ridges. Cook them, a few at a time, in boiling salted water until they rise to the surface. Remove with a slotted spoon and keep warm.

Soften the shallot in olive oil, adding a few sage and rosemary leaves and the anchovy. Stir in the passata and thicken with the cream. Simmer for a minute or two.

Pour the sauce over the gnocchi and serve at once.

POLENTA DELICATA SI FUNGHI

Polenta with Mushrooms

750 ml/1 1/4 pints/3 cups milk
175 g/6 oz/1 1/2 cups corn meal
50 g/2 oz/1/2 cup semolina
350 g/12 oz mushrooms
75 g/3 oz/6 tbspoons butter
2 1/2 teaspoons flour
grated nutmeg
100 g/4 oz/1 cup grated Emmental cheese
2 egg yolks
1 garlic clove
a handful of parsley
2 tbspoons olive oil
ground thyme

SERVES 4
PREP/COOKING: 1 HR

Pour 600 ml/1 pint/2 1/2 cups each of water and milk into a large saucepan and slowly bring to the boil. Mix the corn meal with the semolina. As soon as the liquid boils, add the salt and, after a few moments, gradually sprinkle in the mixed corn meal and semolina. At the beginning stir with a small whisk, then use a wooden spoon. Cook over medium heat for about 40 minutes, stirring frequently.

Clean the mushrooms, trim the stems and wipe the mushrooms with a damp cloth. Slice them thinly. In a small saucepan melt 2 tablespoons of butter, add the flour and stir with a wooden spoon. Moisten with the remaining boiling milk poured in a trickle and, stirring constantly, bring to the boil. Remove from the heat, season with salt and nutmeg, then add the cheese and egg yolks, stirring hard after each addition.

Finely chop the garlic clove with the parsley and soften the mixture in a third of the butter and 2 tablespoons of oil, without browning. Add the mushrooms and leave for not more than 5 minutes, seasoning with salt and pepper and a pinch of thyme.

Remove the polenta from the heat and fold in the remaining butter, softened and cut into small pieces, then pour it on to a round serving plate and make a hollow in the centre. Pour in the cheese sauce, spread over the mushroom slices and sprinkle with a little chopped parsley.

'Budino' di polenta al formaggio

Polenta and Cheese Pudding

450 ml/¾ pint/2 cups milk
salt
1½ vegetable stock cubes
350 g/12 oz/3 cups quick-cooking polenta
50 g/2 oz/4 tbspoons butter

olive oil
100 g/4 oz/1 cup grated Parmesan cheese
25 g/1 oz/¼ cup flour
2 egg yolks
100 g/4 oz Fontina cheese
celery leaves

SERVES 6–8
PREP/COOKING: 40 MINS

Heat 1½ litres/2 pints/1½ quarts of water and 150 ml/5 fl oz/⅔ cup of milk together. Add a little salt and crumble in a stock cube. As soon as the mixture begins to boil, sprinkle in the polenta, stirring first with a whisk and then a wooden spoon. Cook for about 20 minutes, then remove from the heat. Mix in 25 g/1 oz/2 tablespoons of butter in small knobs and half the Parmesan cheese, stirring constantly. Put the polenta into a greased mould with fluted sides. Cover with a cloth while you prepare the sauce.

Melt the remaining butter in a saucepan. Remove from the heat and stir in the flour to make a smooth roux. Boil the remaining milk and add to the roux, a little at a time. Return to the heat and, stirring constantly, bring the sauce to the boil and flavour with half a stock cube.

Remove from the heat and add the 2 egg yolks, the remaining Parmesan cheese and the Fontina cheese cut into small pieces. Mix well, then pour the boiling sauce over the polenta which has been turned out on to a deep dish.

Place chopped celery leaves in the centre of the polenta pudding and serve immediately.

POLENTA BIANCA ALLA PROVOLA E SPINACH

White Polenta with Smoked Cheese and Spinach

100 g/4 oz/1 cup white maize flour
salt and pepper
1 shallot
4 tbspoons olive oil

250 g/8 oz spinach, cooked and squeezed dry
50 g/2 oz/4 tbspoons butter
350 g/12 oz smoked provola cheese

SERVES 6
PREP/COOKING: 1½ HRS

Pour 275 ml/9 fl oz/a generous cup water into a saucepan and bring to the boil. Add a small handful of salt, then scatter in the maize flour, mixing hard so that no lumps form. As soon as the mixture comes to the boil, lower the heat and cook for about 45 minutes, stirring frequently.

Meanwhile, preheat the oven to 240°C/475°F/gas 9. Peel and finely chop the shallot and soften in the olive oil. Add the spinach, leave to absorb the flavour for a few minutes, then season with salt and pepper. Butter an ovenproof dish and pour in the cooked polenta. Dot over the remaining butter, and cover with the spinach and thin slices of cheese. Cook in the hot oven for about 15 minutes.

Remove from the oven and allow to cool for about 10 minutes, then serve the polenta straight from the dish. This makes an excellent complete meal served with a slice or two of cooked ham.

FISH & SEAFOOD

Fish and seafood have pride of place in a country largely surrounded by water, and the way in which they are cooked is second to none anywhere in the world. In these pages, you'll find a wonderful selection of marine delicacies that have authentically Italian style and simplicity.

Cozze tarantine

Taranto-style Mussels

450 g/1 lb tomatoes
1 kg/2¼ lb mussels
1 garlic clove
olive oil
350 g/12 oz potatoes
250 g/8 oz courgettes/
  zucchini
350 g/12 oz onions
salt and pepper
2 tbspoons grated
  Pecorino cheese
a few sprigs fresh parsley

SERVES 4
PREP/COOKING: 1¾ HRS

Parboil the tomatoes and then skin and slice them thinly, discarding the seeds. Scrape and rinse the mussels and place them in a frying pan with the sliced garlic clove and 2 tablespoons of olive oil. Cover the pan and heat briskly to open the shells. Discard any mussels that don't open. Discard the empty half of each shell and place the half containing the mussel on a plate. Strain the cooking juices into a bowl. Peel, wash and slice the potatoes, not too thinly. Top and tail the courgettes and cut them into slices about 3 mm/⅛ inch thick. Slice the onions very finely.

Preheat the oven to 170°C/325°F/gas3. Grease a large ovenproof pan or dish with plenty of olive oil and line the bottom of it with a quarter of the onion rings. Arrange all the potato slices on top in one layer. Add another layer of onion rings and sprinkle with salt. Arrange half the mussels on top of the onion rings. Add half the tomatoes and season with pepper and a tablespoon of grated Pecorino cheese. Add another layer of onion rings, then all the courgette slices and then the rest of the onions. Sprinkle with salt. Add another layer of mussels and top with the remaining tomatoes and a little pepper.

Sprinkle with the remaining grated Pecorino cheese and pour on all the strained mussel juices and 5–6 tablespoons of oil. Add a few sprigs of parsley and cover the pan with a lid or with foil. Bake in the oven for about 1 hour or until the potatoes and courgettes are tender.

Pagellini alla ghiotta

Stuffed Bream

*8 small fresh bream, gutted and cleaned
1–2 sprigs fresh parsley
2–3 leaves fresh basil
2 tbspoons capers
2 anchovy fillets in oil
a little oregano

7 tbspoons fresh white breadcrumbs
1 egg
salt and pepper
1 egg, hard-boiled
olive oil
50 ml/2 fl oz/1¼ cup dry white wine

SERVES 4
PREP/COOKING: 1¼ HRS

Rinse the bream under running water and dry thoroughly. Finely chop 1 sprig of parsley, the basil, capers and drained anchovy fillets. Stir in a little oregano and 4 tablespoons of the breadcrumbs and bind the mixture with beaten egg. Season with salt and pepper. Stuff the bream with the prepared mixture and sew up with kitchen string.

Preheat the oven to 190°C/375°F/gas 5. Mix the remaining breadcrumbs with the crumbled yolk of the hard-boiled egg and a tablespoon of olive oil. Arrange the bream in a well-greased ovenproof serving dish. Brush them with olive oil and sprinkle with a little salt. Top with the breadcrumbs and egg mixture and a little finely chopped parsley. Sprinkle with olive oil and cook in the oven for 25–30 minutes. Pour on the white wine and cover with foil. Return to the oven for about 10 minutes to finish cooking, then serve immediately.

Calamari ripieni di magro

Stuffed Squid

8 medium squid
3 handfuls of fresh parsley
3 garlic cloves
100 g/4 oz prawns/shrimp
100 g/4 oz/1 cup breadcrumbs
2 tbspoons grated Pecorino cheese
2 eggs

olive oil
salt and pepper
1 small onion
100 ml/4 fl oz/1½ cup dry white wine
150 ml/5 fl oz/⅔ cup fish stock
1 teaspoon cornflour

SERVES 4
PREP/COOKING: 1½ HRS

Separate the tentacles from the body of each squid. Empty the body pouches and discard the dark outer skins. Discard the eyes and 'beaks' and wash and drain both the tentacles and pouches.

Finely chop a handful of parsley and 2 large garlic cloves and place in a bowl. Peel and chop the prawns and add to the bowl. Stir in the breadcrumbs, cheese, eggs and 3 tablespoons of olive oil. Season with salt and pepper and blend thoroughly. Stuff the pouches of the squid with the mixture and stitch up the opening.

Finely chop the onion, the remaining garlic clove and a small handful of parsley, and fry gently in 4 tablespoons of olive oil. Add the stuffed squid and their tentacles and fry gently for a few minutes, turning once. Pour over the wine and allow it to evaporate rapidly over a brisk heat. Dissolve the cornflour in the fish stock and add to the pan.

Shake the pan to make sure that nothing is sticking and then cover it. Lower the heat and simmer for about 40 minutes, shaking the pan occasionally and adding a little more fish stock if necessary. By the end of the cooking, the squid should be fairly dry and the sauce well reduced.

Transfer to a warmed dish and serve garnished with some parsley.

MOSCARDINI, POMODORI E OLIVE

Octopus with Tomatoes and Olives

1 kg/2 1/4 lb small octopuses	olive oil
1 celery stalk	450 g/1 lb tomatoes
1 small onion	1 piece lemon rind
1 sprig fresh parsley	salt and pepper
2 small garlic cloves	8 stoned green olives
	celery leaves

SERVES 4–6
PREP/COOKING: ABOUT 2 1/2 HOURS

Remove the 'beak', eyes and viscera from the octopuses' body pouches and discard them. Wash and drain the octopuses. Trim the celery and chop it finely with the onion, parsley and garlic. Heat 4 tablespoons of olive oil in a saucepan and lightly fry the chopped vegetables. Wash and chop the tomatoes and liquidise them. Add them to the pan, stir the mixture and bring it slowly to the boil.

Beat the octopus tentacles with a wooden meat mallet, slice tentacles and bodies, and stir them into the boiling sauce. Add a piece of lemon rind. Season with a little salt and pepper and bring the mixture back to the boil. Lower the heat, cover the pan and cook for about 1 3/4 hours, stirring occasionally. If the sauce reduces too much, pour on a little boiling water.

Stir in the olives and cook for 15 minutes more. Test and adjust the seasoning according to taste. Serve topped with a few finely chopped celery leaves.

TRIGLIE E MELUZZETTI ALL'ACCIUGA

Red Mullet and Hake with Anchovies

5 small red mullet, together weighing about 350 g/12 oz, gutted and cleaned
5 baby hake, together weighing about 350 g/12 oz
olive oil
1 garlic clove
1 sprig parsley
2 anchovy fillets
2 tbspoons breadcrumbs
oregano
salt and pepper
1 tbspoon lemon juice
1 lemon, sliced
a little dry white wine

SERVES 5
PREP/COOKING: 45 MINS

Rinse the fish well under running water and dry. Oil an ovenproof dish which is large enough to hold all the fish without any overlap. Preheat the oven to 190°C/375°F/gas 5.

Finely chop a large garlic clove, the parsley and well-drained anchovy fillets, and place them in a shallow bowl. Add the breadcrumbs, a little oregano and a generous pinch of salt and pepper. Mix to blend.

In another shallow bowl, beat the lemon juice with 3 tablespoons of olive oil and a large pinch of salt to form a smooth sauce. Dip the fish one by one in the sauce and then sprinkle them with the breadcrumb mixture. Arrange the fish on the ovenproof dish, alternating the two different types of fish.

Place half-slices of lemon between the heads of the fish and sprinkle with a little olive oil. Cook in the oven for about 15 minutes, pouring on a little white wine halfway through cooking. Serve hot.

Spiedini di Pesce Spada

Swordfish Skewers

1 red and 1 yellow bell pepper, each weighing about 300 g/10 oz	flour olive oil 1 garlic clove
2 thick slices of swordfish, together weighing 550 g/ 1 1/4 lb	100 ml/4 fl oz/1/2 cup dry white wine salt

SERVES 4
PREP/COOKING: 1 HR

Grill the peppers, turning them often, to scorch the skins. Wrap them individually in kitchen towels and set them aside for a few minutes. Peel away the skins, cut them in half, remove the seeds and stem, then cut them into 1 1/2 inch squares.

Remove the skin from the swordfish and cut each slice into 16 small pieces of similar size. Thread eight pieces on a long wooden skewer, alternating with the pepper squares, and beginning and ending with a pepper square. Make four skewers. Roll each skewer in the flour until well covered, shaking off the excess.

Heat 5 tablespoons of oil flavoured with a slightly crushed garlic clove in a large frying pan and arrange the skewers side by side in the pan. Let the skewers of fish brown well, then sprinkle with the white wine and season with some salt. Let the wine evaporate almost completely and serve on a heated plate.

Filetti di nasello infuocati

Hake with Tomato Sauce

---

3 hake, each weighing about 350 g/12 oz
salt and pepper
milk
flour
olive oil
250 g/8 oz firm ripe tomatoes
175 ml/6 fl oz/¾ cup fish stock

2 basil leaves
granulated sugar
1 garlic clove
½ green pepper, scorched and peeled
salt and pepper
1 teaspoon cornflour

SERVES 6
PREP/COOKING: 1 HR

Gut, clean and fillet the hake. Dip the fillets first in lightly salted cold milk, then roll them in flour. Heat 5 tablespoons of olive oil in a pan large enough to hold all the fish in one layer. When the oil is hot, add the fillets and brown, adding salt and pepper to taste. As soon as they are cooked, remove from the pan and arrange them in a fan on a heat-proof dish, without overlapping them. Cover with foil and keep them warm.

Chop and purée the tomatoes, then whisk them together with the fish stock. Strain the mixture through a fine sieve into the pan used to fry the fillets. Add the basil leaves, a pinch of sugar, a slightly crushed garlic clove, salt, pepper, and finely chopped pepper. Simmer for about 10 minutes, then thicken the sauce with a teaspoon of cornflour dissolved in 5 tablespoons of cold water; stir and simmer for a few more minutes. Discard the garlic and basil. Pour the sauce over the fish fillets and serve at once, garnishing as you wish.

Gamberoni dorati

Golden King Prawns

12 fresh king prawns/
  langostinos
1 small leek
1 small celery stalk
1 small carrot
1 garlic clove
a few sprigs fresh parsley
4 tbspoons dry white
  wine

salt
flour
1 large egg
breadcrumbs
oil for frying
1 bay leaf
1 lemon

SERVES 4
PREP/COOKING: 40 MINS + 1 HR MARINATING

Peel the prawns and lay them in a shallow bowl. Finely slice the leek, celery and carrot and arrange on top of the prawns. Coarsely chop the garlic with the parsley and add these to the mixture. Pour over the wine and lightly sprinkle with salt. Cover the dish with cling film and leave to marinate for 1 hour in a cool place or the least cold part of the refrigerator.

Remove the prawns from the marinade, shaking off the other ingredients without wiping them, then dip them first in the flour, next in the beaten egg and finally in the breadcrumbs. Ensure that they are coated all over with these ingredients. Heat the oil with a bay leaf in a large pan and, when it is hot, pour in the prawns and fry until they are golden brown all over. Use two forks to turn them over carefully while cooking.

Drain the prawns from the oil and put them on a plate covered with a double layer of paper towels to absorb any excess oil. Then arrange on a serving dish, sprinkle lightly with salt and garnish with slices of lemon.

Orata 'san marco'

Bream San Marco

1 large bream, weighing about 1 1/2 kg/3 1/4 lb, gutted and cleaned	100 ml/4 fl oz/1/2 cup dry white wine
1 small onion, thinly sliced	100 ml/4 fl oz/1/2 cup fish stock
1 small carrot, thinly sliced	2–3 whole black peppercorns
1 small celery stalk, thinly sliced	olive oil
3 tbspoons butter	a handful of fresh parsley
1 garlic clove	3 anchovy fillets in oil
1 small bay leaf	1 tablespoon mustard juice of 1/2 lemon

SERVES 6
PREP/COOKING: 1 HR

Rinse and dry the bream. Sauté the onion, carrot and celery in 1 tablespoon of the butter. Add the lightly crushed garlic clove and the bay leaf and pour over the white wine and fish stock. Add the whole peppercorns, half-cover the pan and simmer gently until almost all the liquid has been absorbed.

Preheat the oven to 200°C/400°F/gas 6. Arrange half the vegetables on a large sheet of buttered aluminium foil. Lay the fish on top and cover with the remaining vegetables. Season with a pinch of salt and a little olive oil. Wrap the foil around the fish, place on a baking tray and cook in the oven for about 30 minutes or until it is cooked through.

Meanwhile, finely chop the parsley and anchovy fillets and place them in a bowl. Add a generous dash of the mustard, lemon juice and 4 tablespoons of olive oil. Mix carefully and adjust the seasoning to taste.

Take the fish out of the oven, unwrap it and cut off the head and tail. Discard the vegetables. Divide the fish in half and remove all the bones. Arrange the two halves on a warmed dish, cover with the prepared sauce, garnish and serve hot.

Acciughe 'in savore'

Savoury Anchovies

750 g/1 1/2 lb very fresh anchovies
flour
frying oil
salt
2 large onions
2 large garlic cloves
1 sprig fresh rosemary
1 bay leaf
3–4 peppercorns

a piece of cinnamon stick
olive oil
150 ml/5 fl oz/2/3 cup white wine vinegar
450 ml/3/4 pint/2/3 cup white wine
salt
1 fish stock cube
1 leek, green part only

SERVES 4–6
PREP/COOKING: 1 1/2 HRS + 36 HRS MARINATING

Clean and gut the fish if necessary. Wash them rapidly under running water and drain carefully. Flour them, a few at a time, and shake off any excess flour. Heat plenty of oil in a deep frying pan and fry the anchovies until they are browned all over. Drain from the oil and lay on a plate covered with a double layer of kitchen towels to absorb the excess oil. Lightly sprinkle with salt. Meanwhile, finely slice the onions. Make a small muslin bag and place inside the lightly crushed garlic, rosemary, bay leaf, peppercorns and cinnamon. Secure. Heat 3 tablespoons of olive oil in a frying pan and put in the bag of herbs and then the onions. Fry gently, stirring. When the onions begin to brown, pour in the vinegar and wine. Mix and bring slowly to the boil, then turn down heat and cover. Simmer for about 15 minutes. Add salt 5 minutes before removing the pan from the heat. Crumble in the stock cube. Remove the bag of herbs and squeeze it out. Place the anchovies and the boiling marinade in a deep dish and leave to cool, first at room temperature and then in the least cold compartment of the refrigerator for at least 36 hours. Be sure to cover the dish. Slice the leek into thin rings and use for garnish.

Frittura 'Misto Mare'

Fried Mixed Seafood

150 ml/5 fl oz/2/3 cup
  mayonnaise
juice of 1/2 lemon
1 teaspoon mustard
paprika
1 sprig parsley, finely
  chopped

2 dill pickles, finely chopped
1 tbspoon capers, finely
  chopped
oil for frying
350 g/12 oz mixed seafood
250 g/8 oz squid rings

SERVES 4
PREP/COOKING: 30 MINS

Mix the mayonnaise and lemon juice and season with the mustard and a pinch of paprika. Add the chopped parsley, pickles and capers to the mayonnaise. Blend to make a smooth sauce. Check and adjust the seasoning to taste. Pour into a serving bowl or jug.

Heat plenty of oil in a deep frying pan and fry the mixed seafood and squid briskly until crisp and golden (2–3 minutes should be enough). Drain well on kitchen towels and arrange on a warm plate. Garnish and serve with the prepared sauce.

Spigola farcita, al forno

Baked Stuffed Sea Bass

1 small onion	salt and pepper
2 garlic cloves	10 prawns/shrimp
a few sprigs parsley	15 mussels
50 ml/2 fl oz/¼ cup olive oil	breadcrumbs
100 g/4 oz cod fillet	1 sea bass, weighing about 1¼ kg/2¾ lb
1 slice white bread soaked in milk	2–3 bay leaves
1 egg	3–4 tbspoons dry white wine

SERVES 8
PREP/COOKING: 1½ HRS

Chop the onion, 1 garlic clove and parsley, and sauté in half the oil. Leave to cool. Cut the cod fillet into small pieces, drain the milk from the bread and then place the sautéed mixture, the cod, bread, egg and a pinch of salt and pepper in the blender. Blend briskly for a couple of minutes. Shell the prawns, dice them and add to the blended mixture.

Scrape and wash the mussel shells and place them in a pan with a tablespoon of oil, the remaining garlic clove and a few leaves of parsley. Cover the pan and place over high heat to open the shells. Shell the mussels and add to the blended mixture. Strain the mussels' cooking juices through muslin and reserve. If the stuffing seems too liquid, add some breadcrumbs. Preheat the oven to 200°C/400°F/gas 6.

Clean and gut the bass if necessary, then rinse under running water and dry it. Stuff the bass with the prepared mixture and sew up the opening. Brush the fish with olive oil and coat it thoroughly in breadcrumbs.

Place the bay leaves in the bottom of a well-oiled ovenproof pan, put the fish in the pan and bake in the oven for about 30 minutes, turning the fish once or twice during cooking. Sprinkle it with 3–4 tablespoons each of white wine and the cooking liquid from the mussels. Serve the fish cut into large slices.

Telline in umido aromatico

Aromatic Stewed Clams

1 kg/2¼ lb clams
salt and pepper
a handful of fresh parsley
1 garlic clove
4 fresh basil leaves

50 ml/2 fl oz/¼ cup
olive oil
350–450 g/¾–1 lb firm
ripe tomatoes
extra basil leaves for garnish

SERVES 4
PREP/COOKING: 40 MINS + 1 HR SOAKING

Wash the clams well under cold running water then soak them in a bowl of cold salted water for about 1 hour to release any sand. Meanwhile, finely chop the parsley with the garlic and the basil. Put the herbs in a large pan with the olive oil and cook over moderate heat. Do not allow to brown.

Blanch the tomatoes in boiling water, peel and chop them. Add them to the pan and stir with a wooden spoon. Cook for about 10 minutes, then drain the clams thoroughly and put these in too. Stir, and cover the pan for a few minutes until the clams have opened (discard any that do not open). Then remove the lid and simmer gently, stirring from time to time. After 5–6 minutes, season with freshly ground pepper, taste and correct the seasoning if necessary. Serve in a warmed bowl or serving dish, garnished with fresh basil.

COZZE AL SAPORE DI MARE

Mussels with a Sea Tang

3 kg/6 lb mussels
salt and pepper
4–6 shallots
1/2 celery heart
300 g/10 oz mushrooms
a handful of fresh parsley
1 tbspoon chopped chives

40 g/1 1/2 oz/3 tbspoons
  butter
150 ml/5 fl oz/2/3 cup dry
  white wine
nutmeg
1 teaspoon cornflour
a few drops lemon juice

SERVES 6
PREP/COOKING: 1 1/2 HRS

Scrape the mussels with a small knife under running water, then leave them in a bowl of salted cold water for at least 30 minutes. Discard any that open. Meanwhile, finely chop the shallots with the celery, mushrooms and parsley. Add the finely chopped chives and fry in 2 tablespoons of butter taking care not to let the ingredients brown. Put the mussels into the pan, pour in the wine, season generously with freshly ground black pepper and a little grated nutmeg. Cover the pan and allow the mussels to open over a high heat, shaking the pan from time to time.

Remove from the heat as soon as the mussels have opened (discard any that do not open). Take the mussels from their shells and place on a serving dish. Filter the liquid from the pan through a piece of muslin, then heat the liquid until it has reduced by half. Add the rest of the butter, softened, in small pieces. Dissolve the cornflour in 2 or 3 tablespoons of cold water and a few drops of lemon juice and add this too. Simmer gently for a few seconds then pour over the mussels and sprinkle generously with chopped parsley. Serve immediately.

'Capriccio' marino

Mixed Shellfish

12 scallops
250 g/8 oz prawns/shrimp
450 g/1 lb mussels
50 ml/2 fl oz/¼ cup olive oil
3 garlic cloves
a little lemon juice
1 small onion
a small bunch of fresh parsley

25 g/1 oz/2 tbspoons butter
50 ml/2 fl oz/¼ cup brandy
75 ml/3 fl oz/⅓ cup dry white wine
½ fish stock cube

SERVES 4
PREP/COOKING: 45 MINS

Open the scallops using an oyster knife and remove them from their shells. Carefully separate the membranes that surround the scallops and rinse them under running water to remove any sand.

Carefully peel the prawns. Scrub the mussel shells and rinse under running water; discard any that open. Place the mussels in a pan with 2 tablespoons of olive oil, 2 cloves of garlic and a few drops of lemon juice. Cover the pan and heat briskly to open the shells (discard any that do not open). Remove the mussels from their shells and place on a plate. Strain the cooking juices.

Finely chop the onion, the remaining garlic and a small handful of parsley and fry gently in the butter, and remaining olive oil. Add the scallops, prawns and mussels, and cook for a few minutes. Pour over the brandy and dry white wine. Season with the crumbled cube. Add 3–4 tablespoons of the strained mussel cooking juices and simmer until a light sauce has formed. Stir in a little chopped parsley and serve.

SGOMBRO IN SALSA FORTE

Mackerel with Piquant Sauce

6 whole mackerel gutted, and cleaned
flour
1 garlic clove
olive oil
10 black peppercorns, coarsely crushed
dry white wine
1 onion, finely chopped
1 yellow pepper, seeded and sliced
70 g/2½ oz black olives
200 g/7 oz/1 cup tomato passata, (sieved tomatoes)

SERVES 6
PREP/COOKING: 30 MINS

Wash the mackerel inside and out, dry then roll in flour, shaking off any excess.

Crush the garlic, using the flat edge of a knife. In a shallow pan, heat 4 tablespoons of oil, add the garlic and coarsely crushed peppercorns and cook for about a minute. Brown the mackerel on both sides, then season to taste and moisten with a very little wine (approximately 2 or 3 tablespoons).

Remove the fish from the pan and keep warm. Add the onion and yellow pepper to the pan with the whole olives. Mix and sweat until the vegetables are tender, then add the tomato passata. Bring to the boil, add the mackerel again and cook over medium heat for 10 minutes.

Transfer the fish to a serving platter, surround with the olives, spoon over some of the sauce and serve the rest separately, in a sauceboat.

Pesce spada al cartoccio

Swordfish 'En Papillotte'

3 large ripe tomatoes, peeled	300 g/10 oz mussels
1 garlic clove	200 g/7 oz clams
a small bunch of fresh parsley	100 g/4 oz shelled prawns/shrimp
4 swordfish steaks or fillets	2 basil leaves
olive oil	1 sprig thyme
	1 egg white

SERVES 4
PREP/COOKING: ABOUT 1 HOUR

Preheat the oven to 190°C/375°F/gas 5. Fold a 50 x 70 cm/20 x 28 inch rectangle of baking parchment in half and cut it out into a heart shape. Prepare three more hearts in the same way.

Wash the tomatoes and cut into small pieces. Place in a bowl with the finely chopped garlic and parsley. Rinse the swordfish slices and flour lightly. Heat 3 tablespoons of oil in a frying pan and add the fish. Brown for 2 minutes on each side.

Scrub and wash the mussels and wash the clams, removing beards and sand, and discarding any that are open. Put them in a saucepan and set over high heat until they open. Discard any that do not open. Heat 2 tablespoons of oil in a frying pan, put in the prawns and herbs then, after 2–3 minutes, add the mussels and clams with their strained juices, and the tomatoes. Cook for 5 minutes.

Lay one parchment heart on a flat plate, and on it arrange a piece of fish. Season and add some of the mussel and prawn sauce. Brush the edges of the parchment heart with egg white.

Close the heart-shaped papillotte and place it on a lightly-oiled baking sheet. Make three more hearts in the same way, place them on the baking sheet and trickle over a little oil. Bake in the preheated oven for about 20–25 minutes, until well puffed up. Transfer to warmed plates and serve immediately.

Pescatrice in salsa aromatica

Monkfish with Aromatic Sauce

1 small onion	1 teaspoon tomato paste
1 small celery stalk	1 teaspoon cornflour
1 small carrot	1/2 fish stock cube
25 g/1 oz/2 tbspoons butter	salt
3 tbspoons olive oil	1 monkfish weighing about 1 1/2 kg/1 1/2 lb, head removed
2 garlic cloves	1 sprig rosemary
2 bay leaves	2 or 3 sage leaves
100 g/4 oz prawns/shrimp unpeeled	celery leaves for garnish
250 ml/8 fl oz/1 cup dry white wine	

SERVES 6
PREP/COOKING: 1 1/4 HRS

Preheat the oven to 200°C/400°F/gas 6. Finely slice the onion, celery and carrot. Heat in a saucepan with the butter and 2 tablespoons of olive oil. Add a lightly crushed garlic clove and a small bay leaf. Fry gently but do not brown. Add the prawns and sauté for a few minutes. Pour in half the wine and simmer until the wine has almost evaporated. Dissolve the tomato paste and the cornflour in about 150 ml/5 fl oz/2/3 cup of cold water, pour into the pan and stir. Crumble in the stock cube and simmer until the liquid has reduced by half. Remove the bay leaf and blend the mixture at maximum speed for a couple of minutes. Filter through a fine strainer, taste and add salt if required. Keep the sauce hot.

Clean, skin and gut the fish (the fishmonger will do this), then brush with olive oil, sprinkle with salt and place in a dish large enough to hold the fish. Surround with a sprig of rosemary, sage leaves, the remaining garlic and bay leaf. Put in the oven for about 30 minutes, moistening with the remaining white wine. Place the fish on a preheated serving dish and pour over some of the sauce. Serve the rest in a sauceboat.

CAPPE CHIONE ALLA MARINARA

Marine–style Clams

24 fresh clams	1 garlic clove
salt	3 tbspoons olive oil
1 bay leaf	2 egg yolks
8 white peppercorns	50 ml/2 fl oz/¼ cup
2–3 sprigs fresh parsley	whipping cream
1 small onion	

SERVES 6
PREP/COOKING: 40 MINS + 2 HRS SOAKING

Soak the clams in plenty of lightly salted cold water for a long time, frequently turning them and changing the water at least twice. Finally wash them well, one by one, under running water, placing them in a saucepan as they are done.

Cover them with cold water and add the bay leaf, peppercorns and almost all the parsley. Gradually bring to the boil, keeping the lid on but stirring from time to time. Take them off the heat, lift them out, rinse again in the cooking water if there is any trace of sand, and then keep them covered in a large deep serving dish.

Chop the onion and garlic finely and fry them gently in the oil, taking care not to brown them. Pour in the white wine and half a glass of the clams' cooking water strained through a cloth. Simmer for 5 or 6 minutes, then thicken with the egg yolks beaten together with the cream. Taste the sauce (which will be fairly runny), adjust the seasoning as you wish, pour it over the clams, sprinkle with chopped parsley and serve at once.

CARPACCIO DI TROTA

Carpaccio of Trout

200 g/7 oz tender lettuce
2 trout fillets,
  cleaned, about 550 g/
  1 1/4 lb
150 g/5 oz tomatoes
50 g/2 oz button mushroom
  caps
100 g/4 oz cucumber

FOR THE DRESSING
salt and pepper
4 tbspoons lemon juice
fresh chives
extra virgin olive oil

SERVES 4
PREP: 15 MINS + MARINATING

Carefully trim the lettuce and wash it in plenty of water, then drain and dry well. Make a bed of the leaves on a serving plate. Check that the trout fillets are perfectly clean then, using a very sharp knife, slice them very thinly, like smoked salmon. Arrange the slices on the bed of lettuce. Wash and dry the tomatoes and mushroom caps, and peel the cucumber. Dice all these vegetables very finely and sprinkle them over the fish.

To make the dressing, in a bowl, mix a pinch of salt with the lemon juice. Add a pinch of pepper, some snipped chives and 10 tablespoons of extra virgin olive oil. Whisk the dressing until very smooth and pour it over the carpaccio.

Cover the plate with cling film, put in a cool place and leave to marinate for about 30 minutes before serving it.

'Picaia' di merluzzo

Stuffed Cod

4 fresh cod fillets, weighing about 800 g/1 ¾ lb in all
salt and pepper
3 large garlic cloves
large bunch of fresh parsley
100 g/4 oz/¾ cup fine breadcrumbs
50 g/2 oz/½ cup grated Parmesan cheese
2 eggs
olive oil

SERVES 6–8
PREP/COOKING: 1½ HRS

Preheat the oven to 375°F/190°C/gas 5. Lightly beat the cod fillets and overlap them a little so as to form a rectangle with an even edge. Sprinkle with salt and pepper. Finely slice a large garlic clove and scatter over the cod. Wash and dry the parsley and chop it very finely together with the remaining garlic cloves. Place in a bowl. Add the breadcrumbs and Parmesan cheese, a pinch of salt and a generous sprinkling of freshly ground pepper. Mix well and add the eggs and 2 tablespoons of olive oil. Work into a smooth mixture and spread this evenly over the fish.

Using the blade of a long knife, raise the slab of fish, from the shorter edge, and roll it up tightly enough to keep the stuffing inside. Wrap the roll in a double sheet of oiled foil, sealing the ends and then. the upper edges. Tie up with kitchen string, as for a roast. Place the roll in a casserole that is just the right size and bake in the oven for about 45 minutes, carefully turning the roll from time to time.

Serve either hot by itself or cold with mayonnaise.

CEFALI CON CREMA DI MOLLUSCHI

Grey Mullet with Shellfish

350 g/12 oz mussels
250 g/8 oz clams
4 grey mullet, together weighing about 1 kg/2 lb
2 garlic cloves
a handful of fresh parsley
1 bay leaf
olive oil
1 small onion
150 ml/5 fl oz/^{2}/$_3$ cup sparkling white wine
a pinch of cornflour
^{1}/$_4$ fish stock cube
breadcrumbs
salt and pepper
1 sprig rosemary

SERVES 4
PREP/COOKING: 1 HR + 1 HR SOAKING

Scrape the mussel shells with a knife and then leave to soak in cold water for about 1 hour, together with the clams; discard any that do not open. Gut and clean the mullet if necessary, then rinse and dry thoroughly.

Place the mussels and clams in a pan with 2 lightly crushed garlic cloves, a few sprigs of parsley and a small bay leaf. Pour in 2 tablespoons of olive oil, cover the pan and heat gently to open the shells (discard any that do not open). Remove from the heat and leave to cool. Remove the molluscs from their shells and strain the juices.

Finely chop the onion and a small handful of parsley and fry gently in 4 tablespoons of olive oil. Add the molluscs and cook for a few minutes. Pour over half the sparkling wine and 4–5 tablespoons of the strained juices in which the cornflour has been dissolved. Season with the crumbled stock cube and simmer for a few minutes. Place in the blender and blend vigorously. Pour the blended shellfish back into the pan and keep hot.

Coat the mullet in breadcrumbs. Heat 5 tablespoons of olive oil and a sprig of rosemary in a pan and fry the mullet until golden brown on both sides. Sprinkle with salt and pepper and pour over the remaining sparkling wine. Allow the wine to evaporate, then transfer the fish to a warmed dish. Top with the creamed shellfish and serve at once.

TROTELLE RIPIENE, IN FORNO

Baked Stuffed Trout

4 trout, cleaned and gutted
butter for greasing
50 ml/2 fl oz/¼ cup
   white wine

FOR THE STUFFING
2 whiting, filleted
salt and pepper

50 ml/2 fl oz/¼ cup
   whipping cream
a small bunch of fresh
   parsley
1 egg
1 med. red pepper,
   seeded and diced
butter

SERVES 4
PREP/COOKING: 1 HR 10 MINS

Preheat the oven to 200°C/ 400°F/gas 6. Slit the trout open from top to bottom along the belly and the back then, with a sharp knife, fillet the fish without removing the heads, skin or tails. Using a needle and fine white thread, sew up the two fillets of each trout following the line of the belly, and sew up a small section of the back fillets, starting from the tail end. The trout should now have a large opening along their backs. Place the prepared trout on a plate, cover with cling film and chill in the refrigerator.

    To make the stuffing, purée the whiting flesh in a food processor and place in a bowl. Season with salt and pepper, then stir in the cream, some finely chopped parsley leaves and the egg. Blend again until smooth. Sweat the red pepper in a frying pan with a knob of butter, then add it to the stuffing.

    Take the trout out of the refrigerator and fill each one with about a quarter of the stuffing. Butter a baking dish and arrange them in one layer. Pour over the wine, cover with foil, and bake for about 35 minutes. Transfer the fish to a warm serving platter, garnish and serve.

UMIDO DI FRAGOLINI

Casserole of Baby Squid

1 kg/2¼ lb baby squid, cleaned and gutted	flour
olive oil	50 ml/2 fl oz/¼ cup full-bodied red wine
2 garlic cloves	1 x 400 g/14 oz tin chopped tomatoes
1 tbspoon capers	
dried oregano	1 small bunch fresh parsley

SERVES 4
PREP/COOKING: 1 HR

Wash the baby squid in cold water. Leave to drain and, in the meantime, heat 4 tablespoons of olive oil in a shallow pan. Crush the garlic and add it to the pan, together with the chopped, drained capers and a pinch of oregano. Add the well-drained fish, cook for a few minutes, stirring with a wooden spoon, then discard the garlic. Sift a tablespoon of flour over the mixture, mixing it in with a wooden spoon as you do so. Pour on the wine, let it evaporate, then add the chopped tomatoes. Bring to the boil, season and pour over a glass of boiling water.

Cover and cook over low heat for about 50 minutes. Sprinkle the dish with coarsely chopped parsley and serve piping hot.

TROTA AL CARTOCCIO VERDE

Trout in Green Jackets

2 trout, cleaned and gutted
salt and pepper
fresh dill
1 small bunch fresh parsley
sage leaves
1 bay leaf
large green lettuce leaves
extra virgin olive oil

SERVES 2
PREP/COOKING: 50 MINS

Wash and dry the fish, then season inside and out with salt and pepper and put a sprig of dill into each fish. Finely chop the parsley, about 10 sage leaves and the bay leaf, and scatter this mixture over the fish.

Wrap the fish in large lettuce leaves, and secure them with a few turns of thread. Lay the fish on the rack of a steamer, fill the bottom with simmering water and steam for about 30 minutes.

Remove the fish from the pan, untie the lettuce and place them on a serving plate. Drizzle over a trickle of olive oil and serve at once, piping hot.

MOSCARDINI AL VERDE

Baby Octopus in Green Sauce

800 g/1 ¾ lb baby octopus
olive oil
1 garlic clove
1 med. onion
white wine (optional)

1 small bunch fresh parsley
2 pearl or pickling onions
50 g/2 oz lettuce
juice of ½ lemon
1 tbspoon green olive paste

SERVES 4
PREP/COOKING: 45 MINS

Thoroughly clean the octopus then rinse them. Heat a pan of water and, when it starts to boil, toss in the octopus and cook for about 4 minutes. Lift them out with a slotted spoon and spread them out to dry on kitchen towels.

In a shallow pan, heat 4 tablespoons of oil. Finely chop the garlic and onion, place in the pan and add the octopus. Cover, lower the heat to moderate and cook, stirring frequently, for about 20 minutes, until the octopus are fairly dry. If the pan becomes too dry, moisten with a little water or white wine.

Meanwhile, wash, drain and finely chop the parsley leaves, the pearl onions and trimmed lettuce. Add this mixture to the octopus with the lemon juice and the olive paste. Stir and cook for about another 10 minutes. Transfer the octopus in sauce to a serving dish and serve immediately.

BIANCO DI PESCE AL VAPORE

Steamed Whiting

50 ml/2 fl oz/¼ cup
  dry white wine
1 shallot, peeled and halved
celery leaves
650 g/1 ½ lb whole whitings
1 tablespoon grated lemon
  rind

fresh thyme
fresh sage
lettuce leaves
salt and pepper
extra virgin olive oil

SERVES 4
PREP/COOKING: 1 HR

First prepare the cooking broth: put about 1½ litres/2½ pints/1½ quarts water, the wine, shallot and a few celery leaves into a fish kettle and bring to the boil.

Wash the whitings and place on the rack of the fish kettle over the by now boiling liquid. Season, then scatter on the lemon rind and a few thyme and sage leaves. Cover and steam the fish for about 30 minutes.

Take the fish kettle off the heat, place the fish on a platter and remove the skin, heads and bones. Flake the flesh, following the natural grain.

On a serving platter or individual plates, make a bed of well washed and dried lettuce leaves. Arrange the flaked fish on the lettuce, season, dress with a trickle of olive oil and serve sprinkled with a little lemon rind, some sprigs of thyme and one or two sage leaves.

SALMONE IN FILETTI, GRATINATO

Fillets of Salmon au Gratin

650 g/1 1/2 lb salmon fillets
100 ml/4 fl oz/1/2 cup dry white wine
fresh thyme
fresh marjoram
salt and pepper
olive oil

1 shallot
1 x 400 g/14 oz tin chopped tomatoes
6 slices white bread
1 small bunch fresh parsley

SERVES 6
PREP/COOKING: 1 HR + 2 HRS MARINATING

Wash the fillets, then remove any skin and lay them on a long, deep platter. Pour on the wine and cover thickly with sprigs of thyme and marjoram, season and leave to marinate for about 2 hours.

Preheat the oven to 190°C/375°F/gas 5. Transfer the marinated salmon fillets to a baking dish and strain and reserve the marinating liquid. Mix the liquid with 4 tablespoons of oil and pour over the fish. Cook in the oven for about 25 minutes.

Meanwhile, peel and finely chop the shallot and colour it lightly in 1 tablespoon of oil in a saucepan. Add the chopped tomatoes without their juice, season and cook over high heat for about 15 minutes until the mixture has reduced and thickened.

Crumb the bread in a blender. Take the salmon fillets out of the oven and sprinkle them with the breadcrumbs and a trickle of oil, then cook under a hot grill until the breadcrumbs have formed a golden crust. Transfer the fish to a warmed serving platter, scatter over some finely chopped parsley and pour over the sauce. Serve at once.

ORATE ALLA SENAPE

Sea Bream with Mustard Sauce

4 small sea bream, cleaned and gutted
salt and pepper
fresh basil
fresh rosemary
1 med onion
1/2 garlic clove

olive oil
150 ml/5 fl oz/2/3 cup dry white wine
a little light fish stock
50 g/2 oz/4 tbspoons wholegrain mustard

SERVES 4
PREP/COOKING: 40 MINS

Preheat the oven to 190°C/375°F/gas 5. Wash the fish, inside and out, and dry well. Season and place a few basil and rosemary leaves inside. Arrange the bream well spaced out in a flameproof baking dish. Finely chop the onion and garlic and sprinkle these over the fish. Moisten with a trickle of olive oil.

Cook in the preheated oven for 10 minutes, then baste the bream with the wine and a ladleful of stock. Cook for another 10 or 15 minutes, then take the baking dish out of the oven and remove the fish.

Put the baking dish on the hob, bring the cooking juices to the boil and stir in the mustard. Stir, simmering for 1 or 2 minutes, then pour the sauce over the bream and serve.

TROTELLE CON CARCIOFI

Trout with Artichokes

4 trout, cleaned and gutted	2 artichokes
fresh rosemary	lemon juice
fresh sage	2 med. onions
fresh parsley	1 carrot
salt and pepper	50 ml/2 fl oz/¼ cup
olive oil	dry white wine

SERVES 4
PREP/COOKING: 40 MINS

Preheat the oven to 200°C/400°F/gas 6. Wash the fish, inside and out, then dry with kitchen paper. Inside each fish, place a sprig of rosemary, a sage leaf and a parsley stalk. Season, then lay the trout in a baking dish, trickle over a little olive oil and cook in the oven for 10 minutes.

Trim the artichokes, removing the tough outer leaves and the spiny parts. Cut them in half and, if necessary, discard the chokes. Place the prepared artichokes in water acidulated with a little lemon juice. Peel the onions, trim, scrub and wash the carrot, then drain and dry the artichokes. Chop all the vegetables.

In a frying pan, heat 3 tablespoons of oil, put in the chopped vegetables and sweat over moderate heat until tender. Moisten with the wine, bring to the boil then, before it evaporates, briefly remove the trout from the oven and pour the mixture over them.

Return the baking dish to the oven and cook for a further 15 minutes. Serve the trout straight from the dish, with all the vegetables and herbs.

COZZE AI PISTILLI DI ZAFFERANO

Mussels with Saffron

1 1/5 kg/2 1/2 lb mussels
olive oil
1 garlic clove
1 small red chilli pepper, chopped
1 shallot
1 bay leaf

250 ml/8 fl oz/1 cup whipping cream
a small pinch of powdered saffron
1 teaspoon saffron strands, soaked for 10 minutes in a tbspoon of water
salt and pepper

SERVES 4
PREP/COOKING: 35 MINS

Scrub the mussels, remove the beards and any impurities from the shells, then wash thoroughly under running water. Discard any that are open. In a shallow pan, heat 3 tablespoons of oil with a halved and lightly crushed clove of garlic and the chilli pepper. Add the mussels, cover and set the pan over high heat until they open (discard any that do not open). When they have opened, take the pan off the heat and remove the top shell of each mussel, leaving them still attached to the half shell. Keep warm.

Meanwhile, strain any mussel liquor, return it to the heat, add the finely chopped shallot, bay leaf, cream and the powdered saffron. Cook this sauce, stirring with a wooden spoon, until thick and reduced by about half.

Now add the mussels, immersing them in the sauce. Add the saffron strands, cover and cook over high heat for 5 minutes. Season then divide the mussels between individual plates and serve.

TRANCI DI NASELLO AROMATICI

Aromatic Hake Steaks

550 g/1 1/4 lb hake steaks
3 slices white bread
1/2 tbspoon capers
fresh rosemary
fresh sage
celery leaves

2 anchovy fillets
green olive paste
olive oil
salt and pepper
50 g/2 oz/4 tbspoons butter

SERVES 4
PREP/COOKING: 35 MINS

Preheat the oven to 200°C/400°F/gas 6. Rinse the fish and dry carefully on kitchen towels.

Crumb the bread in a blender and transfer to a bowl. Drain and finely chop the capers, the leaves from a sprig of rosemary, a sage leaf, 3 celery leaves and the anchovy fillets and add these to the bowl. Stir, then add about 2 tablespoons olive paste, 3 tablespoons of olive oil and a pinch of salt and pepper. Stir to amalgamate all the ingredients properly, then coat the fish with the paste, pressing it down well to make sure the hake steaks are completely and uniformly covered.

Heat the butter in a large frying pan and brown the fish steaks on both sides, without cooking them through. Transfer the fish to a baking dish, spacing them out well, and finish cooking in the oven for about 10 minutes. Serve very hot.

BOCCONCINI DI MARE AL LIMONE

Light Seafood Stew with Lemon

---

3 salmon fillets
4 large cuttlefish or squid, about 350 g/12 oz
salt and pepper
250 g/8 oz king prawns/shrimp

1 shallot
olive oil
50 ml/2 fl oz/¼ cup dry Martini
rind of 1 lemon, chopped

SERVES 4
PREP/COOKING: 40 MINS

Wash and dry the salmon fillets and cut into bite-sized pieces. Clean the cuttlefish or squid, removing the ink sacs. Wash carefully and cut into thin strips. Wash the prawns, peel, and break off the heads. Peel and finely chop the shallot, and colour it in 3 tablespoons of oil. Add the cuttlefish or squid and cook over medium heat for about 5 minutes. Season and add the pieces of salmon and continue to cook for 6 or 7 minutes. Finally, add the prawns and cook all the seafood for another 5 minutes.

Before removing the mixture from the heat, add the Martini and the lemon rind. Pour the stew into a warmed serving dish. If you wish, garnish with slices of tomato and celery leaves. Serve immediately.

SFOGE IN SAOR

Soused Sole

800 g/1 ¾ lb sole, gutted and cleaned
flour
olive oil
salt
2 large onions, very thinly sliced

white wine vinegar
50 g/2 oz/½ cup pine nuts
50 g/2 oz/½ cup raisins
chopped fresh parsley

SERVES 4
PREP/COOKING: 45 MIN + MARINATING

To skin the sole, make small incisions at the head and tail on both sides of the fish. Lift up a flap of skin and pull it sharply towards you (if it is too slimy, grip it with a cloth). Turn over the sole and repeat on the other side. Dip the skinned sole in flour, shaking off the excess. Fry in deep hot oil until golden on both sides, then drain on a double thickness of kitchen towels. Season with salt.

Discard the frying oil and clean the frying pan to eliminate any burned bits. Pour in half a glass of fresh oil and soften the sliced onions, without letting them take on any colour. Add 2 tumblers of vinegar, simmer for 2–3 minutes, then turn off the heat and add the pine nuts and raisins. Arrange the sole in an earthenware dish and cover completely with the sousing liquid. Cover the dish with cling film and leave to marinate in the refrigerator for a day, or, better still, 48 hours.

Just before serving, sprinkle the dish with a pinch of chopped parsley, if you like.

ZUPPA DI SCORFANO E CANOCCHIE

Salmon and Prawn Stew

450 g/1 lb salmon fillets
250 g/8 oz cooked shelled prawns/shrimp
350 g/12 oz mussels
350 g/12 oz clams
olive oil
2 garlic cloves
fresh rosemary
1 med. onion
2 celery stalks
2 carrots
100 ml/4 fl oz/$^1/_2$ cup dry white wine

SERVES 6–8,
PREP/COOKING: 1 HR 20 MINS

Wash and dry the salmon fillets and prawns. Clean the mussels and clams, removing any beards or impurities and discarding any that are open. Put the mussels and clams in separate pans, each with 2 tablespoons of oil, a chopped garlic clove and a sprig of rosemary. Cook until they are open (discard any that do not open). Remove the mussels and clams from the two pans and filter the juices through a sieve to remove any residues.

Carefully trim and chop the onion, celery and carrots and sweat in a large saucepan with 3 tablespoons of oil until soft. Add 250 ml/8 fl oz/1 cup water and the wine and bring to the boil. Cut the salmon fillets into good-sized chunks and add to the broth. Cook over medium heat, turning them only occasionally, for about 5 minutes.

Carefully add in the prawns, mussels and clams and heat through for 5 minutes. Arrange in a suitable dish and serve immediately.

Grigliata di gamberoni al ragù di peperoni

Grilled Langoustines with Sweet Pepper Sauce

8 langoustines
salt and pepper
olive oil

FOR THE SAUCE
1 small onion

olive oil
1/2 each red and yellow pepper
50 g/2 oz/1/2 cup pine nuts
fresh basil

SERVES 4
PREP/COOKING: 30 MINS

Shell the langoustines, leaving the heads on, and arrange them on a plate. Season and moisten with a trickle of olive oil. Cover the plate with another inverted plate and leave to marinate in the refrigerator for about 15 minutes.

Meanwhile prepare the sauce. Peel and thinly slice the onion and sweat with 2 tablespoons of oil. Wash and seed the red and yellow peppers, remove the membrane and cut them into tiny dice. Add them to the pan with the onion and sauté over high heat for about 2 minutes. Season then add the pine kernels and a few washed and drained basil leaves, roughly torn with your hands. Cook, stirring, for about 1 minute, then put in the chopped tomatoes. Lower the heat, cover the pan and cook for about 10 minutes to reduce the sauce.

Heat the grill and, when it is searing hot, drain the langoustines and grill them for about 8 minutes, turning them over halfway through. As soon as they are ready, divide them between individual plates and serve piping hot, accompanied by the pepper sauce.

Trota salmonata al cartoccio
Salmon Trout 'En Papillotte'

300 g/10 oz mussels
olive oil
1 garlic clove
150 g/5 oz uncooked
    prawns/shrimp
1 shallot
1 x 200 g/7 oz tin chopped
    tomatoes

1 salmon trout, about
    1 kg/2¼ lb, cleaned and
    gutted
fresh sage
fresh mint
fresh rosemary
1 egg white

SERVES 6
PREP/COOKING: 45 MINS

Preheat the oven to 200°C/400°F/gas 6. Scrub the mussels and wash thoroughly. Discard any that are open. Put them in a pan with 2 tablespoons of olive oil and the chopped garlic clove. Cover and heat until the mussels have opened. Take the pan off the heat and remove the top mussel shells, leaving the mussels attached to the half shell. Strain any cooking juices into another pan and keep them warm.

Shell the shrimp, peel and dinely chop the shallot and sweat it in a shallow pan with 2 tablespoons of oil. Add the prawns and cook over high heat until browned all over, then season with salt and pepper and misten with the mussel juices. Bring to the boil, stir, then add the chopped tomatoes and simmer until the sauce is well thickened.

Meanwhile, wash, dry and fillet the fish, then lay the fillets side by side on a sheet of heavy baking parchment. Finely chop a few sage, mint and rosemary leaves and sprinkle them over the fillets. As soon as the prawn sauce is ready, pour it evenly over the fillets, then add the mussels on their half shells and season to taste. Place another sheet of parchment over the fish, brush the edges with egg white, and seal the packet lightly. Lightly oil a baking sheet and slide on the *papillotte*. Trickle over a little oil, then bake in the preheated oven for about 20 minutes. Transfer the *papillotte* to a suitable platter and serve.

Rombo gratinato

Gratin of Turbot

1 ½ kg/3 ½ lb turbot,
  gutted and cleaned
fish stock (see method)
100 g/4 oz sole fillets
75 ml/3 fl oz/⅓ cup
  whipping cream
salt and pepper
thyme
butter for greasing

FOR THE SAUCE
25 g/1 oz/¼ cup flour
25 g/1 oz/2 tbspoons butter
250 ml/8 fl oz/1 cup
  fish stock
salt
1 slice white bread made
  into breadcrumbs, and
  butter, for gratinating

SERVES 6
PREP/COOKING: 1 ½ HRS

Halve the turbot lengthways and fillet it. Cut the fillets into six equal slices. Use all the bones and head to make about 1 litre/1 ¾ pints of fish stock, and reserve it. Purée the sole fillets in a food processor and transfer to a bowl. Add the cream, a pinch of salt and pepper, and stir thoroughly. Preheat the oven to 200°C/400°F/gas 6. Sprinkle the slices of turbot with a pinch of thyme, then cover them with the sole mixture. Arrange in a well-buttered ovenproof dish, adding a ladleful of stock. Cover with foil and bake for about 10 minutes. Take the turbot out of the liquid, cover and set aside (all this can be done a day in advance).

Just before serving, prepare the sauce. Mix the flour and butter to a paste and whisk in the fish stock. Season with salt. Put the pan on the heat and simmer for 6–7 minutes, whisking continuously. Lay the turbot slices on a buttered ovenproof dish and sprinkle with the breadcrumbs. Dot with a little butter and place under the grill just to give the top a light golden colour. Serve hot, with the sauce.

FILETTI DI PESCE PERSICO FIORENTINA

Florentine-style Fillet of Perch

1 kg/2 lb fresh young spinach	200 ml/7 fl oz/1 cup milk
coarse cooking salt	1 garlic clove
50 g/2 oz/4 tbspoons butter	2 sage leaves
olive oil	16 small or 8 large fillets of perch, weighing about 1 kg/2 lb in all, divided in half lengthways
salt and pepper	breadcrumbs
nutmeg	parsley
flour	

SERVES 4
PREP/COOKING: 1¼ HOURS

Preheat the oven to 190°C/375°F/gas 5. Wash the spinach thoroughly under running water. Cook for about 5 minutes in an uncovered saucepan with only the water that remains on the leaves after washing and a little coarse cooking salt, until the leaves are tender. Drain the spinach and cool under running water. When it has cooled, squeeze it dry and chop it.

Heat half the butter and 2 tablespoons of olive oil in a large frying pan and, as soon as the fat is hot, put in the spinach and fry lightly. Sprinkle in a little flour and heat the milk before pouring that in too. Stir and simmer for a few seconds, then transfer the contents of the pan to a heatproof dish. Keep warm in the oven with the door open.

Flour the fish and shake them to remove any excess. Clean and dry the pan that was used for the spinach and melt the rest of the butter and 3 tablespoons of olive oil in it, flavouring with the lightly crushed garlic and the sage leaves. Fry the fish until golden brown and season with a little salt and a pinch of pepper.

Remove from the pan and arrange on the bed of spinach. Strain the juices in the pan and pour over the fish. Sprinkle lightly with breadcrumbs and bake for a couple of minutes. Serve garnished with parsley.

TROTE AL PANGRATTATO AROMATICO

Trout in Herbed Breadcrumbs

4 cleaned trout, about 250 g/8 oz each
2 large sprigs fresh rosemary
1 sprig fresh parsley
1 sprig fresh sage
1 garlic clove
4 slices fresh white bread
salt and pepper
juice of $1/2$ lemon
a little olive oil
lemon slices for garnish

SERVES 4
PREP/COOKING: 50 MINS

Wash and dry the trout on kitchen towels. Finely chop the leaves of 1 rosemary sprig, the parsley, 3 sage leaves and the garlic clove. Crumble the bread into breadcrumbs, then mix the breadcrumbs with the chopped herbs and place on a large plate or tray.

Preheat the oven to 190°C/375°F/gas 5. Slit the trout lengthways, remove the backbone, and open them out. Sprinkle the insides with a little salt and pepper. Rub with a little lemon juice and brush with a little olive oil.

Coat the fish thoroughly in the herbed breadcrumbs, place them on a lightly greased baking tray and cook in the oven for about 20 minutes or until golden brown. Arrange the trout on a warmed dish, garnish with parsley and slices of lemon, and serve immediately.

GIRANDOLE DI PESCI

Fish Whirls

1 x 100 g/4 oz slice red pepper, diced
25 g/1 oz/1/2 small onion, chopped
salt and pepper
fresh thyme
olive oil
100 g/4 oz button mushrooms
20 g/3/4 oz/1 1/2 tbspoons butter, plus extra for greasing
2 shallots
parsley
dry white wine
2 hard-boiled egg yolks
chervil
chives

3 egg whites
2 slices white bread, made into crumbs
8 very thin slices of monkfish, about 250 g/8 oz
8 small fillets of sole, about 200 g/7 oz
8 small slices of fresh salmon, about 200 g/7 oz
butter for greasing

FOR THE BRUNOISE
1 courgette/zucchini
1 small carrot
1 small leek
butter
salt

SERVES 4
PREP/COOKING: 45 MINS

Brown the diced pepper with the chopped onion, salt and a sprig of thyme in 1 tablespoon of oil. Cook for 15 minutes, then purée. Stew the mushrooms in the butter with a chopped shallot, parsley, salt, pepper and a dash of wine. Take off the heat and purée. Rub the hard-boiled egg yolks through a sieve and mix them with some chopped chervil, thyme, chives and salt and pepper. Bind each of these mixtures with an egg white, and add a slice of crumbed bread to the pepper and mushroom mixtures.

Preheat the oven to 180°C/350°F/gas 4. Spread the monkfish slices with the pepper mixture, the sole with flavoured egg, and the salmon with the mushroom mixture. Roll up each slice and secure with a cocktail stick. Arrange the fish whirls in a buttered baking dish and add a chopped shallot and half a glass of wine. Cook in the oven for about 8 minutes.

Meanwhile, cut the courgette, carrot and leek into very fine dice (brunoise). Soften in about 20 g/^{3}/$_4$ oz/1 ^{1}/$_2$ tablespoons butter and scatter them over the fish whirls as soon as these come out of the oven. Serve immediately.

Carpaccio caldo di pesce

Hot Fish Carpaccio

2 slices white bread
200 g/7 oz very thin slices of fresh salmon
200 g/7 oz very thin slices of swordfish
200 g/7 oz very thin slices of monkfish
salt and pepper
chopped fresh parsley and mint
butter

SERVES 4
PREP/COOKING: 15 MINS

In a food processor, reduce the bread to fine white crumbs. Arrange the slices of fish in a large oven-to-table dish, alternating according to the pinkness of the flesh. Season with salt and pepper and sprinkle with the breadcrumbs mixed with 1/2 tablespoon of chopped parsley and mint.

Dot with small flakes of butter and place under the grill for 2 minutes, then serve, garnishing the dish as you like.

Arrosto di Trota Salmonata

Baked Stuffed Salmon Trout

900 g/2 lb salmon trout
200 g/7 oz sole fillets
100 ml/4 fl oz/½ cup whipping cream
1 egg white
75 g/3 oz prawns/shrimp, cooked and shelled
25 g/1 oz shelled and skinned pistachios
olive oil

FOR THE SAUCE
500 g/1 lb mussels
1 garlic clove
olive oil
25 g/1 oz/¼ cup flour
50 g/2 oz/4 tbspoons butter
250 ml/8 fl oz/1 cup fish stock (see method)
1 shallot, chopped
½ glass dry white wine
2 egg yolks
50 ml/2 fl oz/¼ cup whipping cream

SERVES 8
PREP/COOKING: 2 HRS

Fillet the trout and keep the bones to make a stock. Purée the sole fillets in a food processor and place in a bowl. Work in the cream and egg white, and season with salt and pepper. When the mixture is smooth, add the prawns and chopped pistachios.

Preheat the oven to 200°C/400°F/gas 6. Brush a sheet of greaseproof paper with butter and lay the trout on it. Spread the sole mixture all over the trout. Cover with the second fillet, brush with melted butter and season with salt and pepper. Enclose the fish in the paper and tie the opening with several turns of string. Lay it in an ovenproof dish, trickle on a little oil and bake in the hot oven for about 40 minutes.

Meanwhile, make stock with the trout bones, appropriate vegetables and 700 ml/1 ¼ pints/3 cups water, then strain it. Scrub the mussels and remove any impurities; discard any that open. Open them in a tablespoon of very hot oil, flavoured with the garlic (discard any that do not open). Shell them and strain the juices. Make a sauce with 25 g/1 oz /2 tablespoons butter, the flour and 250 ml/8 fl oz/1 cup stock. Brown the shallot in the remaining butter, then add the mussels. Pour on the wine and 100 ml/4 fl oz/$1/2$ cup mussel juices. Reduce the sauce by half, stir it into the stock and thicken with the egg yolks and cream. Season to taste. Take the trout out of the oven, leave to rest for 10 minutes, coat with the sauce and serve.

TORTA DI TONNO

Tuna Tart

400 g/14 oz/3½ cups flour, plus extra for dusting
250 g/8 oz butter, softened and diced, plus extra for greasing
1 egg

FOR THE FILLING
450 g/1 lb potatoes
400 g/14 oz tomatoes
250 g/8 oz courgettes/zucchini
1 slice of fresh tuna (400 g/14 oz)
olive oil
freshly ground black pepper
a pinch of oregano
1 small bunch fresh parsley

SERVES 8
PREP/COOKING: 1½ HRS + RESTING THE PASTRY

Sift the flour on to a work surface and make a well. Put in a pinch of salt and butter. Incorporate the butter, then add the egg and knead a little, rolling it into a ball. Wrap in cling film and place in the refrigerator for 30 minutes.

Butter and flour a 25 cm/10 inch springform cake tin. Roll out the dough on the floured surface to about 3 mm/⅛ inch thick and use to line the tin, leaving enough overhanging to fold in to make a ring after the tin has been filled.

Peel the potatoes and cut the tomatoes and courgettes into rounds. Skin the tuna and cut into bite-sized pieces. Cover the base of the tin with about half the potatoes, then make an even layer of half the courgettes then the tomatoes. Trickle over a little olive oil.

Arrange the pieces of tuna on the tomatoes in a single layer. Continue to make layers of the vegetables, finishing with tomatoes. Season, and moisten with about 3 tablespoons of olive oil.

Fold the overhanging pastry inwards, pinch up the edges and bake in the oven preheated to 200°C/400°F/gas 6 for about 1 hour. Take the tart out of the oven, sprinkle with finely chopped parsley leaves and serve.

Pisci spata a ghiotta

Delicious Swordfish

25 g/1 oz/¼ cup raisins
flour
4 swordfish steaks, about
    550 g/1 ¼ lb
olive oil
salt and pepper
1 medium onion
2 garlic cloves
1 celery stalk

25 g/1 oz/¼ cup
    pine nuts
1 tablespoon capers
green olives
400 g/14 oz ripe but firm
    tomatoes, peeled and
    deseeded
2 bay leaves

SERVES 4
PREP/COOKING: 50 MINS

Soak the raisins in tepid water. Meanwhile, lightly flour the fish and fry in a pan of hot oil. Season with salt and pepper and, when the steaks are well browned, take them out of the pan and keep warm. Finely chop the onion with the garlic cloves and celery. Soften the vegetables in the oil you used for the fish, adding the pine nuts, the squeezed-out raisins, drained capers and a handful of olives. Brown the mixture well, then finally add the tomatoes. Season the sauce to taste, cover and cook over medium heat for about 10 minutes.

Preheat the oven to 200°C/400°F/gas 6. Arrange the swordfish in an ovenproof dish, coat it with the sauce, season again, and add the bay leaves. Add enough tepid water to cover the fish, then cook in the oven for about 15 minutes. Take the fish out of the oven as soon as it is ready and serve with fresh crusty bread.

PISCISTUOCCU A MISSINISA

Sicilian Dried Cod

1 kg/2¼ lb dried salt cod, already softened	50 g/2 oz capers
olive oil	100 g/4 oz courgette/zucchini sliced
1 med. onion, thinly sliced	50 g/2 oz carrot, sliced
400 g/14 oz chopped tomatoes	50 g/2 oz celery stalk, trimmed and cut into sticks
500 g/1 lb potatoes, sliced into rounds	black and cayenne pepper
100 g/4 oz black olives	salt

SERVES 6
PREP/COOKING: 2½ HRS

Remove any fish bones from the salt cod, then cut the fish into even pieces. In a heavy frying pan or terracotta casserole, soften the sliced onion in a little oil. Purée and strain half the tomatoes and add them to the pan with a glass of water. Cover and bring to the boil, then add the pieces of cod, sliced potatoes, olives, capers, courgette and carrot, the rest of the chopped tomatoes and finally the celery. Season with plenty of black pepper and a pinch of cayenne, cover and cook over medium heat for about 2 hours, adding a ladleful of hot water from time to time.

When the cod is cooked, taste it and add salt if necessary. Serve the dish very hot with its sauce (there should be plenty). Accompany the cod with crusty bread, sprinkled with a little olive oil, then toasted in the oven.

PESCATRICE AL ROSMARINO

Baked Monkfish with Rosemary

650 g/1 1/2 lb monkfish tail	olive oil
salt and pepper	100 ml/4 fl oz/1/2 cup dry white wine
fresh rosemary	1 small bunch fresh parsley

SERVES 6
PREP/COOKING: 40 MINS

Preheat the oven to 190°C/375°F/gas 5. Wash and dry the monkfish and place it in a flameproof baking dish. Season and add a few sprigs of rosemary. Moisten with 4 tablespoons of oil and the wine, then bake in the oven for about 25 minutes.

Meanwhile, finely chop the leaves from a branch of rosemary and the parsley. When the fish is cooked, take it out of the oven, remove from the baking dish and keep warm. Remove the sprigs of rosemary from the cooking juices, and put in the chopped herbs. Place the dish on the heat, bring the sauce to the boil and cook for about 2 minutes.

To serve, cut slices from the fish and place on a platter, accompanied by the sauce. If you wish, garnish with a few tender lettuce leaves, a sprig of rosemary and half a lemon, cut into a flower.

Dentice aromatico

Aromatic Sea Bream

*1 sea bream, about 1.2 kg/
   2½ lb
salt and pepper
chopped fresh herbs
   (thyme, sage, marjoram)
8 large lettuce leaves
100 g/4 oz unsmoked
   bacon rashers
8 anchovy fillets, chopped
olive oil
450 g/1 lb tomatoes
50 ml/2 fl oz/¼ cup dry
   white wine*

**SERVES 4
PREP/COOKING: 45 MINS**

Preheat the oven to 220°C/425°F/gas 7. Rinse the bream under running water, then dry by patting it with a double thickness of kitchen towel. Season inside and out with salt, then with a pinch of chopped herbs.

Blanch the lettuce leaves in boiling water. Refresh and lay out half on a tea-towel. Arrange half the bacon on top, then finally put on the sea bream. Cover the fish with the remaining bacon rashers and wrap it in the rest of the lettuce leaves, to make a green parcel.

Place the fish on a greased baking tray and scatter over the chopped anchovies, then trickle on a little olive oil. Put the baking tray in the preheated oven and cook for about 10 minutes.

Blanch the tomatoes, peel and dice then add to the fish as it cooks and sprinkle with the white wine. Season with salt and pepper. After about 20 minutes, remove the fish from the oven, drain it, place on a serving platter and keep warm. Rub the sauce through a vegetable mouli, then pour it over the fish.

Serve immediately.

MEAT

The *piatto di mezzo* or 'middle dish' is the Italian term for the central course of a full meal. Italian cooking is noted for its many ways with veal, but here are also recipes for beef, lamb (treated in Italy as a special-occasion dish), pork, poultry and game, a northern speciality. These dishes range from simple roasts to elaborate recipes with sumptuous sauces suitable for the grandest occasion.

POLPETTINE VELLUTATE

Very Smooth Rissoles

350 g/12 oz lean pork
100 g/4 oz veal
100 g/4 oz sausage
50 g/2 oz mortadella sausage
3 slices white bread soaked in stock
a handful of fresh parsley
1 garlic clove
lemon rind
1 large egg or 2 small ones
50 g/2 oz/1½ cup grated Parmesan cheese
salt and pepper
ground nutmeg
olive oil
breadcrumbs
75 g/3 oz/6 tbspoons butter
1 small onion
2 small pieces dried mushroom (porcini)
25 g/1 oz/¼ cup flour
600 ml/1 pint/2½ cups light stock
celery leaves

MAKES 16 RISSOLES.
PREP/COOKING: 1½ HRS

Mince the meats and the bread finely. Chop a handful of parsley with half a garlic clove and a piece of lemon rind, add to the meats, mix thoroughly with the egg and the Parmesan cheese, salt lightly and season with a little pepper and ground nutmeg.

Form into 16 rissoles, moistening your hands with a little olive oil. Press the rissoles in breadcrumbs, then arrange in a buttered casserole and sprinkle with 25 g/1 oz/2 tbsp melted butter. Leave in a cool place for about 10 minutes. Preheat the oven to 200°C/400°F/gas 6.

Chop the onion and soften it in the remaining butter in a small pan. Add the dried mushrooms and, after a few seconds, the sifted flour, stirring to prevent lumps from forming. Slowly add the hot stock and, still stirring, bring the sauce to the boil. Lower the heat and let it simmer for 15 minutes.

Put the rissoles in the hot oven and cook them for about 15 minutes. Cover with the strained sauce, sprinkle with the finely chopped celery leaves and serve them immediately.

GAROFOLATO DI BUE

Leg of Beef with Cloves

2 garlic cloves parsley marjoram 50 g/2 oz salt pork, cut into lardons 1 kg/2¼ lb leg of beef 40 g/1½ oz/3 tbspoons each carrot, celery and onion, chopped	75 g/3 oz raw ham olive oil salt and pepper 3 cloves, ground in a pestle and mortar nutmeg robust red wine 400 g/14 oz/1¾ cups tomato passata

SERVES 6–8
PREP/COOKING: 2½ HRS

Chop 1 garlic clove with the leaves from a bunch of parsley and marjoram. Roll the lardons in this mixture and insert them into the meat, then tie the beef up with kitchen thread.

In a flameproof casserole dish, make a bed of the chopped vegetables and the ham, chopped with a garlic clove and a few parsley leaves. Lay the meat on this bed, moisten with a trickle of oil and colour lightly over moderate heat. Season with salt and pepper, the ground cloves and a grating of nutmeg. When the meat is uniformly browned, moisten with a glass of wine and evaporate this over high heat. Add the tomato passata and enough cold water to cover the meat. Lower the heat, cover and continue to cook for about another 2 hours or until the meat is tender but not pulpy, and the sauce nicely thickened.

Remove from the heat and serve, cut into thick slices, with the sauce.

Filetto alla Pizzaiola

Roast Beef with Tomato and Garlic Sauce

1 large ripe tomato, weighing about 150 g/5 oz	50 g/2 oz Mozzarella cheese
olive oil	butter
1 garlic clove	350 g/12 oz fillet of beef, finely sliced
a few fresh basil leaves	
salt	

SERVES 4
PREP/COOKING: 20 MINS

Preheat the oven to 190°C/375°F/gas 5. Cut the tomato in half horizontally, remove the seeds and then dice. Heat 2 tablespoons of olive oil and fry the garlic. Add the tomato, basil leaves and a pinch of salt. Fry over high heat without overcooking. Dice the Mozzarella cheese. Liberally butter a baking tray and place the slices of beef on it, setting them well apart. Pour over a trickle of olive oil and place in the oven for about 2 minutes. The meat should remain almost pink.

Remove from the oven and sprinkle with the cubes of Mozzarella cheese and tomato. Reheat in the oven just long enough for the cheese to melt a little. Arrange the beef on individual warmed plates and serve at once.

Filetto con funghi e grana

Fillet of Beef with Mushrooms and Parmesan

---

100 g/4 oz roast lean fillet of beef cut into very thin slices
1 medium mushroom (preferably cep)
25 g/1 oz Parmesan cheese, flaked
celery leaves

½ garlic clove
anchovy paste
mild mustard
herb vinegar
salt and pepper
olive oil

SERVES 1
PREP: 20 MINS

Arrange the fillet slices in a ring on a plate which you have chilled in the refrigerator. Trim the mushroom and wipe it with a damp cloth. Cut into slices and arrange the best ones on the slices of meat, the others in the centre of the plate. Pile the flaked cheese on top and surround with the celery leaves.

Rub the bottom of a bowl lightly with half a garlic clove, put in 2 cm/¾ inch anchovy paste, a little mustard on the end of a teaspoon, 3–4 drops of herb vinegar and a pinch each of salt and pepper. Combine the ingredients with a fork and dilute with a tablespoon of olive oil. Pour this dressing over the slices of meat and serve.

Polpettoncino alle olive

Meatloaf with Olives

2 slices white bread
milk
400 g/14 oz minced beef
50 g/2 oz/1½ cup grated
 Parmesan cheese
1 egg

salt and pepper
nutmeg
4 stuffed olives
breadcrumbs
olive oil
frisée

SERVES 4–6
PREP/COOKING: 1 HR

Soak the 2 slices of bread in a little milk. Preheat the oven to 190°C/375°F/gas 5.

Squeeze the bread well then add it to the meat and mince both together. Place the mixture in a bowl, add the Parmesan cheese, the egg, a pinch of salt, a grinding of pepper and one of nutmeg. Mix well with a wooden spoon. The mixture should be rather firm. Shape it into a loaf about 17.5 cm/7 inches long, pressing the olives into the mixture.

Roll the meatloaf gently in the breadcrumbs to coat it, then place in a lightly oiled rectangular baking pan, sprinkle with a little olive oil and bake for about 35 minutes until the surface is lightly browned.

Remove the loaf from the oven and let it rest for about 10 minutes before cutting it into slices. Arrange on a serving dish and garnish with tender leaves of frisée.

'DELIZIE' CIPOLLATE, ALLA GRIGLIA

Grilled Meatballs with Onion

1 small onion	2 slices fresh white bread
1 garlic clove	cold beef stock
butter	350 g/12 oz minced beef
1 sprig fresh rosemary	salt and pepper
1 sage leaf	olive oil
a few young, fresh fennel leaves	breadcrumbs

SERVES 4
PREP/COOKING: ABOUT 1 1/4 HOURS

Preheat the oven to 200°C/400°F/gas 6. Finely chop the onion and garlic and fry gently in 25 g/1 oz/2 tablespoons of butter, taking care not to let them brown. Remove from the heat and place in a bowl to cool.

Meanwhile, chop the rosemary leaves together with the sage and a little fennel. Add the herbs to the cold onion. Soak the bread in the stock, then squeeze well and add to the bowl together with the minced beef, salt and pepper.

Combine all the ingredients together until smooth and make 16 equal-sized meatballs. Brush them all over with olive oil, then coat evenly with breadcrumbs.

Grill the meatballs quickly, turning them over once. Arrange them in a greased ovenproof dish, pour over a trickle of olive oil, then bake for 10–12 minutes or until they are cooked through. Serve on a bed of vegetables cooked in butter, garnished with fennel leaves.

CONTROFILETTO FREDDO, FARCITO

Stuffed Cold Beef

100 g/4 oz/2 med. stalks sliced celery
1 small pimiento
1 tbspoon capers
1 x 75g/3 oz jar artichoke in oil
thick mayonnaise
1 teaspoon mustard
24 thin slices cold roast beef
olive oil

SERVES 6
PREP: 30 MINS

Drain the celery, dry it carefully on kitchen towel and place it in a bowl. Drain and dry the pimiento in the same way, cut it into short, thin strips and mix it with the celery. Add the finely chopped capers and artichoke, cut into small pieces.

Bind the mixture with mayonnaise and fold in the mustard. Taste and adjust the seasonings.

Spread the slices of meat on a work surface and place some of the prepared mixture on each slice. Roll the meat up and arrange the rolls on a plate. Brush each roll with a very little olive oil and garnish as desired.

Serve with a fresh mixed green salad and a simple vinaigrette dressing.

'Fusello' d'autunno

Autumn Stew

2 large carrots
1 celery stalk, trimmed
1 small onion
1 large garlic clove
olive oil
50 g/2 oz/4 tbspoons butter
650 g/1 ½ lb stewing beef
flour
100 ml/4 fl oz/½ cup
    Marsala wine
1 litre/1 ¾ pints/1 quart
good meat stock

2 tbspoons concentrated
    tomato purée
1 bay leaf
2 red chillies
2 juniper berries, lightly
    crushed
1 clove
1 small piece cinnamon
    stick
250 g/8 oz baby onions
¼ stock cube
nutmeg

SERVES 4
PREP/COOKING: 3 HRS

Peel the carrots, cut them in half lengthways and cut them into 2½ cm/1 inch lengths. Then, using a small knife with a curved blade, pare the edges and chop the trimmings together with the celery, onion and garlic. Heat in a large shallow saucepan in 4 tablespoons of olive oil and 25 g/1 oz/2 tablespoons of butter. Fry gently over moderate heat. Remove and leave aside.

Cut the beef into large cubes, flour them and brown them in the pan, stirring occasionally with a wooden spoon. Pour in the Marsala and let it evaporate, keeping the heat moderate and the pan uncovered.

Boil the stock. When nearly all the Marsala has been absorbed in the other pan add the tomato purée and stir, then pour in the boiling stock. Turn the heat down to simmer. Put the bay leaf, chillies, juniper berries, clove and cinnamon in a small muslin bag, and add to the pan. Cover and simmer for about 2 hours, stirring from time to time and adding a little boiling water if necessary.

When the meat is half-cooked, heat a frying pan containing the rest of the butter and 1 teaspoon of olive oil. Put in the carrot mixture and the baby onions and fry gently for a few minutes. Pour in 150 ml/5 fl oz/^{2}/$_3$ cup of boiling water and crumble in the stock cube. Add a little grated nutmeg. Cover and cook over moderate heat until all the liquid has disappeared and the vegetables are tender. Add this to the stew 10 minutes before the end of cooking, stirring carefully. Serve with polenta.

Manzo al vino rosso

Beef in Red Wine Carbonade

800 g/1 ¾ lb braising beef flour
50 g/2 oz/4 tbspoons butter
1 large onion
600 ml/1 pint/2 ½ cups robust red wine
salt and pepper

SERVES 6
PREP/COOKING: 2 HRS

Trim the meat of any sinews and fat, then cut it into largish cubes. Coat the cubes of beef with flour and shake off the excess.
Melt the butter in a flameproof casserole and brown the meat. When it is well browned on all sides, take it out of the pan. Cut the onion into small pieces and brown it in the same casserole. Return the meat to the casserole, cover and cook over very low heat for about 1 ¾ hours, adding the wine a little at a time, and stirring frequently so that the meat does not stick to the bottom of the casserole dish. Season with a pinch of pepper and a good handful of salt (originally this recipe was made with beef preserved in salt).

Apart from salt and pepper, you could season the 'carbonade' with a pinch of aromatic herbs and a little sugar; the strong taste of the wine can be diluted with a ladleful of boiling stock; or substitute bitter beer for the wine (as they do in the Belgian version of this dish), or, failing that, add vinegar to the cooking liquid.

Serve the beef straight from the casserole, accompanied by some steaming polenta, cooked slowly in a copper cauldron, or lightly puréed potatoes.

Filetto di Manzo ai Funghi

Fillet of Beef with Mushrooms

50 g/2 oz onion
70 g/2½ oz pancetta
olive oil
fresh sage
fresh rosemary
1⅕ kg/2½ lb beef fillet
10 large cultivated
  mushrooms

juice of ½ lemon
salt and pepper
dry white wine
50 ml/2 fl oz/¼ cup
  whipping cream

SERVES 8–10
PREP/COOKING: 1 HR

Preheat the oven to 220°C/425°F/gas 7. Peel and chop the onion and place in a roasting pan. Dice the pancetta and add it, together with 4 tablespoons oil and a small bunch of sage and rosemary. Place the casserole over high heat and soften all the contents, then add the beef and colour it evenly all over, turning it with a fork but taking care not to pierce it (so that the juices do not run out).

Meanwhile peel and halve the mushrooms. Add them to the well-browned beef and sprinkle them with the lemon juice. Season with salt and pepper and cook in the hot oven for about 20 minutes, or longer depending on how you like your meat cooked; it should still be more or less rare when served. Baste the meat frequently with its cooking juices and half a glass of wine during cooking.

When the beef is cooked to your liking, drain it, place on a serving dish and keep warm. Discard the aromatic herbs, then place the roasting pan on the heat. Add the cream, allow the sauce to thicken slightly, then season the beef with salt.

Serve immediately, with a selection of steamed and crisp green vegetables.

BRASATO AL BAROLO

Braised Beef in Barolo

1 kg/2¼ lb boned shin of beef in one piece	bouquet garni (parsley, sage, bay leaf, rosemary)
2 carrots, scraped and cut into large chunks	peppercorns
	salt
2 med. onions, each stuck with 2 cloves	ground cinnamon
	nutmeg
2 garlic cloves	1 x 75 cl bottle of Barolo
1 celery stalk, cut into lengths	25 g/1 oz/2 tbspoons butter
	brandy

SERVES 6
PREP/COOKING: 5 HRS + MARINATING

Put the meat in a bowl with the carrots, onions, whole garlic cloves, celery, bouquet garni, 5–6 peppercorns, a pinch each of salt and cinnamon and a grating of nutmeg. Pour on the wine, cover the bowl and leave to marinate in a cool place for at least 6 hours (overnight is better).

To cook the braised beef, drain the meat from the marinade. Heat the butter in a flameproof casserole, put in the beef and brown it carefully over high heat. Sprinkle with a small glass of brandy and flame it. As soon as the alcohol has evaporated, add the vegetables and the strained wine from the marinade. Cover the casserole and cook over very low heat for about 4 hours, or until the meat is very tender.

Just before the end of cooking, pass the sauce, including the bouquet garni, through a vegetable mouli back over the beef. Cook for a further 10 minutes, then serve the beef in thick slices, very hot with its sauce and puréed potatoes or polenta, whichever you prefer.

TAPULON

Braised Beef with Cabbage and Barbera

40 g/1 1/2 oz salt pork
40 g/1 1/2 oz/3 tbspoons butter
olive oil
3 garlic cloves, crushed
2 bay leaves
450 g/1 lb savoy cabbage
600 g/1 1/4 lb braising beef

fennel seeds
1 teaspoon ground cloves
peppercorns
1 glass of Barbera wine
hot beef stock
salt

SERVES 4
PREP/COOKING: 1 HR

Sweat the beaten salt pork with the butter and 2 tablespoons of oil in a large saucepan. Add the crushed garlic cloves and bay leaves and brown them. Shred the cabbage, cut the meat into 5 cm/2 inch cubes and add them to the pan. Mix, season with a pinch of fennel seeds, the ground cloves and a grinding of pepper, and brown the cubes of meat over high heat until it is very dry and completely sealed.

Moisten with a glass of Barbera and, when this has evaporated, add a ladleful of hot stock. Taste, add salt if necessary, then cover the pan and cook over medium heat for about 1 1/2–2 hours, or until the meat is tender. Check from time to time to make sure that the meat does not dry out too much; add a ladleful of hot stock if it does. The 'tapulon' should be neither too dry nor too moist. Serve it immediately.

STRACOTTO DI STINCO DI MANZO SPEZIATO

Braised Beef Shank

900 g/2 lb boned beef shank	100 g/4 oz/1 large onion, peeled
600 ml/1 pint/2½ cups robust red wine	olive oil
cinnamon, sticks and ground peppercorns	flour
6 cloves	salt and pepper
	hot stock

SERVES 6
PREP/COOKING: 2¼ HRS + MARINATING

Cut the meat into cubes, trim off any sinews and fat and place in a bowl. Pour in the wine and add 2 cinnamon sticks, ½ tablespoon peppercorns and 6 cloves. Cover the bowl with cling film and leave to marinate in a cool place for about 12 hours.

When you are ready to cook the meat, roughly chop the onion, place in a casserole with 3 tablespoons oil, and soften. Drain the meat from the marinade and remove any peppercorns sticking to it. Lightly flour the meat, then brown the pieces in the casserole with the onion, turning them to colour on all sides. Season with a pinch each of salt, pepper and ground cinnamon. Strain the marinade and pour it into the pan with the meat, then add 3 ladles of hot stock. Cover and cook over very moderate heat for about 2 hours, or until the meat is tender. If the sauce seems too liquid at the end of cooking, increase the heat and reduce it. If it seems too thick, dilute it with a little more stock.

Serve the beef very hot, straight from the casserole, accompanied by some steaming polenta or lightly puréed potatoes, whichever you prefer.

Filetti di manzo su crostini

Fillet of Beef on Croûtons

4 slices white bread
4 slices of beef fillet, about 450 g/1 lb
olive oil
salt and pepper
1 shallot, finely chopped

3 pickled gherkins
mustard
100 ml/4 fl oz/1½ cup whipping cream
beef stock

SERVES 4
PREP/COOKING: 30 MINS

Using a 5 cm/2 inch round pastry cutter, cut out four circles of bread, then toast them lightly in the oven or under the grill.

Gently bat out the beef into four even medallions. In a frying pan, heat 2 tablespoons oil, then brown the meat for about 1½ minutes on each side. Season with salt and pepper and keep warm. In the same pan, and in the meat juices, soften the chopped shallot. Add the gherkins, cut into rounds, and 2 teaspoons mustard. Finally, add the cream and half a ladle of stock. Stir with a wooden spoon and cook until the sauce has thickened.

Lay the beef medallions on the croûtons, arrange on a serving plate, coat with the sauce and serve. Some crunchy green beans and a mixed leaf salad go well with this dish.

Medaglioni di carne con i carciofi

Meat Patties with Artichokes

2 fresh artichokes
a little lemon juice
1 small onion, finely
  chopped
1 small garlic clove, finely
  chopped
1 sprig fresh parsley,
  chopped
olive oil
150 ml/5 fl oz/2/3 cup
  dry white wine
100 ml/4 fl oz/1/2 cup
  meat stock
a pinch of thyme

50 g/2 oz/4 tbspoons
  butter
1/2 beef stock cube
2 slices white bread, soaked
  in milk
200 g/8 oz ground beef
100 g/4 oz ham
25 g/1 oz/1/4 cup grated
  Parmesan cheese
1 egg
ground nutmeg
flour
1 sprig fresh sage

SERVES 4
PREP/COOKING: 1 HR

Top and tail the artichokes and remove the tough outer leaves. Cut them in half lengthways, scoop out and discard the chokes. Place the artichokes in a bowl of water with the lemon juice. Sauté about one-third of the onion, the garlic and the parsley in 3 tablespoons of oil. Drain the artichokes, cut into small pieces and add to the pan. Cook gently for a few minutes then add half the wine. When it has been absorbed, add the boiling stock. Season with salt, pepper and thyme. Cover, lower the heat and cook for about 15 minutes.

Meanwhile sauté the remaining onion in a tablespoon of butter. Blend in the crumbled stock cube. Drain the bread and process it in a food processor with the beef and ham. Place in a bowl and add the sautéed onion, grated cheese, egg and a little pepper and nutmeg.

Blend thoroughly and divide into four patties. Coat in flour.

Heat the remaining butter, 2 tablespoons of oil and 2 sage leaves and fry the patties over low heat until browned on both sides. Add the remaining wine and cook until the liquid has reduced by about two-thirds. Serve topped with the artichokes.

POLPETTINE SAPORITE AL VINO ROSSO

Meatballs in Red Wine

300 g/10 oz boneless beef
70 g/2½ oz raw ham
4 slices white bread, soaked in milk
1 tbspoon grated Parmesan cheese
chopped parsley
salt and pepper
flour
50 g/2 oz onion
25 g/1 oz celery
25 g/1 oz carrot
4 tbspoons olive oil
1 bay leaf
1 clove
fresh sage
200 ml/7 fl oz/1 cup robust red wine
350 g/12 oz chopped tomatoes
hot beef stock

SERVES 6
PREP/COOKING: ABOUT 1½ HOURS

Pass the beef and ham through a mincer and place in a bowl. Squeeze out the bread and add it, together with the Parmesan cheese, a pinch of chopped parsley, and salt and pepper to taste. Amalgamate the mixture and form it into balls, flattening them slightly. Roll in a little flour.

Chop together the onion, celery and carrot; soften the chopped vegetables in the oil with the bay leaf, clove and a small bunch of sage. Add the meatballs, brown them over high heat, then moisten with the wine. When this has partially evaporated, add the chopped tomatoes and half a ladleful of hot stock. Reduce the heat, cover and cook the meatballs for about 50 minutes.

Serve hot, accompanied by a potato purée and a green vegetable, such as spinach or broccoli.

Punta di Maiale alle Verze

Breast of Pork with Cabbage

1 garlic clove
chopped mixed herbs (sage, rosemary, parsley)
salt and pepper
900 g/2 lb breast of pork
70 g/2½ oz onion, chopped
olive oil

300 ml/½ pint/1¼ cups dry white wine
900 g/2 lb savoy cabbage
hot chicken stock
100 g/4 oz/½ cup tomato passata
2 bay leaves

SERVES 8
PREP/COOKING: 2 HRS 20 MINS

Preheat the oven to 200°C/400°F/gas 6. Finely chop the garlic and mix it with 2 tablespoons chopped herbs. Season with salt and pepper, then rub this mixture liberally over the meat. Roll it up and tie like a rolled roast with kitchen thread. Place the meat in a roasting pan just large enough to hold it and the chopped onion, moisten with a trickle of oil, then roast in the hot oven for about 1 hour 20 minutes, basting the meat from time to time with the wine.

Meanwhile, trim the cabbage and pull off the leaves; boil for 2 minutes in salted water. Drain and add to the meat after the stated cooking time; cover with foil and return to the oven for about another 30 minutes.

Drain the meat, transfer to a serving plate and keep warm. Add a ladleful of hot stock, the tomato passata and bay leaves to the cooking juices, place over moderate heat and cook for about 15 minutes.

Partially slice the meat, coat generously with the sauce and serve with the cabbage.

BRACIOLE DI MAIALE ALL'ACETO BALSAMICO

Pork Chops with Balsamic Vinegar

6 pork chops, each weighing about 175 g/6 oz
2 tbspoons mild mustard
flour
1 sprig fresh sage
1 garlic clove
butter
olive oil

100 ml/4 fl oz/1/2 cup dry white wine
1/2 chicken stock cube
1 tbspoon balsamic vinegar
a few sprigs fresh parsley for garnish

SERVES 6
PREP/COOKING: 40 MINS

Remove excess fat from the chops, then beat them lightly, taking care not to split the meat. Put the mustard in a bowl and coat the chops with it on both sides. Then coat them with flour, shaking them gently to remove any excess.

Finely chop 2 sage leaves and the garlic. Melt 25 g/1 oz/2 tablespoons butter with 3 tablespoons of oil in a large frying pan and soften the sage and garlic gently, taking care not to brown them. Now put the chops in the pan and allow them to cook and brown. Moisten them with the white wine. Then add the crumbled half stock cube.

When the meat has absorbed almost all the wine, moisten it with the balsamic vinegar and keep the pan on the heat for a few moments more. Serve very hot, garnished with fresh parsley.

Costolette di Maiale all'Uva

Pork Chops with Grapes

48 perfectly ripe green
  grapes
4 pork chops
a little flour
butter
olive oil
1/2 bay leaf

50 ml/2 fl oz/1/4 cup
  dry white wine
a piece of chicken stock
  cube
50 ml/2 fl oz/1/4 cup
  brandy

SERVES 4
PREP/COOKING: 1 HR

Using a short, sharp knife, peel and pip the grapes if necessary. Remove any sinews and membranes from the chops. Beat the chops lightly and flour them all over, shaking off any excess.

Heat 25 g/1 oz/2 tablespoons butter and 1 tablespoon oil in a large frying pan and flavour with the bay leaf. Put the chops into the hot fat and brown on both sides, turning them over without piercing them. Splash over a little white wine from time to time.

When the wine has almost entirely evaporated, put in the grapes. Turn up the heat, crumble in the piece of stock cube and shake the frying pan frequently from side to side to allow all the chops to absorb the flavour. Pour in the brandy and set it alight.

Finally, arrange the chops on a serving dish with the grapes on one side, together with the sauce from the pan. Serve at once.

INVOLTINI DI FEGATO E MAIALE

Pork and Liver Roulades

1 small onion
1 garlic clove
butter
150 g/5 oz calves' liver
25 g/1 oz capers
1 teaspoon anchovy paste
1 tbspoon breadcrumbs

salt and pepper
16 thin slices of pork fillet, weighing about 450 g/1 lb
flour
100 ml/4 fl oz/1½ cup dry white wine

SERVES 4
PREP/COOKING: 45 MINS

Chop the onion finely together with the garlic and fry in a knob of butter. Chop the liver and place in a bowl. Add the fried onions, thoroughly drain and chop the capers and add these, mix in a heaped teaspoon of anchovy paste and a heaped tablespoon of breadcrumbs. Add salt and pepper and mix thoroughly.

Beat the slices of pork as thinly as possible and spread a little of the liver mixture on one side of each piece. Roll up the meat, sealing the stuffing well inside and tie up with kitchen thread like a small parcel. Flour the roulades, shaking off any excess.

Melt a knob of butter in a frying pan and fry the roulades, browning them well on all sides. Add very little salt, then pour over the wine. Shake the pan vigorously to prevent the meat from sticking to the bottom, then cover. The wine will evaporate leaving a delicious sauce. Serve hot, with boiled new potatoes and a green vegetable.

Costolette di Maiale all'Origano

Pork Cutlets with Oregano

4 pork cutlets, each weighing 150 g/5 oz
flour
olive oil
butter
1 garlic clove
1 sprig fresh basil
1 tbspoon spiced white wine vinegar
50 ml/2 fl oz/¼ cup dry white wine
1 x 250 g/8 oz tomatoes, puréed
½ chicken stock cube
pepper
oregano
2 tbspoons capers, well drained

SERVES 4
PREP/COOKING: 40 MINS

Remove any tendons and sinews from the cutlets, then beat them lightly. Coat them one at a time in the flour, shaking off any excess.

Put 2 tablespoons of oil and the butter in a frying pan wide enough to contain the cutlets in a single layer. Heat the fats with the lightly crushed garlic clove and the basil; remove the flavourings when they have browned. Arrange the cutlets in the pan and brown them over vigorous heat. Moisten them with the vinegar, then add the white wine. Cook until the liquid is reduced by two-thirds.

Add the tomatoes, season with the crumbled stock cube and a grinding of pepper, flavour with a pinch of oregano and sprinkle over the capers. Shake the pan to prevent the sauce sticking and reduce it, turning the cutlets once only.

Arrange on a hot serving dish, pour over the sauce and garnish according to taste. Serve immediately.

ARISTA DI MAIALE IN CROSTA DI PANE

Loin of Pork in a Bread Crust

1.4 kg/3 lb loin of pork
300 g/10 oz cooked ham, thinly sliced
chopped fresh sage
chopped fresh parsley
salt and pepper
olive oil
900 g/2 lb bread dough (can be made from a packet)

2 eggs
20 g/³⁄₄ oz/3 tbspoons grated Parmesan cheese
50 g/2 oz/4 tbspoons butter
25 g/1 oz toasted flaked almonds

SERVES 12
PREP/COOKING: 2¹⁄₂ HRS

Preheat the oven to 200°C/400°F/gas 6. Using a long, very sharp knife, make deep vertical and horizontal cuts in the meat and open it up into a rectangle. Cover the rectangle with one-third of the ham slices, then roll up the meat to make a roast, and tie with several turns of kitchen thread. Place in a roasting pan, season generously with the chopped herbs and salt and pepper, and trickle on some olive oil. Roast in the hot oven for 50 minutes. Remove and set aside to cool.

Meanwhile, put the bread dough in the bowl of an electric mixer. Add 1 egg, the Parmesan cheese and 3 tablespoons oil. Knead slowly with the dough hook to make a smooth, elastic dough. Leave to rise in a warm place until the pork is completely cooked. Roll out the dough to make a rectangle slightly larger than the meat.

Chop the remaining ham, then mix with the butter to make a mousse. When the meat is cooked and cold, cut off the thread, roll out the dough to a thickness of 1 cm/¹⁄₂ inch and lay the meat on the dough. Spread the meat and dough with the ham mousse, then roll up the dough and brush with beaten egg. Preheat the oven to

190°C/375°F/gas 5. Place the roll on a baking tray lined with baking parchment. Form the pastry trimmings into a plait and lay it on the roll. Brush again with egg and sprinkle with almonds. Bake in the oven for about 40 minutes, or until the dough is cooked and golden.

Involtini di Lonza

Pork Sausage Parcels

1 aubergine/eggplant
12 slices wide pork sausage
100 g/4 oz Provola cheese
oil for frying
12 fresh basil leaves
2 anchovy fillets in oil, broken up
flour

olive oil
butter
1 small onion, sliced
3 tbspoons Marsala wine
100 ml/4 fl oz/½ cup chicken stock
salt and pepper

SERVES 6
PREP/COOKING: 1¼ HRS

Peel the aubergine and cut it into 12 equal slices about 3mm/⅛ inch thick. Arrange the slices on a tilted plate, sprinkle with salt and leave for about 30 minutes for the juices to drain off.

Lightly beat the slices of sausage with a meat mallet. Cut the Provola cheese into 12 equal pieces. Rinse the slices of aubergine under running water, drain and dry them. Fry them in plenty of oil, then drain thoroughly.

Arrange the slices of sausage on a tray, keeping them well apart from each other, and place a slice of aubergine on each side of sausages. Place a leaf of fresh basil, a piece of Provola cheese and a small piece of anchovy fillet one on top of the other in the centre of each piece of aubergine. Roll the meat tightly around the other ingredients and secure with kitchen thread. Coat the parcels in flour.

Heat 3 tablespoons olive oil and a large knob of butter in a large frying pan. Add the sliced onion, discarding it as soon as it has browned. Fry the parcels until golden brown. Pour in the Marsala wine and the boiling stock. Season with salt and pepper and cook until the liquid has reduced to form a thick sauce. Remove from the heat, discard the kitchen thread from the parcels and serve immediately.

POLPETTINE AL POMODORO

Rissoles with Tomato Sauce

2 slices white bread, soaked in milk	ground nutmeg
450 g/1 lb sausage meat	olive oil
100 g/4 oz ham, diced	1 med. onion
75 g/3 oz/¾ cup grated Parmesan cheese	1 garlic clove
2 eggs	450 g/1 lb firm ripe tomatoes
salt and pepper	5–6 fresh basil leaves
	sugar

SERVES 6
PREP/COOKING: 1¼ HRS

Drain the bread and mince with the sausage meat and ham. Place the minced mixture in a bowl and stir in the grated Parmesan cheese, the eggs, a pinch of salt and pepper and a little ground nutmeg. Mix thoroughly to form a smooth paste. Make 24 rissoles from the mixture, shaping them with your hands, and place them on an oiled baking pan. Sprinkle with a little oil and leave to stand in a cool place for at least 15 minutes.

Meanwhile finely slice the onion and fry it gently with the lightly crushed garlic clove in 4 tablespoons of oil. Stir in the coarsely chopped tomatoes, a few basil leaves, a little salt and pepper and a pinch of sugar. Bring slowly to the boil and then lower the heat, half-cover the pan and cook for about 15 minutes, stirring occasionally.

Preheat the oven to 200°C/400°F/gas 6. Process the sauce in a liquidiser and pour it back into the pan. Test and adjust the seasoning according to taste. Bake the rissoles in the oven for 12–13 minutes, transfer to the sauce in the pan and cook gently for a further 4–5 minutes. Place in a warmed dish, garnish with fresh basil and serve.

COTECHINO IN GALERA

Cotechino in a Galley

1 cotechino (fresh pork sausage, salted and spiced), about 600 g/ 1 1/4 lb	40 g/1 1/2 oz/1/2 med. onion
	olive oil
	chicken stock
1 large slice of leg of pork. 300 g/10 oz	dry Lambrusco wine
	salt
270 g/7 oz sliced raw ham	

SERVES 6–8
PREP/COOKING: 2 1/4 HRS

Prick the cotechino in several places with a toothpick, put it in a pan of cold water and cook over medium heat until half-cooked. Drain and remove the skin.

Cover the pork with the slices of ham and lay the cooled cotechino in the centre. Roll it up in the meat and tie up the roll with kitchen thread.

Chop the onion and soften it in 2 tablespoons oil. Add the meat roll, but do not let it colour. Pour in a mixture of equal quantities of stock and wine sufficient to cover the meat. Salt lightly, cover the pan and cook over medium heat for 1 hour.

To serve, cut off the thread and cut the roll into quite thick rounds. Transfer to a serving dish with the very hot sauce and serve with puréed potatoes.

COTECHINO IN SALSA CON VERDURE

Cotechino in Béchamel Sauce with Vegetables

2 cotechino sausages
150 g/5 oz/1 med. leek
100 g/4 oz/2 med. carrot
100 g/4 oz/2 med. celery
150 g/5 oz mushrooms
olive oil
vegetable or chicken stock
salt

FOR THE BECHAMEL
SAUCE
25 g/1 oz/2 tbspoons butter
25 g/1 oz/4 tbspoons flour
300 ml/1/2 pint/1 1/4 cups
   hot milk
salt
3 egg yolks

SERVES 6
PREP/COOKING: 2 HRS

Prick the cotechino in several places with a toothpick, place in a pan of cold water and cook over very moderate heat for about 1 1/2 hours. (You can even do this a day in advance.)

To serve the cotechino, trim and wash the leek and cut into rounds. Scrape the carrot and slice it; peel the celery and cut into thin strips. Trim the mushrooms to remove any dirt, wash, drain and slice thinly. Sweat the leek, carrot and celery in the butter and 1 tablespoon oil. When they are lightly browned, add the mushrooms and soften all the vegetables, adding a small ladleful of stock. Season with a little salt.

Meanwhile, make the béchamel. Make a roux with the butter and flour, then stir in the hot milk. Cook over moderate heat for about 5 minutes, then remove from the heat, season with salt and thicken with the egg yolks.

Remove the skin from the cooked cotechino and cut into rounds. Spread the vegetables over the bottom of an ovenproof serving dish. Arrange the cotechino rounds on top, then cover thickly with the béchamel. Place under a hot grill for a couple of minutes, to brown the dish. Serve immediately.

AGNELLO E CARCIOFI IN UMIDO

Lamb and Artichoke Stew

800 g/1 ¾ lb boned leg of lamb
1 med. onion
2 garlic cloves
1 sprig fresh sage
butter
olive oil
100 ml/4 fl oz/½ cup Marsala wine
250 g/8 oz tomatoes, peeled and finely chopped
150 ml/5 fl oz/⅔ cup meat stock
1 teaspoon cornflour
1 lemon
3 med. artichokes
a few sprigs fresh parsley
a pinch of ground thyme

SERVES 6
PREP/COOKING: 2 HRS

Cut the lamb into small pieces. Finely chop two-thirds of the onion, a garlic clove and 2 sage leaves and fry them in 2 tablespoons of butter and 2 tablespoons oil. Add the lamb and cook for at least 5 minutes, stirring frequently. Add the wine and cook until it has been absorbed, shaking the pan occasionally. Stir in the tomatoes and the cold stock in which the cornflour has been dissolved. Add a small piece of lemon rind, a pinch of salt. Cover and cook for 1 ¼ hours, adding stock if necessary.

Meanwhile, cut off the stalks and tips of the artichokes, remove the tough outer leaves and place the artichokes in a bowl of water with the juice of half the lemon. Thinly slice the remaining onion, finely chop the garlic clove and a small handful of parsley, and sauté them in the remaining butter and 2 tablespoons oil.

Discard the chokes from the artichokes, and cut each into six pieces. Add to the pan. After a few minutes stir in 150 ml/5 fl oz/⅔ cup boiling water, a little salt and thyme. Cover and cook the artichokes over moderate heat until *al dente*. When the meat has been cooking for about 1 hour, add the artichokes. Pour into a serving dish. Serve immediately.

STUFADIN DI AGNELLO

Braised Lamb

20 g/¾ oz dried mushrooms (porcini)
1½ kg/3½ lb boned lamb
1 large onion
50 g/2 oz/4 tbspoons butter
olive oil
1 celery stalk, cut into even pieces
1 large carrot, scraped, washed and cut into small chunks
salt and pepper
dry white wine

SERVES 6
PREP/COOKING: 2½ HRS

Soften the mushrooms in tepid water. Remove any sinews and skin from the lamb, then cut the meat into even pieces. Peel and chop the onion and soften in a casserole with the butter and a tablespoon of oil Add the pieces of lamb and brown them, then add the mushrooms, celery and carrot. Season with salt and plenty of pepper, cover and cook gently over the lowest possible heat for about 2 hours.

Towards the end of cooking, take the lamb out of the liquid and add half a glass of wine to the sauce. When this has evaporated, serve the lamb, straight from the casserole if you wish. Polenta makes a particularly good accompaniment to this dish.

Spezzatino di Agnello, Fiorito

Lamb Stew with Flowers

800g/1 ¾ lb boned leg or shoulder of lamb
150 ml/5 fl oz/⅔ cup dry white wine
2 large sage leaves
1 sprig rosemary
2 garlic cloves
butter
olive oil
1 small onion
100 ml/4 fl oz/½ cup Marsala wine
petals of 7–8 edible white daisies (optional)
1 piece lemon rind
150 ml/5 fl oz/⅔ cup meat stock
250 g/8 oz tomatoes, skinned
salt and pepper
1 teaspoon cornflour
extra fresh daisy petals

SERVES 4–6
PREP/COOKING: 1 ½ HRS + OVERNIGHT MARINATING

Dice the lamb into 4 cm/1 ½ inch cubes. Put in a bowl and pour over the wine. Add the sage, rosemary and 1 crushed garlic clove. Cover the bowl with cling film and leave to marinate overnight in a cool place.

The following day, remove the lamb from the marinade and pat it dry on kitchen towels. Heat 25 g/1 oz/2 tablespoons of butter and 2 tablespoons of oil in a large frying pan and finely chop the onion together with the remaining garlic clove. Fry these without browning them, put in the meat cubes and lightly brown them all over. Pour over the Marsala and let it reduce almost completely. Then put in the daisy petals and a piece of lemon rind, which should later be discarded.

After a few minutes, pour over the boiling stock and purée the tomatoes before adding them too. Stir and season. Dissolve the cornflour in 3 tablespoons of cold water and stir into the pan. Simmer the stew for about 1 hour, adding a little more boiling stock if necessary.

Serve on a warm dish, garnished with daisy petals.

CIBREO DI REGAGLIE

Chicken Livers with Egg and Lemon

400 g/14 oz chicken livers
25 g/1 oz/2 tbspoons butter
chicken stock
salt and pepper
3 eggs
white flour
juice of 1/2 lemon

SERVES 4
PREP/COOKING: 45 MINS

Clean the livers, eliminating any greenish spots. (If you get your chicken livers from a butcher and can get them, the cockscombs can be used in this recipe too.) Toss the livers into boiling water for 2 minutes, then drain. If you are using the cockscombs, they should be boiled with the chicken livers then skinned and chopped. Coarsely chop the livers, keeping them separate. Melt the butter, add the cockscombs, if you are using them, and when they are lightly browned, moisten with a glass of stock. Cover and cook over moderate heat for about 30 minutes, then add the chopped livers. Season with salt and pepper and cook for a few minutes more.

Meanwhile, beat the eggs with a teaspoon of flour, the lemon juice and a small ladleful of hot stock, adding the stock a little at a time so that the eggs do not curdle.

Take the livers and cockscombs off the heat, mix in the eggs to thicken slightly, and serve.

FEGATO AGLI AROMI

Liver with Herbs

4 large slices calves' liver, together weighing 350 g/ 12 oz
2 fresh sage leaves
½ sprig rosemary
a bunch of fresh parsley
a handful of fresh basil
salt and pepper
2 slices fresh white bread
butter
olive oil

SERVES 4
PREP/COOKING: 30 MINS

Remove the thin membrane and any nerves from the slices of liver. Finely chop together 2 sage leaves, the rosemary sprig, a small bunch of parsley and 4 basil leaves; put the chopped mixture in a bowl and add a generous grinding of pepper. Crumble bread finely and mix with the herbs. Spread the mixture over a plate and roll the slices of liver in it, one by one, coating them as evenly as possible and shaking off any excess.

Heat 25 g/1 oz/2 tablespoons of butter and 3 tablespoons oil in a large frying pan and when hot put in the liver slices; brown and cook them on both sides, adding salt only when the meat is cooked. While they are cooking, do not prick the slices of liver but turn them carefully with a spatula.

Finally arrange them on a serving dish and serve immediately, garnishing them with a few parsley sprigs and more fresh basil leaves.

Animelle di Vitello ai Funghi

Sweetbreads with Mushroom Sauce

2–3 dried cep mushrooms	1 garlic clove
450 g/1 lb calves' sweet breads	a little parsley
salt	olive oil
juice of 1 lemon	4 tablespoons Marsala wine
50 g/2 oz/4 tbspoons butter	a piece of chicken stock cube
breadcrumbs	thyme
100 g/4 oz fresh mushrooms	100 ml/4 fl oz/½ cup single cream
1 small onion	½ teaspoon cornflour

SERVES 4
PREP/COOKING: ABOUT 1½ HRS

Soak the dried mushrooms in cold water for about 1 hour. Wash the sweetbreads and simmer them for about 20 minutes in a saucepan of lightly salted boiling water to which 2 tablespoons of strained lemon juice have been added. Remove from the water with a slotted spoon and place in a bowl of cold water. When they are cool enough to handle, remove the membrane, veins and any nerves. When the sweetbreads are completely cold, remove from the water and drain thoroughly. Dry, and cut into fairly thick slices.

Melt half the butter and brush the slices of sweetbread with this. Then coat them evenly with breadcrumbs, shaking off any excess.

Trim and wash the fresh mushrooms. Finely chop the onion with the garlic, and a few parsley leaves. Heat 3 tablespoons of oil in a frying pan and gently fry this mixture until the onion is lightly coloured. Then drain the dried mushrooms thoroughly, setting aside the water in which they soaked, and finely chop before adding these to the frying pan too. Finely slice the fresh mushrooms and add them to the other ingredients after a short time. Fry for a few minutes, then pour in 4 tablespoons of water from the dried mushrooms and the Marsala. Crumble in a piece of stock cube and add a pinch of thyme. Simmer until the liquid has reduced by at least two-thirds before dissolving the cornflour in the cream and adding this to the sauce. Stir in and simmer gently for a few minutes.

Meanwhile, fry the slices of sweetbread in the rest of the butter and a tablespoon of olive oil until golden brown on both sides. Sprinkle with salt when they are cooked. Arrange on a warmed serving dish and pour over the mushroom sauce. Sprinkle with a little chopped parsley and serve.

Rognoncino ai funghi

Kidney With Mushrooms

1 slice bread
butter
1 large mushroom cap
  (preferably cep)
olive oil
½ garlic clove
100 g/4 oz calves' kidney,
  fat removed, thinly sliced

flour
50 ml/2 fl oz/¼ cup meat
  stock
1 tbspoon whipping
  cream
chopped parsley

SERVES 1
PREP/COOKING: 20 MINS

Preheat the oven to 200°C/400°F/gas 6. Remove the crust from the bread; brush with 2 teaspoons of melted butter, then brown it in the oven for 3–4 minutes. Divide it into four triangles, lay them on a plate and keep hot.

Wipe the mushroom cap with a damp cloth and slice it. Heat a small frying pan with a knob of butter, half a tablespoon of oil and half a garlic clove (which you then discard). Put the kidney and mushroom in the pan and brown them lightly over high heat for a couple of minutes.

In another frying pan melt the remaining butter, mix in a little flour, then moisten with the hot stock. Bring to the boil, stirring all the time, then add the kidney and the mushroom cream and keep over a very low heat for 2–3 minutes, taste and adjust the seasoning if necessary.

To serve, spoon on to a warmed plate, sprinkle with a pinch of chopped parsley and garnish with the four croûton triangles.

FEGATO DI VITELLO ALL' AGRODOLCE

Sweet and Sour Calves' Liver

6 slices calves' liver
50 g/2 oz/4 tbspoons butter
1 sprig fresh sage
salt
1 tbspoon pine nuts
10 capers
1 macaroon biscuit
1 dry biscuit (zweiback)
1 teaspoon white wine vinegar
juice of 1/2 lemon
4–5 tbspoons chicken stock
mild mustard
a little flour
olive oil
1/2 garlic clove
a little chopped parsley

SERVES 6
PREP/COOKING: 40 MINS

Trim the slices of liver, removing membrane and tendons but reserving the scraps.

Heat a small frying pan with 25 g/1 oz/2 tablespoons butter and a small sage leaf. As soon as it is hot, add the scraps of liver, brown them lightly, then put them with the other contents of the pan into a mortar. Add a large pinch of salt, the pine nuts, capers, macaroon, dry biscuit and the vinegar. Pound to a pulp, adding the strained lemon juice.

Put the mixture into a small saucepan, dilute with the boiling stock and flavour with the mustard. Bring to the boil over low heat, stirring all the time, then taste and adjust the seasoning. Keep warm.

Flour the liver slices, shaking to remove any excess. Melt the remaining butter and 3 tablespoons of oil, flavoured with 2 sage leaves and half a garlic clove, in a frying pan that will just hold the liver. Brown the liver slices lightly on both sides until they are cooked through (about 3–5 minutes).

Salt them after cooking, then arrange them in a dish. Pour over the sauce, sprinkle over some parsley and serve.

Cosciotto di Capriolo 'Alpestre'

Venison Alpine-style

1 haunch or leg of venison, well hung	2 large onions
	about 100 g/4 oz butter
1 carrot	25 g/1 oz flour
1 celery stalk	at least 450 ml/3/4 pint/
1 sprig fresh rosemary	2 cups good meat stock
3–4 fresh sage leaves	1 teaspoon sugar
1 bay leaf	olive oil
2 garlic cloves	salt and pepper
100 ml/4 fl oz/1 1/2 cup white wine vinegar	

SERVES 6
PREP/COOKING: 2 HRS + 24 HRS MARINATING

Wash and dry the venison, then remove the bone. Sew the meat up and arrange in a dish. Slice the carrot and celery and place around the meat, with the chopped rosemary and sage leaves. Put in a bay leaf and add the garlic cloves, crushed. Pour in the vinegar and cover the dish. Leave to marinate for 24 hours, turning the haunch three or four times.

The next day slice the onions and fry in 50 g/2 oz/4 tablespoons of butter in a saucepan. Mix 25 g/1 oz/2 tablespoons of butter with an equal amount of flour and, when the onions begin to brown, stir this in. Mix and fry for a few seconds, then stir in 150 ml/5 fl oz/2/3 cup of boiling stock. Mix well and add the sugar. Cook the gravy for a few minutes.

Heat the remaining butter with 3 tablespoons of oil in a frying pan. Remove the venison from the marinade, dry and flour it all over and seat it in the hot fat. Carefully drain it and place it in the onion sauce. Add salt and pepper and pour in 150 ml/5 fl oz/2/3 cup of boiling stock. Cover and cook over low heat for about 1 1/2 hours, adding more boiling stock if necessary. Remove the meat from the saucepan. Blend the juices and pass them through a fine strainer. Serve the meat hot, with the sauce.

Lombo di capriolo in umido

Venison Stew

3–4 shallots
1 sprig fresh rosemary
100 g/4 oz streaky raw ham
100 g/4 oz butter
12 venison loin chops
50 ml/2 fl oz/¼ cup red wine vinegar
100 ml/4 fl oz/½ cup robust red wine

1 litre/1¾ pints/1 quart good meat stock
2–3 juniper berries
1 clove
1 piece cinnamon stick
1 bay leaf
meat extract
25 g/1 oz/¼ cup flour
2 tbspoons Marsala wine

SERVES 6
PREP/COOKING: 1¾ HRS

Finely chop the shallots together with the rosemary leaves and the ham and put in a saucepan. Add about half the butter and fry gently for a few seconds without browning. Add the venison chops and brown gently. Turn them over carefully with a fork, without pricking the surface. Pour over the vinegar and allow it to evaporate almost entirely before pouring in the wine. When that in turn has completely evaporated, pour in about 600 ml/1 pint/2½ cups of boiling stock. Add the juniper berries, clove, cinnamon, bay leaf and ½ teaspoon of meat extract. Cover the pan and simmer for about 1 hour, diluting with more stock if necessary.

Meanwhile prepare a sauce by heating the rest of the butter and incorporating the flour with a wooden spoon. Pour in 300 ml/½ pint/1¼ cups of boiling stock gradually, as if for a béchamel sauce. Remove the juniper berries, clove, bay leaf and cinnamon from the stew and pour the sauce into the stew. Shake the pan so that the sauce blends well with the meat juices, then put in the Marsala wine and simmer for a further 20 minutes.

Serve hot, with polenta or potatoes.

Coniglio al forno, con verdure

Baked Rabbit with Vegetables

4–6 rabbit pieces, about 800 g/1 3/4 lb	2 large garlic cloves
olive oil	1 sprig fresh sage
1 bay leaf	1 chicken stock cube
1 small onion	salt and pepper
1 small carrot	300 ml/1/2 pint/1 1/4 cups dry white wine
1 small celery stalk plus a few leaves for garnish	2 teaspoons cornflour
50 g/2 oz/4 tbspoons butter	parsley

SERVES 4
PREP/COOKING: 1 3/4 HRS

Put the rabbit pieces into a greased large frying pan, and add half a bay leaf. Cover the pan, put it over low heat and draw out some of the moisture from the meat. Drain well and leave to dry on a plate covered with a double sheet of kitchen towel. Preheat the oven to 200°C/400°F/gas 6.

Slice the onion very thinly and cut the carrot and the celery into thin rounds. Mix these vegetables together and put them in the bottom of a small buttered baking pan just large enough to contain the rabbit pieces. Add the large garlic cloves, lightly crushed, and 2 or 3 sage leaves. Pack the pieces of rabbit closely on top of the vegetables and season with the crumbled stock cube and a generous grinding of pepper. Moisten with the white wine in which you have dissolved the cornflour, then dot with the remaining butter cut into small pieces.

Seal the pan with foil, and bake in the oven for 1 hour or a little longer, until the rabbit is tender and the gravy reduced. Serve sprinkled with chopped parsley and garnished with a few celery leaves.

Coniglio ripieno al forno

Roast Stuffed Rabbit

1 rabbit, complete with its offal (liver, lungs, heart)
salt and pepper
olive oil
1 garlic clove
1 small onion
a bunch of aromatic herbs (basil, bay leaf, rosemary)

450 g/1 lb vermicelli
25 g/1 oz/¼ cup grated Pecorino cheese
100 g/4 oz Mozzarella cheese, diced

SERVES 6
PREP/COOKING: 1 HR 40 MINS

Preheat the oven to 180°C/350°F/gas 4. Wash and dry the rabbit and season inside and out with salt and pepper. Wash the liver, lungs and heart and cut into small pieces. Chop the garlic and onion and soften in a tablespoon of oil, then put in the offal pieces and brown them. Add the bunch of herbs, season with salt and pepper and cook until tender.

Cook the vermicelli in plenty of boiling salted water until it is *al dente*, drain, then toss in the onion mixture to flavour. Season with the Pecorino and diced Mozzarella cheeses and salt and pepper. Twirl small portions of pasta round a fork and stuff the rabbit with these. Sew up the opening, lay the rabbit in a roasting pan and trickle over a little olive oil. Roast in the preheated oven for about 1 hour 10 minutes.

When the rabbit is cooked, cut it into thick slices with a very sharp knife, and serve with a fresh salad or with baby vegetables roasted in the oven.

ROTOLO DI CONIGLIO CON CAPPERI

Rolled Roast Rabbit with Capers

1 rabbit, weighing about 1¼ kg/3 lb
salt and pepper
2 plump chicken legs
3 slices white bread, soaked in milk
50 g/2 oz green olives, stoned and chopped
1 tbspoon capers, drained
1 egg
a bunch of sage
a bunch of rosemary
1 garlic clove
olive oil
dry white wine

SERVES 6–8
PREP/COOKING: 1½ HRS

Preheat the oven to 200°C/400°F/gas 6. Wash and dry the rabbit thoroughly and then, using a pointed, very sharp knife, bone it completely, taking care not to pierce the flesh; you should end up with a regular rectangular shape. Season with salt and pepper. Bone the chicken legs, remove the skin, then pass both the chicken and the well-squeezed bread through a mincer and transfer to a bowl. Mix in the olives, capers, egg, and season with salt and pepper.

Spread the rabbit flesh with this stuffing, then roll it up like a rolled roast. Tie with several turns of kitchen thread and lay in a roasting pan. Add a bunch of sage and rosemary, the garlic clove and 4 tablespoons oil. Roast in the hot oven for about 1 hour, basting the meat from time to time with its cooking juices and a little wine (about half a glass will be enough).

When the rabbit is cooked, remove the thread and slice the roll. Degrease and strain the sauce and serve it and the rabbit hot, accompanied by roast potatoes, if you wish.

Coniglio al limone

Rabbit with Lemon

1 rabbit, weighing about 1 1/2 kg/3 1/2 lb
100 g/4 oz leek
2 shallots
olive oil
1 sprig of thyme
salt and pepper
dry white wine
juice of 2 lemons

SERVES 6
PREP/COOKING: 1 HR

Wash the rabbit thoroughly and cut into even pieces. Dry with kitchen paper.

Trim and peel the leek and slice it with the shallots. Soften the vegetables in 3 tablespoons oil, then add the rabbit pieces. Brown well over high heat, then flavour with the thyme, a pinch each of salt and pepper and a glass of wine. Cover, reduce the heat and cook for about 30 minutes. Add the lemon juice and cook for a further 20 minutes or so.

When the rabbit is tender, transfer to a serving dish and serve hot, coated with the strained sauce.

PICCIONI ALLA PERUGINA

Pigeon, Perugia-style

4 pigeons
100 g/4 oz sliced raw ham
1 onion
cloves

3 bay leaves
olive oil
hot chicken stock
vinegar

SERVES 4
PREP/COOKING: 1 HR

Singe the pigeons by passing them quickly over a high flame to burn off any remaining feathers or wing tips. Wrap the birds in the slices of ham. Stud the onion with 3–4 cloves, halve it and place in a flameproof casserole. Add the bay leaves and a pinch each of salt and pepper, pour over 4 tablespoons oil, then place on the heat and brown the onion before adding the pigeons. Brown them evenly, then add a ladleful of hot stock and reduce it. Add half a glass of vinegar, then reduce the heat to the minimum, cover the casserole with a very tight-fitting lid to seal it almost hermetically, and cook the pigeons for about 50 minutes. They should be tender but not mushy.

Serve hot, with the strained cooking juices.

Lepre alla trentina

Hare, Trento-style

1 hare, about 1 1/2 kg/ 3 1/2 lb	vinegar
2 litres/3 1/2 pints/2 quarts red wine	cloves
rosemary	1 teaspoon sugar
sage	a pinch of ground cinnamon
bay leaves	olive oil
juniper berries, crushed	50 g/2 oz salt pork
1 onion	flour
lemon rind	breadcrumbs
	chicken stock

SERVES 6
PREP/COOKING: 2 HRS + MARINATING

Clean the hare and reserve the offal. Joint the hare and marinate it for 48 hours in two-thirds of the wine, the herbs, bay leaves, juniper berries, 1/2 onion, lemon rind and vinegar. In another bowl, marinate the offal in the remaining wine with lemon rind, cloves, sugar and cinnamon.

Drain the hare pieces and roll them in flour and breadcrumbs, shaking off any excess. Strain the marinade. Chop the salt pork and brown it in a tablespoon of oil with the rest of the onion and the hare. When they are well-coloured, add the chopped offal and a glass of stock. Season with salt and pepper and cook over medium heat, moistening with a little strained wine, for about 50 minutes – 1 hour or until the hare pieces are cooked through and tender.

Serve hot, with the pan juices.

FAGIANO AL PORTO E MASCARPONE

Pheasant with Port and Mascarpone

pheasant, about 900 g/2 lb
500 ml/18 fl oz/2½ dry
  white wine
peppercorns
salt
2 bay leaves
150 g/5 oz onion

olive oil
2 chicken livers
200 ml/7 fl oz/scant 1 cup
  port
200 ml/7 fl oz/scant 1 cup
  chicken stock
75 g/3 oz mascarpone

SERVES 4
PREP/COOKING: 1 HR + OVERNIGHT MARINATING

The night before, clean, wash and dry the pheasant and place in a bowl. Pour over the white wine, add a tablespoon of peppercorns, cover and leave in a cool place to marinate overnight.

To cook the pheasant: drain it well, reserving the strained marinade liquid, salt it lightly inside and put the bay leaves in the cavity. Tie up the bird with several turns of thread to prevent it from falling apart during cooking.

Peel and finely chop the onion and brown it in a casserole with 4 tablespoons oil. Add the pheasant and colour it well on all sides. Trim the chicken livers, discarding any membrane, then add to the casserole. Pour in the port and half the reserved marinade liquid, reduce by half, then add the stock. Melt the mascarpone into the cooking liquid, cover, lower the heat and cook gently for about 1 hour. Check the pheasant from time to time, basting it with a little sauce each time. If it dries out too much, add a few more ladles of stock.

When the pheasant is cooked, remove the bay leaves and purée the sauce in a blender. Serve the pheasant, carved into slices, with the very hot sauce.

POLLO ALLA CONTADINA

Country-style Chicken

100 g/4 oz mushrooms	1 bay leaf
100 g/4 oz baby onions	200 ml/7 fl oz/scant 1 cup
1 chicken, weighing about	dry white wine
1 kg/2¼ lb	2 tbspoons Marsala wine
flour	1 teaspoon tomato purée
butter	1 chicken stock cube
olive oil	

SERVES 4
PREP/COOKING: ABOUT 45 MINS

Peel the mushrooms and wash them well; also wash and peel the onions. Divide the chicken into eight pieces. Flour them, shaking off any excess, then brown them in a large frying pan in 25 g/1 oz/2 tablespoons butter and 2 tablespoons oil. Add the onions and the quartered mushrooms, flavour with a bay leaf, then fry them for a few moments.

Pour in the white wine and Marsala, in which you have dissolved the tomato purée and the stock cube. Stir the mixture and cover the pan. Cook over a moderate heat for about 30 minutes.

Serve hot, with a selection of vegetables.

POLLO ALLA COPPA, GRATINATO

Chicken with Ham au Gratin

50 g/1 1/2 lb chicken meat, skinned and boned
flour
75 g/3 oz/6 tbspoons butter
salt and pepper
150 ml/5 fl oz/2/3 cup dry white wine
50 g/2 oz thinly sliced raw ham
1 teaspoon chopped fresh parsley
25 g/1 oz/1/4 cup grated Parmesan cheese
150 ml/5 fl oz/2/3 cup milk
nutmeg

SERVES 6
PREP/COOKING: 1 1/4 HRS

Cut the chicken (preferably leg and thigh meat) into pieces about 6 cm/2 1/2 inches long. Flour lightly shaking off any excess and brown on all sides in 50 g/2 oz/4 tablespoons of the butter, adding salt and pepper. Pour in the wine and allow to evaporate over high heat. Shake the pan to prevent the meat from sticking.

Cut the ham into short thin strips. Remove from the heat and cut the chicken pieces into short but thicker strips and arrange, alternating with the ham, in a large buttered, ovenproof dish. Sprinkle the chopped parsley and Parmesan cheese over the meat.

Preheat the oven to 200°C/400°F gas 6. Make a béchamel sauce by melting the remaining butter in a pan, stirring in 25 g/1 oz/2 tablespoons of flour and adding the milk; season with salt and grated nutmeg. Pour the sauce over the meat and bake for about 20 minutes, until the surface is golden brown. Serve immediately.

COSCE DI POLLO AL GINEPRO

Chicken Legs with Juniper

butter
1 large onion
salt and pepper
4 chicken legs, together weighing about 1 kg/ 2½ lb
1 bay leaf

olive oil
4 juniper berries
small glass gin
200 ml/7 fl oz/1 cup dry white wine
1 teaspoon cornflour

SERVES 4
PREP/COOKING: 50 MINS

Preheat the oven to 200°C/400°F/gas 6. Butter the base of a casserole dish capable of holding the chicken legs in a single layer. Slice the onion very thinly and place half of it in the bottom of the dish. Season with salt and pepper and place the chicken legs on top, putting the bay leaf between them. Scatter the remaining onion over the top, moisten with the oil, and season with salt and pepper and the juniper berries, broken into small pieces.

Cook in the oven for about 40 minutes. After 15 minutes, pour over the gin, then the white wine in which you have dissolved the cornflour. Finish cooking, basting often, but without turning.

Serve hot, with crusty bread.

FUSI DI POLLO FARCITI

Stuffed Chicken Drumsticks

6 chicken drumsticks
3 sprigs fresh sage
1 garlic clove
3–4 slices smoked bacon
1 small onion
1 small carrot
1 small celery stalk
olive oil

butter
salt and pepper
50 ml/2 fl oz/1/4 cup dry white wine
150 ml/5 fl oz/2/3 cup chicken stock
1/2 tablespoon cornflour

SERVES 6
PREP/COOKING: 1 1/2 HRS

Preheat the oven to 200°C/400°F/gas 6. Rinse and dry the chicken drumsticks. Slit the skin, take out the bones and remove the sinews, turning the meat inside out, without cutting it up. Then push the meat back into shape and insert half a small sprig of fresh sage, a thin strip of garlic clove and a sliver of smoked bacon into each boned drumstick. Stitch up the opening on the drumstick. Cover the base of a flameproof dish with the finely chopped onion, carrot and celery. Arrange the drumsticks on top. Finally, add 2 tablespoons oil, dot with butter and season lightly with salt and pepper.

Bake in the preheated oven for about 45 minutes; turn the drumsticks a couple of times and, halfway through the cooking time, add the dry white wine. Remove the drumsticks from the dish, place the dish on top of the stove and add the stock, with half a tablespoon of cornflour dissolved in it; allow the sauce to simmer for a few minutes, stirring it constantly.

Strain the gravy over the drumsticks and serve. Arrange them, if you like, on top of buttered peas, with a little parsley for garnish.

PETTI DI POLLO FARCITI E DORATI

Stuffed Chicken Breasts in Breadcrumbs

6 chicken breasts
12 thin bacon slices
1 sprig fresh sage
1 garlic clove
75 g/3 oz/¾ cup grated
　Parmesan cheese
2 eggs plus 2 yolks
salt
breadcrumbs
butter

flour
100 ml/4 fl oz/½ cup milk
½ chicken stock cube
50 g/2 oz/½ cup grated
　Emmental cheese
50 ml/2 fl oz/¼ cup single
　cream
nutmeg
pepper
olive oil

SERVES 6
PREP/COOKING: 1 HR

Beat the chicken breasts lightly. Place 2 slices of bacon on one side of each breast, a small leaf of sage and a sliver of garlic, then close them up into their original shape. Roll them first in the Parmesan cheese, then in two of the beaten eggs, lightly salted, and finally in the breadcrumbs, making sure that they are thoroughly coated each time. Trim the edges using a large knife, then lay the chicken breasts on a tray.

Melt 25 g/1 oz/2 tablespoons butter in a small saucepan, add the flour and stir with a wooden spoon. Slowly pour in the cold milk and bring the mixture to the boil, stirring continuously, and season with the crumbled stock cube. Remove the sauce from the heat, mix in the Emmental, the egg yolks and the cream, mixing well after each addition. Season the sauce with a pinch of ground nutmeg and pepper, then keep warm.

Heat two frying pans, and in each one put a knob of butter, 4 tablespoons oil and 2 sage leaves. As soon as the fat is hot, fry the breaded chicken breasts. Remove them from the frying pans and lay them on a plate covered with kitchen paper to drain. Transfer to a warm serving dish, garnish to taste, pour the prepared sauce over them and serve at once.

Petti di pollo al marsala, con funghi

Chicken Breasts with Mushrooms in Marsala

350 g/12 oz small mushrooms	salt and pepper
1 small onion	150 ml/5 fl oz/2/3 cup Marsala wine
6 chicken breasts	1/2 teaspoon tomato purée
50 g/2 oz/4 tbspoons butter	1 garlic clove
olive oil	meat extract
flour	a little chopped parsley

SERVES 6
PREP/COOKING: 50 MINS

Trim the mushrooms, wipe with a damp cloth and slice thinly. Chop the onion very finely and put it in a frying pan large enough to hold the chicken breasts in one layer. Add 25 g/1 oz/2 tablespoons butter and a tablespoon of oil, then fry very gently until the onion is soft.

Remove any sinews from the chicken breasts and flatten them with a meat mallet; flour them, shaking off any excess. Brown them lightly in a pan with the fried onion; season with salt and pepper and moisten them with three-quarters of the Marsala in which you have dissolved the tomato purée.

When the Marsala has formed a creamy sauce and the chicken is cooked, remove the pan from the heat, arrange the chicken breasts on a serving dish, and pour over the boiling sauce, strained through a fine sieve. Cover the dish with foil and keep it hot.

Put the remaining butter in the frying pan together with a tablespoon of oil, and flavour with the lightly crushed garlic. Add the thinly sliced mushrooms and sauté them gently for a few minutes. Then pour over the remaining Marsala in which you have dissolved a little meat extract. Add salt and pepper to taste and let the mushrooms absorb all the liquid.

Arrange them alongside the chicken breasts, sprinkle over some chopped parsley and serve.

POLLO AL VINO ROSSO

Chicken in Red Wine

25 g/1 oz dried mushrooms (porcini)
1 chicken, weighing about 1 1/4 kg/3 lb
flour
75 g/3 oz/6 tbspoons butter
olive oil
100 g/4 oz onion
2 slices unsmoked bacon
2 tbspoons brandy
50 ml/2 fl oz/1/4 cup red wine
salt and pepper
350 g/12 oz frozen short crust pastry, thawed

SERVES 6
PREP/COOKING: 1 1/4 HRS

Soak the mushrooms in warm water for 1 hour. Meanwhile cut the chicken into serving portions. Coat with flour and fry in 25 g/1 oz/2 tablespoons butter and a tablespoon of oil. When they are browned, remove from the pan, drain on kitchen paper and keep warm.

Chop and fry the onion in a further 25 g/1 oz/2 tablespoons butter. Drain and squeeze dry the mushrooms and slice them into strips with the bacon slices. Add to the onion in the pan and fry for a few minutes. Return the chicken to the pan, then sprinkle over the brandy. Leave it to evaporate before adding the wine. Stir, reduce the heat to low and season with salt and pepper. Cook gently for 30 minutes, half-covered, and add a little warm water if necessary.

Grease a 23 cm/9 inch flan tin with a loose bottom with the remaining butter. Roll out the pastry to a circle about 4 cm/1 1/2 inches larger than the tin, then use this to line it. Prick all over with a fork, cover with waxed paper and baking beans and cook in the oven preheated to 190°C/425°F/gas 7 for 20 minutes. Remove the beans and paper and cook for a further 5 minutes until the pastry is browned and crisp. Arrange the pastry shell on a serving dish. Carefully spoon over the chicken sauce. Serve hot.

Galletti amburghesi, in tegame

Chicken with Herbs

3 very small chickens or
  poussins
olive oil
1 sprig fresh rosemary
2 fresh sage leaves

½ garlic clove
salt and pepper
100 ml/4 fl oz/½ cup
  dry white wine

SERVES 6
PREP/COOKING: 1 HR

Cut the chickens in half (preferably using poultry shears) along the backbone (to one side of it) and flatten them gently with a meat mallet, taking care not to break or shatter the bones.

Place 4–5 tablespoons of oil, the rosemary, sage leaves and garlic clove in a very large frying pan and fry gently for a few minutes. Add the chickens, open side upwards. Sprinkle with salt and pepper, cover the pan and cook over low heat for 10 minutes.

Turn the chickens, sprinkle with salt and pepper again and pour over the white wine. Cover the pan and cook briskly for a further 20 minutes.

Arrange on a warmed dish and serve immediately.

Sopracosce con noci e olive

Chicken with Walnuts and Olives

6 chicken legs
a little flour
butter
3 fresh sage leaves
1 sprig fresh rosemary
100 ml/4 fl oz/½ cup dry white wine

150 ml/5 fl oz/⅔ cup chicken stock
10 green olives, stoned
10 walnuts
cornflour
single cream
a little chopped parsley

SERVES 6
PREP/COOKING: 40 MINS

Tie each chicken leg in three places with kitchen thread and coat lightly in flour, shaking off any excess. Heat a large knob of butter in a large frying pan with the sage and the sprig of rosemary. Fry the chicken pieces briskly until crisp and golden on all sides. Pour on the white wine and let the liquid evaporate before adding the stock. Cook over moderate heat for about 20 minutes.

Meanwhile quarter the olives and break the walnuts up into fairly large pieces. As soon as the chicken is cooked and the liquid has reduced, remove the meat from the pan and discard the thread. Place the chicken on a plate and keep hot. Discard the sage and rosemary and add the olives and walnuts to the pan. Dissolve a teaspoon of cornflour in a little cold water and stir it into the mixture together with 5 tablespoons of cream. Blend thoroughly.

Replace the chicken in the pan and soak in the sauce for a few minutes. Transfer to a hot serving dish, coating the meat with the sauce. Sprinkle with a little chopped parsley, if desired, and serve.

FARAONA ALL' ALLORO

Guinea Fowl with Bay Leaves

1 guinea fowl, weighing about 1 1/2 kg/3 1/4 lb	50 ml/2 fl oz/1/4 cup olive oil
salt and pepper	350 ml/12 fl oz/1 1/2 cups white wine
75 g/3 oz onion	
1 garlic clove	hot chicken stock
50 g/2 oz pancetta	
8 bay leaves	

SERVES 4
PREP/COOKING: 1 HR 20 MINS

Singe the guinea fowl over a high flame to remove any remaining feathers or feather ends. Wash and dry the bird, then season both inside and out with salt and pepper.

Chop the onion, garlic, pancetta and bay leaves. Soften this mixture in the oil, then add the guinea fowl and brown it all over, turning it frequently. Sprinkle over about half of the wine. Lower the heat, cover and cook the guinea fowl for about 1 hour (the meat should be falling off the bones), basting it from time to time with the remaining wine and a ladleful of hot stock.

Serve straight from the casserole, with the sauce.

Anatra in salsa

Duck in Sauce

70 g/2½ oz sliced pancetta
25 g/1 oz/2 tbspoons butter
sage
rosemary
2 ducks, about 2⅕ kg/ 4¾ lb each

1 lemon
salt and pepper
3 anchovies
1 garlic clove
200 g/7 oz Italian sausage
white wine vinegar

SERVES 6
PREP/COOKING: ABOUT 3 HRS

Preheat the oven to 180°C/350°F/gas 4. Chop the pancetta and brown it in the butter with a few sage leaves and a sprig of rosemary. Take the pan off the heat and add the ducks, the lemon cut into wedges, salt and pepper. Roast in the oven for about 2 hours, basting the ducks frequently with their juices.

Meanwhile, finely chop the anchovies with the garlic and, separately, the Italian sausage. Place all the chopped ingredients in a saucepan and sweat over very moderate heat for about 10 minutes, then moisten with half a glass of vinegar; mix and turn off the heat.

As soon as the ducks are cooked, cut them into serving pieces and arrange in an ovenproof dish. Pour over the sauce, then place in the switched-off but still warm oven for about 20 minutes to give the ducks a fine flavour.

'COSCETTE' DI TACCHINO IN CASSERUOLA

Casserole of Turkey 'Haunches'

> 2 turkey wings
> 25 g/1 oz/1 small stalk celery
> 25 g/1 oz carrot
> 50 g/2 oz onion, peeled
> 50 g/2 oz/4 tbspoons butter
> 1 garlic clove
> 200 g/7 oz chopped tomatoes
> hot chicken stock
> salt and pepper
> paprika
> chopped fresh parsley and sage
> 70 ml/2 1/2 fl oz/1/3 cup whipping cream

SERVES 4
PREP/COOKING: 1 HR 40 MINS

Cut off the turkey wing tips, then cut the meat away from the bones, pushing the flesh upwards so that the wings look like 'haunches'.

Chop the celery, carrot and onion, and then soften them in the butter, together with a whole garlic clove. Add the turkey and brown gently, then add the chopped tomatoes, 2 ladles of hot stock, salt, pepper, paprika, and half a tablespoon of chopped herbs. Cover and cook over very moderate heat for about 1 hour, then pour in the cream and cook for about 15 minutes more.

Serve the 'haunches' with the cooking liquid and, if you like, some steamed polenta.

FESA DI TACCHINO IN CROSTE

Turkey Breast in Pastry

200 g/7 oz smoked bacon (in one piece)
900 g/2 lb turkey breast
butter
rosemary
sage
1 celery stalk
1 carrot
1 onion
olive oil
150 ml/5 fl oz/²/3 cup dry white wine

1 small lettuce
250 g/8 oz frozen puff pastry, thawed
200 g/7 oz cooked ham
4 tbspoons mustard
1 egg, beaten
1 teaspoon cornmeal
100 ml/4 fl oz/¹/2 cup single cream

SERVES 6–8
PREP/COOKING: 2 HRS

Preheat the oven to 190°C/375°F/gas 5. Slice the bacon into strips and cover the turkey with the strips and a little softened butter, then sprinkle over some chopped rosemary and sage. Tie up the turkey securely with kitchen thread. Wash and chop the celery, carrot and onion.

Put the turkey into a roasting pan, add the vegetables, salt and pepper to taste and 150 ml/5 fl oz/²/3 cup oil. Brown for 10 minutes over high heat. Transfer to the oven and cook for 30 minutes; after 15 minutes, pour over the wine and turn the meat over. Turn the oven up to 200°C/400°F/gas 6. When the turkey is cooked, remove from the oven and allow to cool.

Wash and finely slice the lettuce. Roll the pastry into a thin rectangle about 30 x 35 cm/12 x 15 inches. Put it on a greased baking tray and arrange on it half the ham, half the lettuce and the turkey. Spread mustard over the meat, then cover with the rest of the ham and lettuce. Bring the pastry up around the turkey to enclose it completely, securing it well. Cut away any excess pastry. Brush the top with egg then roll out the excess pastry and use to decorate. Brush the strips with egg then bake for 20 minutes.

Strain the meat cooking juices and reheat, adding the cornmeal and cream to thicken and finish it. Strain again, then serve with the turkey.

Vegetables & Salads

Vegetables & salads are often served as a separate course in Italy. They make ideal vegetarian dishes or imaginative side dishes to meat, fish or poultry main courses. Here are recipes for a wide range of vegetables and salads, ranging from the simple to the more ambitious, from the everyday to the exotic – but always absolutely delicious.

Fagiolini cipollati

Green Bean and Onions

400 g/14 oz French beans, cooked and drained
250 g/8 oz/2 large onions
½ sprig rosemary
1 garlic clove
butter
olive oil

2–3 tbspoons Marsala wine
½ vegetable stock cube
nutmeg
1 teaspoon cornflour
150 ml/5 fl oz/⅔ cup light vegetable stock

SERVES 4
PREP/COOKING: 45 MINS

Slice the onions very thinly and finely chop the rosemary leaves and the garlic. Gently fry the onion in 25 g/1 oz/2 tablespoons of butter and 3 tablespoons oil, taking care not to let them brown. Add the beans.

Pour in the Marsala. Allow to evaporate then crumble in the stock cube and season with a little grated nutmeg. Carefully dissolve the cornflour in the cold stock and pour into the pan. Shake the pan and cover, turn the heat down to the minimum and leave the beans to simmer until the sauce has thickened.

Taste and correct seasoning, then serve.

FAGIOLINI ALLA MODA PAESANA

Country-style Green Beans

350 g/12 oz French beans, cooked and drained
1 small onion
1 small carrot
1 celery stalk
1 large garlic clove
2 slices bacon, diced very small
butter
olive oil
250 g/8 oz tomatoes, skinned
1 small bay leaf
2 or 3 sprigs fresh parsley
2 fresh basil leaves
grated Parmesan cheese
a pinch of sugar

SERVES 4
PREP/COOKING: 45 MINS

Preheat the oven to 200°C/400°F/gas 6. Finely chop the onion, carrot, celery and garlic. Gently fry together with the bacon in 25 g/1 oz of butter and 2 tablespoons of oil. Purée the tomatoes and add to the pan. Tie the bay leaf, parsley and basil together and add these too. Season and add the sugar. Simmer for about 10 minutes with the pan half-covered, then add the beans and leave them to absorb the flavours for about 10 minutes, tossing frequently. Remove the herbs and pour the contents of the pan into an ovenproof dish. Sprinkle with cheese and bake for about 10 minutes. Serve at once.

Verza cipollata

Savoy Cabbage with Onions

350 g/12 oz savoy cabbage
150 g/5 oz/2 small onions
50 g/2 oz cooking fat
rosemary
1 garlic clove

olive oil
1/2 vegetable stock cube
salt and pepper
ground nutmeg
a little dry white wine

SERVES 4
PREP/COOKING TIME: 45 MINS

Bring a large saucepan of water to the boil and salt. Wash and drain the cabbage carefully and boil for about 5 minutes.

Meanwhile, slice the onions thinly. Blend the fat with a few leaves of rosemary and the garlic clove and fry gently in 2 tablespoons of olive oil. Add the onions and cook gently until transparent.

Drain the cabbage, slice thickly and add to the onions. Flavour with the crumbled stock cube, pepper and a pinch of nutmeg, and sprinkle with a little white wine. Cover the pan and allow the wine to evaporate, stirring occasionally. Test and adjust the seasoning according to taste.

Serve immediately.

Bianchi de Spagna con Salsa di Cipolla

White Beans with Onion Sauce

1 x 400 g/14 oz tin haricot beans	1 teaspoon cornflour
1 small onion	50 ml/2 fl oz/¼ cup milk
butter	10 capers
	sprig of fresh parsley

SERVES 4
PREP/COOKING: 30 MINS

Rinse the beans thoroughly under warm running water and drain. Chop the onion almost to a paste. Melt 2 tablespoons butter in a small saucepan and fry the onion without browning over low heat for about 15 minutes. Add a tablespoon of warm water, if necessary, to keep the onion soft and to stop it drying out. Sprinkle the cornflour over the onion and blend in well. Dilute gradually with the cold milk to obtain a smooth, consistent sauce. Season with a pinch of salt and simmer over low heat, stirring constantly, for 5–6 minutes. Remove from the heat and blend at maximum speed until the sauce is completely smooth, then put it in a bowl.

Drain the capers thoroughly, chop them coarsely and add to the chopped parsley. Pour the beans into a serving dish and pour over the onion sauce. Sprinkle with the chopped parsley and capers and serve. This vegetable dish makes a delicate accompaniment to boiled meats.

CORNETTI GIALLI CON SALSA AL FORMAGGIO

Haricot Beans with Cheese Sauce

550 g/1 1/4 lb fresh haricot beans
50 g/2 oz butter
olive oil
flour
200 ml/7 fl oz/1 cup vegetable stock
50 ml/2 fl oz/1/4 cup whipping cream

1 egg yolk
25 g/1 oz/1/4 cup grated Emmental and Parmesan cheese
salt
ground nutmeg

SERVES 4–6
PREP/COOKING: 1 HR

Heat a pan of water. Pod the beans and wash them thoroughly. As soon as the water is boiling drop them in and cook for about 20 minutes; they should be very tender. Drain and sauté them in a pan with a large knob of butter and 2 tablespoons of oil, keeping the heat low and the pan covered. Stir occasionally and cook for about 10 minutes.

Meanwhile, melt the remaining butter in another pan, fold in 15 g/ 1/2 oz/2 tablespoons of flour and stir to prevent lumps from forming; dilute with the hot stock and bring slowly to the boil. Remove the sauce from the heat, stir in the cream beaten with the egg yolk, the grated Emmental and Parmesan cheeses, a little salt and ground nutmeg. Stir well after the addition of each ingredient. Arrange the beans in a shallow dish, pour over the sauce, toss the beans gently and serve.

These beans make an ideal side dish for delicate main courses such as fillet of sole, veal escalopes, chicken and turkey breasts, roast saddle or medallions of rabbit. French beans can be prepared with the same cheese sauce.

CAVOLFIORE ALLA PIZZAIOLA

Cauliflower with Tomato and Garlic Sauce

1 med. cauliflower	salt and pepper
1 small onion	oregano
2 garlic cloves	4 fresh basil leaves
olive oil	100 g/4 oz Mozzarella cheese
400 g/14 oz skinned tomatoes	50 g/2 oz/4 tbspoons butter
a little sugar	grated Parmesan cheese

SERVES 6
PREP/COOKING: 1 HR

Preheat the oven to 200°C/400°F/gas 6. Wash the cauliflower thoroughly and simmer in an uncovered pan for about 12 minutes. Meanwhile, finely chop the onion and garlic and sauté in 4 tablespoons of olive oil. After a few minutes add the puréed tomatoes, a pinch of sugar and a little salt and pepper. Stir, and cook for about 15 minutes, stirring from time to time. Then add a pinch of oregano and the finely chopped basil leaves.

When the cauliflower is cooked and tender, remove it from the pan with a slotted spoon and place it on a dish covered with a double layer of kitchen paper to absorb the moisture. Then place it in a buttered ovenproof dish with high sides that just contains it. Dice the Mozzarella and scatter the pieces between the cauliflower florets. Melt the butter and pour over the cauliflower and sprinkle with grated Parmesan cheese. Place the dish in the oven for about 10 minutes.

Pour some of the tomato sauce over the cauliflower and serve immediately, and pour the remaining sauce into a sauceboat for serving.

CARCIOFI RIPIENI AL PROSCIUTTO

Artichokes Stuffed with Ham

4 artichokes
juice of 1 lemon
salt
a little flour
50 g/2 oz lean ham
butter
100 ml/4 fl oz/½ cup milk

¼ chicken or vegetable stock cube
25 g/1 oz/¼ cup grated Emmental cheese
20 g/¾ oz/3 tbspoons grated Parmesan cheese

SERVES 4
PREP/COOKING: 1¼ HRS

Trim the artichokes and remove the tough outer leaves, but reserve the tender central flesh of the stalks. Cut the artichokes in half lengthways, scoop out and discard the chokes. Place the halves in a bowl of water with half the lemon juice.

Bring a large saucepan of water to the boil. Add salt, the rest of the lemon juice and the flour dissolved in a little cold water. Add the artichokes and stalks and cook for about 20 minutes or until the outer leaves are tender. Drain and cool on kitchen paper.

Preheat the oven to 190°C/375°F/gas 5. Finely chop the artichoke stalks and the ham. Prepare a béchamel sauce with a knob of butter, a tablespoon of flour and the milk. Blend in the crumbled stock cube and the grated Emmental cheese. Stir in the chopped ham and artichoke stalks.

Fill the artichoke halves with the prepared sauce and arrange them in a buttered ovenproof pan. Pour on 25 g/1 oz/2 tablespoons of melted butter, sprinkle with the grated Parmesan cheese and bake in the oven for about 20 minutes or until golden brown. Serve hot.

PATATINE, CARCIOFI E PISELLI IN TEGAME

Casserole of New Potatoes, Artichokes and Peas

4 artichokes	salt and pepper
juice of ½ lemon	thyme
1 small onion	400 g/14 oz new potatoes
1 small garlic clove	50 g/2 oz/4 tbspoons butter
1 sprig fresh parsley	2 sage leaves
olive oil	350 g/12 oz petits pois
dry white wine	2–3 slices bacon
150 ml/5 fl oz/⅔ cup vegetable stock	dried mint

SERVES 6
PREP/COOKING: 2 HRS

Trim the artichokes, remove the outer leaves and put in a bowl of water, with the lemon juice.

Chop half the onion finely with the garlic and some parsley and place in a pan that will hold the artichokes. Add 3 tablespoons each of oil and white wine, and 2 tablespoons stock. Place the artichokes in the pan, stalks upwards, and season with salt, pepper and a pinch of thyme. Put the lid on and place over low heat over a wire mesh. Cook gently until the artichokes are tender and have absorbed most of the liquid.

Scrape the potatoes and boil them in salted water for 3–4 minutes, drain well and place in a large casserole with half the melted butter, 2 tablespoons oil and the sage. Cook over very low heat until tender and slightly browned.

Boil the peas for 3–4 minutes. Chop the remaining onion finely with the bacon and sauté the mixture in the remaining butter, taking care that it does not brown. Add the peas and the remaining boiling stock, and season. Simmer until the peas have absorbed most of the liquid.

Remove the sage, and add the peas to the potatoes. Cut the artichokes into six and add with their cooking juices. Simmer gently for 5 minutes and serve hot.

Gratin di patate, funghi, zucchini

Gratin of Potatoes, Mushrooms and Courgettes

300 g/10 oz potatoes
vinegar
250 g/8 oz courgettes/zucchini
200 g/7 oz cep mushrooms
butter
fresh sage
salt and pepper
150 ml/5 fl oz/2/3 whipping cream
2 egg yolks
1 tablespoon chopped fresh parsley
1 tablespoon grated Parmesan cheese

SERVES 6
PREP/COOKING: 50 MINS

Peel the potatoes, cut into rounds and boil for 2 minutes in plenty of water, acidulated with a tablespoon of vinegar. Drain and set aside. Trim the courgettes and cut into rounds. Carefully clean the ceps, delicately scraping the stalks and wiping the caps with a damp cloth. If you wish, rinse quickly under cold running water. Slice the mushrooms and brown them in a nut of butter, flavoured with a few sage leaves. Season with salt and pepper, then add the courgette rounds. Brown for about 3 minutes, then transfer to a plate. In the same pan, heat another nut of butter, put in the potatoes, season with salt and brown them. Add the other two vegetables. Pour off any excess fat, sauté the vegetables over high heat for 2 minutes, then transfer to a heatproof dish.

In a bowl, mix the cream and egg yolks with the parsley and a pinch each of salt and pepper. Pour this mixture over the vegetables; dot with flakes of butter and sprinkle on the Parmesan cheese. Place under a hot grill (or in a very hot oven) just until a golden crust forms. Serve hot, with steaks or pork chops.

INVOLTINI DI MELANZANE

Aubergine Rolls

450 g/1 lb aubergine/ eggplant
salt
100 g/4 oz leek
200 g/7 oz courgettes/ zucchini
100 g/4 oz celery
100 g/4 oz Emmental cheese
olive oil
fresh white breadcrumbs
chopped parsley

SERVES 6
PREP/COOKING: ABOUT 50 MINS

Cut off the aubergine stems, then wash and dry the aubergines and cut lengthways into thin slices (you should have about 18). Place in a colander, sprinkle with salt and leave to draw out the juices.

Meanwhile, trim and wash the leek, courgettes and celery. Cut them into thin julienne strips. Cut the cheese into similar strips. Heat 3 tablespoons oil in a frying pan and sauté the vegetables over high heat for not more than 3–4 minutes; they should still be crunchy. Season with salt and leave them to cool.

Preheat the oven to 180°C/350°F/gas 4. Place the aubergine slices under a very hot grill, turning them over to soften them without cooking. Divide the julienne of vegetables and cheese between the slices and roll them up. Arrange the aubergine rolls in an ovenproof dish and sprinkle with a pinch of salt, breadcrumbs and chopped parsley. Moisten with a trickle of oil, then cook in the oven for 10 minutes; just long enough for the cheese to melt and a crust to form on the rolls. Serve hot.

Melanzane 'Indorate'

Golden Aubergine Slices

2 med. aubergines/eggplants
2 eggs
salt and white pepper
50 g/2 oz/½ cup grated Pecorino cheese
150 g/5 oz/1 ¼ cup fresh breadcrumbs
flour
frying oil

SERVES 4–5
PREP/COOKING: 40 MINS + 1 HR RESTING

Wash and dry the aubergines and cut them in slices about 1 cm/½ inch thick. Lay on a large tray covered with kitchen towels and sprinkle them with salt to bring out their juices. Leave to rest in a cool place for about 1 hour, then wash and dry the slices.

Beat the eggs in a bowl with a pinch of salt and pepper. Mix the Pecorino cheese with the breadcrumbs. Roll each slice of aubergine in the flour, then dip it in the beaten eggs and finally in the mixture of breadcrumbs and Pecorino cheese, making sure that each coating covers the slices of aubergine completely.

Heat plenty of vegetable oil in a frying pan; place the slices of aubergine in the pan a few at a time and brown. Remove them with a slotted spoon and, after draining, place them on a plate covered with a double sheet of kitchen towel to absorb the excess oil; continue to fry the other slices. Finally arrange the aubergine slices on a serving dish.

PEPERONI GIALLI CON TRITO D'AROMI

Yellow Peppers with Aromatic Sauce

4 yellow peppers
1 garlic clove
anchovy paste
15 capers in vinegar

few sprigs fresh parsley
1 sprig fresh watercress
olive oil

SERVES 4
PREP/COOKING: 40 MINS + AT LEAST 2 HRS RESTING

Wash and dry the peppers, then grill them to scorch the skins, turning them over. Wrap them individually in a double sheet of kitchen towel and leave them to rest for about 10 minutes. Remove the paper and peel them completely, keeping them under running water. Dry and divide each pepper into three large strips, removing the seeds and the stem. Arrange the strips in a bowl, overlapping them slightly, and prepare the dressing.

Crush the garlic clove in a small bowl, add 3 cm/1 1/4 inches of anchovy paste and the finely chopped capers, parsley sprigs and watercress leaves, a pinch of salt and 5 tablespoons of oil. Pour the sauce over the pepper strips, cover the dish with cling film and leave it for at least 2 hours in a cool place.

Serve the peppers sprinkled with chopped parsley in small serving bowls.

TRONCHETTI DI ZUCCHINE

Stuffed Zucchini

> 3 courgettes/zucchini
> 1 slice very fresh white bread
> a little milk
> 100 g/4 oz minced lean beef
> 1 tbspoon pine nuts
> handful of fresh parsley
> 2 garlic cloves
> 25 g/1 oz/1/4 cup grated Parmesan cheese
> 1 egg yolk
> salt and pepper
> ground nutmeg
> olive oil
> 100 ml/4 fl oz/1/2 cup meat stock
> 2 tbspoons tomato juice

SERVES 3
PREP/COOKING: 1 1/4 HRS

Trim, wash and dry the courgettes, then cut each one into three. Remove most of the pulp of each one (keep it for a soup or a cream of vegetables), making sure not to cut the outside green part.

Prepare the stuffing: soak the slice of white bread in a small amount of milk, then squeeze it and crumble it in a bowl. Add the minced beef, the pine nuts, finely chopped parsley mixed with half a garlic clove, the Parmesan cheese and the egg yolk. Mix everything together thoroughly, add salt and pepper and season with ground nutmeg. Use this mixture to stuff the courgettes without overfilling them.

Preheat the oven to 200°C/400°F/gas 6. Heat 4 tablespoons of oil in a frying pan and sauté a garlic clove. When the oil is hot, remove the garlic and throw it away, then place the chunks of courgette in the pan and fry them lightly on each side.

Arrange them in an ovenproof dish, moisten them with the stock mixed with the tomato juice and a tablespoon of olive oil. Cover and cook in the preheated oven for about 40 minutes, uncovering the dish for the last 10 minutes.

Carefully transfer the courgettes to a warmed serving dish and serve.

PISELLINI CON PETITELLA

Peas with Mortadella

3 shallots, finely chopped
butter
olive oil
450 g/1 lb frozen peas

100 g/4 oz mortadella sausage
½ stock cube
ground nutmeg

SERVES 6
PREP/COOKING: 30 MINS

Sauté the shallots in a large knob of butter and 2–3 tablespoons of oil. Cook the peas in salted boiling water for about 4 minutes. Skin the sausage, cut it in half lengthways and slice it thinly into crescents. Drain the peas and add them to the shallots. Stir, season, and add the crumbled stock cube and a little nutmeg.

Pour on 100 ml/4 fl oz/½ cup of water, stir and cover the pan. Allow the peas to absorb all the liquid. Stir in the crescents of mortadella, replace the lid on the pan and cook for a further 2 minutes. Serve in a warmed dish.

Ciammotta

Stewed Potatoes, Peppers, Aubergines and Tomatoes

250 g/8 oz potatoes
250 g/8 oz aubergines/ eggplant
250 g/8 oz peppers
olive oil
200 g/7 oz firm ripe tomatoes
1 garlic clove, chopped

SERVES 4
PREP/COOKING: 1 HR 20 MINS

Peel and roughly dice the potatoes. Trim and wash the aubergine, slice it fairly thinly, then sprinkle with salt and leave for about 30 minutes to draw out the juices.

Meanwhile, remove the core, seeds and white membrane from the peppers and cut the flesh into thin strips. Heat plenty of oil in a deep-frying pan and fry first the potatoes, then the peppers and finally the aubergines, rinsed and dried with kitchen towels. Put all the fried vegetables in a flameproof casserole. Peel and deseed the tomatoes, chop roughly and add to the casserole. Season with the chopped garlic and a pinch of salt, then cover and stew over medium heat for about an hour. The stew should be fairly dry.

CIPOLLETTE AL DRAGONCELLO

Baby Onions with Tarragon

salt and pepper
1 kg/2 lb baby onions
butter
2 tbspoons cooking fat

1 tbspoon caster sugar
2 tbspoons red wine vinegar
tarragon

SERVES 4
PREP/COOKING: 1 1/4 HRS

Heat plenty of water in a saucepan and salt it as soon as it comes to the boil. Peel and trim the onions and cook them in the water for 15 minutes. Drain them and leave them to dry on kitchen towels.

Preheat the oven to 180°C/350°F/gas 4. Melt a large knob of butter and the cooking fat in an ovenproof dish. As soon as the fats are hot, add the sugar and wine vinegar. Once the vinegar has evaporated to form a thick syrupy sauce, add the onions and cook briskly for a few minutes. Season with a little salt and pepper to taste and a generous pinch of tarragon.

Place in the oven and cook for about 40 minutes, turning the onions after 20 minutes. Remove from the oven and serve hot.

Sedano e ginocchio

Braised Celery and Fennel

350 g/12 oz celery heart
1 small leek, white part only
100 g/4 oz fennel bulb
butter
olive oil
salt and pepper
ground nutmeg
2 tbspoons grated
   Emmental cheese

SERVES 4
PREP/COOKING: 1 HR

Bring a large pan of salted water to the boil. Cut the celery into pencil-thick pieces 5 cm/2 inches long, removing any strings. Wash thoroughly and boil for about 15 minutes.

Meanwhile, wash the leek and fennel, and cut the leek into very fine slices and the fennel into wedges. Place them in a pan with a large knob of butter and 2 tablespoons oil and brown them gently, uncovered. Remove the celery from the pan with a slotted spoon and add it to the other vegetables. Stir and continue cooking, still uncovered, adding a little of the celery water from time to time.

Preheat the oven to 180°C/350°F/gas 4. When the vegetables are tender and there is no liquid left, season to taste with salt, pepper and ground nutmeg. Place in an ovenproof dish, sprinkle with the cheese and cook in the oven for about 10 minutes.

Garnish, if you like, with a few fine fennel leaves and serve immediately.

Sedano e carote stufati al vino rosso

Celeriac and Carrots Braised in Red Wine

350 g/12 oz celeriac
350 g/12 oz carrots
40 g/1 1/2 oz pancetta
75 g/3 oz/1 med. onion
olive oil
1/2 teaspoon peppercorns

250 ml/8 fl oz/1 cup robust red wine
salt
1 teaspoon sugar
1 teaspoon tomato purée

SERVES 6
PREP/COOKING: 35 MINS

Peel the celeriac and cut it into strips. Trim and scrape the carrots and cut into rounds. Finely dice the pancetta; peel and chop the onion. Soften the onion and pancetta in 3 tablespoons oil, with the peppercorns. Add the prepared celeriac and carrots and cook over high heat for about 1 minute, mixing with a wooden spoon. Pour in the wine, season with salt, add the sugar and tomato purée, mix and bring to the boil. Lower the heat and cook for about 20–25 minutes, until almost all the wine has been absorbed.

Transfer the vegetables to a serving dish immediately and serve very hot.

LENTICCHE STUFATE AI PISTILLI DI ZAFFERANO

Braised Lentils with Saffron

---

300 g/10 oz/1 ¾ cups lentils
100 g/4 oz/1 large onion
olive oil
20 g/¾ oz raw ham, cut into slivers
50 ml/2 fl oz/¼ cup dry white wine

a pinch of saffron strands
a pinch of powdered saffron
hot chicken stock
salt

SERVES 6–8
PREP/COOKING: 30 MINS + SOAKING THE LENTILS

Soak the lentils for about 6 hours. Peel and halve the onion and place in a saucepan with 3 tablespoons oil and the ham. Drain the lentils and add them to the pan, brown briefly, then moisten with the wine. Add a pinch of saffron strands and the powdered saffron. When the wine has evaporated, pour in just enough hot stock to cover the lentils. Bring to the boil, then lower the heat, cover the pan and cook for about 20 minutes.

Taste, add salt if necessary, then discard the onion and serve hot.

INSALATA DI COZZE, PANE E FAGIOLI

Salad of Mussels, Bread and Beans

1 kg/2¼ lb fresh mussels
olive oil
2 large garlic cloves
a little lemon juice
1 x 400 g/14 oz tin haricot beans
2 slices white bread
2 anchovy fillets in oil
1 teaspoon mustard
2 tbspoons white wine vinegar
salt
fresh chervil or parsley for garnish

SERVES 4–5
PREP/COOKING: 45 MINS

Scrape the mussels under cold running water, discarding any that are open, then put them into a saucepan with a tablespoon of olive oil, a lightly crushed garlic clove and a few drops of lemon juice. Cover and place the pan over a high heat. After a few minutes' cooking and when the mussels have opened, remove them from their shells and leave them to cool in a bowl. Discard any that do not open.

Drain and rinse the beans, then dry on kitchen paper. Add them to the mussels. Heat 3 tablespoons oil and the other garlic clove in a frying pan. Fry the bread until it is lightly toasted, then cut it into 2 cm/¾ inch squares. Mix these with the mussels and beans.

Crush the anchovies with a fork in a bowl, then, still mixing with the fork, add the mustard, a little salt, the vinegar and 5 tablespoons olive oil. Pour the dressing over the salad, mix again and garnish with chervil or parsley. Serve immediately.

INSALATA OLIVETTA

Salad with Olives

1 small head of Belgian endive
1 heart of escarole
1 head of radicchio
2 tbspoons white wine vinegar
salt and pepper
olive oil
25 g/1 oz capers
a little parsley
anchovy paste
50 g/2 oz small black olives in brine
a small piece of leek

SERVES 4–5
PREP TIME: 20 MINS

Trim and wash the endive, the escarole and the radicchio. Drain and dry, keeping the different types separate. Break up the leaves and arrange in a salad bowl.

Prepare the salad dressing: mix the wine vinegar with a pinch of salt and pepper in a bowl, stirring until the salt is dissolved. Add, a tablespoon at a time, 6 tablespoons of olive oil, stirring vigorously to blend the ingredients. Chop the capers and parsley and add to the dressing with 4–5 cm/1 1/2–2 inches of anchovy paste. Blend thoroughly.

To serve, place the olives in the centre of the salad bowl and arrange a few finely cut strips of leek on top of them. Pour over the dressing and toss well to mix everything together.

INSALATA RUSTICA

Country Salad

350 g/12 oz fresh fennel bulb
150 g/5 oz small fresh mushrooms
juice of 1/2 lemon
100 g/4 oz ham
75 g/3 oz Emmental cheese
1 tbspoon black olive paste

1 tbspoon mustard anchovy paste
1 tbspoon red wine vinegar
olive oil

SERVES 4
PREP: 40 MINS

Wash and dry the fennel, keeping the best leaves for the garnish. Peel the mushrooms and remove the earthy bases of the stalks. As you clean them, drop them into a bowl of cold water into which the juice of half a lemon has been squeezed. Cut the ham into short strips and the Emmental into thin slices.

Put the olive paste in a bowl and add the mustard and anchovy paste. Dilute with a tablespoon of vinegar and 75 ml/3 fl oz/4 tablespoons of olive oil, and stir carefully.

Cut the fennel into thin slices, likewise the mushrooms, which have been well drained. Mix all the ingredients together in a salad bowl, pour over the sauce and toss carefully. Use the reserved fennel leaves for garnish.

Insalata di Finocchi

Cheese and Fennel Salad

2 fennel bulbs	1 teaspoon mustard
a few drops lemon juice	1 tbspoon white wine vinegar
1/2 garlic clove	olive oil
75 g/3 oz Emmental cheese	1 chive, chopped
salt and pepper	

SERVES 4–5
PREP: 40 MINS

Clean the fennel bulbs, removing the green leaves, small shoots and the first layer, then cut them in half and place them in cold water to which you have added a few drops of lemon juice.

Meanwhile, rub the inside of a salad bowl with the garlic clove. Cut the cheese into very thin slices and place in the salad bowl.

Put a pinch of salt, a grinding of white pepper, the mustard and wine vinegar into a small bowl; stir with a fork until the salt has dissolved, then dilute with 4 tablespoons of olive oil and mix all the ingredients together well.

Drain the pieces of fennel bulb, dry them, cut them into thin slices and add them to the cheese. Then add the chopped chive too, and toss the salad gently. Now pour over the prepared dressing and toss the salad again before serving.

INSALATA D'ESTATE

Summer Salad

50 g/2 oz cornsalad
a bunch of watercress
1 iceberg lettuce
a bunch of radishes
6 soft but not over-ripe tomatoes
1 large carrot

FOR THE DRESSING
1 spring onion
salt and pepper
1 tbspoon mustard
balsamic vinegar
100 ml/4 fl oz/1/2 cup extra virgin olive oil

SERVES 6
PREP: 30 MINS

Trim the cornsalad, wash, drain well and place in a large bowl. Trim, wash and coarsely chop the watercress and shred the lettuce. Trim and scrape the carrot and slice thinly on a mandoline. Thinly slice a few of the radishes and add them to the bowl with the watercress and lettuce, the quartered tomatoes and sliced carrot.

Mix all the vegetables together and transfer to a salad bowl. Make three or four radishes into 'flowers' and garnish the salad with these.

To make the dressing, chop the onion and place in a bowl with a pinch of salt, a grinding of pepper and the mustard. Dilute with about 3 tablespoonfuls of vinegar, then whisk in the oil until well emulsified. Dress the salad just before serving and toss well to mix.

Insalata della casa

Chef's Salad

3 eggs
2 slices white bread
200 g/7 oz mixed salad leaves
green olives
150 g/5 oz palm hearts, sliced into rounds
70 g/3 oz rocket leaves

FOR THE DRESSING
50 g/2 oz/2 cups parsley leaves
1 tbspoon capers, drained
3 anchovy fillets
2 pickled gherkins
1 slice of white bread
vinegar
100 ml/4 fl oz/1½ cup extra virgin olive oil

SERVES 6
PREP: 30 MINS

Hard-boil the eggs: cook for precisely 10 minutes from when the water comes to the boil, then refresh under running water and shell. Cut the bread into small dice and toast in a hot oven. Trim, wash and drain the salad leaves and arrange in a large bowl. Mix in the toasted bread, about 10 olives, segments of hard-boiled egg and the palm hearts. Coarsely chop the rocket and add it to the salad.

Next make the dressing. In a blender, combine the parsley, capers, anchovies, gherkins and the slice of white bread, softened in vinegar and squeezed dry. Finally, add the olive oil and blend on maximum speed for about 1 minute, to make a dense, perfectly homogenous dressing.

Transfer to a bowl and bring it to the table with the salad. Dress and toss the salad at the table in front of the assembled company.

SNACKS

Over the centuries Italians have perfected the art of the snack and the light supper dish. Probably the most famous of all Italian snacks is the pizza. Here are some recipes for classic pizzas, but you can always experiment with your own toppings, using whatever you happen to have to hand.

Pizette Rustiche ai Formaggi e Noci

Rustic Pizzas with Cheese and Walnuts

75 g/3 oz Pecorino cheese
70 g/2½ oz Mozzarella
  or Gruyère
100 g/4 oz shelled walnuts
50 ml/2 fl oz/⅕ cup dry
  white wine
black pepper

FOR THE PIZZA DOUGH
25 g/1 oz fresh yeast
salt
400 g/14 oz/3½ cups
  flour

SERVES 6
PREP/COOKING: 40 MINS + RISING

First, make the bread dough: crumble the yeast and dissolve it in a little tepid water with half a teaspoon salt. Tip the flour on to a work surface and make a well. Pour the yeast mixture into the centre and add another 200 ml/7 fl oz/1 cup tepid water. Mix well and knead the dough until smooth. Cover with a clean tea towel and leave to rise in a warm place for about 40 minutes.

While the dough is rising, cut the Pecorino and Mozzarella cheeses into minute dice, then place the walnuts on a board and chop them coarsely with a heavy knife. Put the well-risen dough into the bowl of an electric mixer or on to the work surface with the cheeses and walnuts, and knead vigorously (use the dough hook of the mixer) to amalgamate all the ingredients perfectly. Soften the dough with the wine and flavour with a good grinding of black pepper. Cover and leave to rise again in a warm place for about 30 minutes.

Preheat the oven to 200°C/400°F/gas 6. Divide the dough into 12 pieces of about 50 g/2 oz each. Place these in individual well-oiled high-sided moulds. Leave the pizzas to rise again in a warm place for 1 hour before baking them in the hot oven for about 40 minutes. Carefully unmould the pizzas and serve.

Pizza all'uovo

Egg Pizza

flour	½ med. courgette/zucchini
450 g/1 lb pizza dough (see recipe on page 234)	100 g/4 oz Mozzarella cheese
olive oil	a slice of lean ham
400 g/14 oz firm ripe tomatoes	a few fennel leaves
oregano	2 tbspoons grated mild Pecorino cheese

SERVES 4
PREP/COOKING: 45 MINS

Preheat the oven to 200°C/400°F/gas 6. Roll out the dough to 30cm/12 inches. Lightly grease a baking tray and place the dough on it. Press it down just inside the edge all the way round. Blanch the tomatoes quickly in boiling salted water and skin them. Cut in half, remove the seeds, and chop coarsely. Season with salt, pepper and a pinch of oregano. Trim and finely slice the courgette. Bring the water in which the tomatoes were blanched back to the boil and put in the courgette slices for 2 minutes. Remove with a slotted spoon and drain. Dice the Mozzarella into 1 cm/½ inch cubes. Cut the ham into matchstick lengths.

Spread the tomatoes over the surface of the pizza dough and arrange the rounds of courgette around the outside edge. Make a circle of Mozzarella, followed by the ham. Place a few young fennel leaves on the ham. Pour over a trickle of olive oil and sprinkle the pizza tops with the grated Pecorino. Bake for about 15 minutes.

Meanwhile, heat a frying pan with 2 tablespoons of oil. Break the egg into a bowl, keeping the yolk intact. While the oil is hot, put in the egg and cook until the white is firm. Cut the egg out with a pastry cutter 10 cm/4 inches in diameter. Sprinkle very lightly with salt and remove from pan with a spatula. Remove the pizza from the oven and place the egg in the centre. Garnish with more fennel leaves and serve immediately.

Pizza alla Napoletana

Naples-style Pizza

flour
250 g/8 oz pizza dough
(see recipe on page 234)
olive oil
2–3 medium tomatoes, skinned

salt
a pinch of oregano
2–3 large fresh basil leaves
1 garlic clove

SERVES 1–2
PREP/COOKING: 30 MINS

Preheat the oven to 200°C/400°F/gas 6. Roll out the dough to a 20 cm/8 inch round. Lightly grease a baking tray and place the dough on it. With your fingertips, press down the dough just inside the edge to give it a raised edge.

Chop the tomatoes, season with a little salt and a pinch of oregano and spread over the pizza. Wipe the basil leaves with a damp cloth and finely chop them before sprinkling them over the tomato. Finely chop or slice half a garlic clove and sprinkle this on too. Do not spread these ingredients right to the edges of the dough. Drizzle on plenty of good olive oil and bake for about 12 minutes.

Serve the pizza straight from the oven on a flat, warmed plate.

Pizza ai funghi

Mushroom Pizza

350 g/12 oz mushrooms
juice of 1 lemon
olive oil
1 garlic clove
salt and pepper

flour
400 g/14 oz pizza dough
  (see recipe on page 234)
a little chopped parsley

SERVES 4
PREP/COOKING: 45 MINS

Preheat the to 200°C/400°F/gas 6. Peel or wipe the mushrooms and trim the stalks. As they are ready, put them in a bowl of cold water to which the lemon juice has been added.

Heat 3 tablespoons of oil in a frying pan. Crush the garlic and put it in the hot oil. Fry until the garlic browns, then remove from the frying pan. Slice the mushrooms directly into the hot oil and sauté for 3–4 minutes, seasoning with salt and pepper. Roll out the dough to a 30 cm/12 inch round.

Lightly oil a baking tray and place the dough on it. With your fingertips press down the dough just inside the edge to give it a raised edge. Spread the mushrooms over the pizza and pour over a trickle olive oil. Sprinkle with chopped parsley and place in the oven for about 15 minutes.

Serve hot from the oven, cut into quarters.

Pizza rustica con prosciutto e formaggio

Farmhouse Pizza

---

350 g/12 oz frozen puff pastry, thawed
flour
butter
breadcrumbs
100 g/4 oz ham, sliced
1 large firm tomato
50 g/2 oz Mozzarella cheese
a few sprigs fresh parsley

2 large fresh basil leaves
2 eggs
5 tbspoons whipping cream
50 g/2 oz/1½ cup grated Emmental cheese
salt and pepper
nutmeg
a pinch of fresh marjoram

SERVES 8
PREP/COOKING: 1¼ HRS

Preheat the oven to 190°C/375°F/gas 5. Defrost the pastry if frozen. Roll it out on a lightly floured board until it is large enough to line a shallow, buttered 28 x 18 cm/11 x 7 inch pie dish. Prick the pastry with a fork, sprinkle the base with breadcrumbs and then make an even layer of ham.

Now prepare the filling: blanch the tomato in lightly salted boiling water for a few seconds, then skin, cut in half and remove the seeds. Cut the tomato into irregular pieces. Dice the Mozzarella cheese and finely chop the parsley with the basil. In a bowl, whisk the eggs with the cream, the grated Emmental cheese, salt, pepper and a little grated nutmeg. Add a pinch of marjoram and then put the chopped tomato into the bowl together with the diced Mozzarella and the chopped parsley and basil. Mix well and pour into the pie dish. Bake in the lower part of the oven for about 35 minutes and serve hot from the oven.

Pizza capricciosa

Pizza of Many Flavours

flour
400 g/14 oz pizza dough
  (see recipe on page 234)
250 g/8 oz skinned
  tomatoes
salt
a pinch of oregano
25 g/1 oz diced Mozzarella
  cheese
3 fresh basil leaves,
  chopped
20 fresh mussels
6 artichoke hearts in oil, cut
  into quarters
6 black olives, stoned and
  cut into quarters
150 g/5 oz clams
100 g/4 oz baby
  mushrooms in oil
50 g/2 oz capers
2 thin slices ham, cut into
  strips
a few slivers Emmental
  cheese
a little chopped parsley
olive oil

SERVES 4
PREP/COOKING: 40 MINS

Preheat the oven to 200°C/400°F/gas 6. Roll out the dough to a 30 cm/12 inch round. Lightly grease a baking tray and place the dough on it. With your fingertips, press down the dough just inside the edge to give it a raised edge. Remove the seeds from the tomatoes and slice finely. Spread over the pizza. Lightly sprinkle with salt and flavour with a pinch of oregano.

Top the pizza in eight divisions with eight separate toppings: the Mozzarella cheese sprinkled with the chopped basil, mussels, artichoke hearts, olives, clams, the well-drained mushrooms, the well-drained capers and finally the strips of ham and slivers of Emmental. Sprinkle with the parsley and pour over a trickle of olive oil.

Bake for about 15 minutes, and serve at once.

CALZONE DI VERDURA

Vegetable Calzone

50 g/2 oz raisins
15 g/1½ oz yeast
300 g/10 oz/2½ cup flour
salt

450 g/1 lb Belgian endive
  or spinach beet
1 dried chilli
olive oil

SERVES 6
PREP/COOKING: 40 MINS + RISING TIME

Soak the raisins in tepid water. Dissolve the yeast in 100 ml/4 fl oz tepid water. Sift the flour on to a work surface and make a well. Put the dissolved yeast and a pinch of salt in the middle, then mix to a soft, elastic dough and knead energetically for several minutes. Leave the dough to rise at room temperature for about 30 minutes.

Meanwhile, preheat the oven to 180°C/350°F/gas 4. Trim the endive or spinach beet, cut into thin strips and place in a bowl. Squeeze the raisins dry and mix them with the endive, together with a pinch of salt, a crumbled chilli and a trickle of oil. Place the risen dough on the floured work surface and knead for a few more minutes, then roll it out to a thickness of 3 mm/⅛ in.

Lay half the dough (without cutting it) on an oiled baking sheet. Spread over the vegetables, then fold over the unfilled dough and seal the edges. Trickle a little oil along the borders and bake in the hot oven for about 30 minutes.

CALZONE CON LA RICOTTA

Calzone with Ricotta

350 g/12 oz Ricotta cheese
75 g/3 oz spicy salami
100 g/4 oz Mozzarella cheese
2 thick slices ham
2 eggs
25 g/1 oz/¼ cup grated Parmesan cheese
25 g/1 oz/¼ cup grated Pecorino cheese
salt and pepper
450 g/1 lb pizza dough (see recipe on page 234)
olive oil

SERVES 4–5
PREP/COOKING: 1 HR

Preheat the oven to 200°C/400°F/gas 6. Sieve the Ricotta into a bowl. Cut the salami into small cubes and the Mozzarella cheese into larger cubes. Coarsely chop the ham, then add all these ingredients to the Ricotta. Bind with the eggs, the Parmesan and Pecorino cheeses, salt and pepper and mix thoroughly. Taste and, if necessary, adjust the seasoning.

Roll out the dough to a 30 cm/12 inch round. Place the Ricotta mixture over half the circle to within about 15 mm/¾ inch of the edge. Fold the other half of the dough over the filling, sealing the two edges by pinching them together. Place the calzone on a greased baking tray and brush it with olive oil; bake in the oven for about 25 minutes. Serve hot.

FRITTATA AI TARTUFFI

Frittata with Truffles

*100 g/4 oz fresh black
 truffles
6 eggs
50 ml/2 fl oz/¼ cup
 whipping cream*

*salt and pepper
olive oil
juice of ½ lemon, strained*

**SERVES 4
PREP/COOKING: 30 MINS**

Wash the truffles well, scrubbing them with a hard brush; dry thoroughly on kitchen towels, then slice on a mandoline.

Break the eggs, one at a time, first on to a plate to check for freshness, then put them into a bowl. Add the cream, salt to taste, a grinding of pepper and the sliced truffles. Heat a trickle of oil in a cast-iron frying pan, then pour in the egg mixture and cook until set on the bottom. Turn over the frittata to set on the other side, then tip it on to a serving plate so that it does not harden; a perfect frittata should be cooked on the outside and soft on the inside, and the truffles should not be cooked.

Cut the frittata into slices and sprinkle with lemon juice. Serve immediately, before it gets cold. Despite their high price, not all bought truffles are of good quality; check carefully that they have a fine aroma (indicating freshness) before buying.

Peperoni e uova

Sweet Peppers with Scrambled Egg

> 1 med. yellow and 1 med. red pepper
> 250 g/8 oz firm ripe tomatoes
> salt and pepper
> 3–4 large fresh basil leaves
> olive oil
> 1 garlic clove
> 2 eggs
> 1 teaspoon grated Pecorino cheese

SERVES 4
PREP/COOKING: 45 MINS

Wash and dry the peppers and cut them in half lengthways, discarding the stalks and seeds. Cut them again lengthways into strips approximately 2 cm/3/4 inch wide.

Parboil the tomatoes in lightly salted water. Skin them and cut them in half, discarding the seeds. Chop into small pieces. Wipe the basil leaves with a damp cloth.

Heat 4 tablespoons of oil and the lightly crushed garlic clove in a frying pan. Discard the garlic as soon as it has browned. Fry the peppers gently until tender (about 15 minutes), stirring occasionally during cooking. Stir in the tomatoes and basil leaves and season with a little salt and pepper. Cook on a low heat for a further 15 minutes, occasionally adding a little boiling water if the mixture becomes too dry.

Beat the eggs with a pinch of salt and pepper and stir them into the vegetables. Keep stirring until the eggs have scrambled. Remove from the heat and serve sprinkled with the grated Pecorino cheese.

Torta di formaggio e noci

Cheese and Walnut Pie

350 g/12 oz frozen puff
  pastry, thawed
a little flour
a little butter
100 g/4 oz Emmental
  cheese

75 g/3 oz walnuts
2 eggs plus 1 egg white
1 tbspoon Calvados
  brandy
salt and pepper
ground nutmeg

SERVES 4
PREP/COOKING: 50 MINS + ANY DEFROSTING TIME

Roll out half the pastry on a floured surface to a thickness of 3 mm/1/8 inch. Butter a 23 cm/9 inch ovenproof pie dish and line it with the pastry. Cut the Emmental cheese into small pieces and liquidise with the walnuts. Place in a bowl and stir in the 2 eggs, the Calvados, a pinch of salt and pepper and a little ground nutmeg. Pour this mixture into the pie shell.

Preheat the oven to 190°C/375°F/gas 5. Roll out the remaining pastry and cover the pie with it. Brush the edges with the lightly beaten egg white and seal the lid to the sides of the pastry. Bake in the lower part of the oven for about 30 minutes or until golden brown. Serve hot.

Teglia di Carciofi e Quartirolo

Emmental and Artichoke Pie

4 artichokes
juice of 1/2 lemon
1 small onion
1 large garlic clove
a handful of fresh parsley
olive oil
50 g/2 oz/4 tbspoons butter
100 ml/4 fl oz/1/2 cup white wine
150 ml/5 fl oz/2/3 cup vegetable stock
a pinch of thyme

25 g/1 oz/1/4 cup flour
150 ml/5 fl oz/2/3 cup milk
50 g/2 oz/1/2 cup grated Parmesan cheese
2 eggs
250 g/8 oz Emmental cheese, thinly sliced
450 g/1 lb frozen puff pastry, thawed
1 tbspoon breadcrumbs

SERVES 8
PREP/COOKING: 1 1/2 HRS

Clean the artichokes, remove the leaves, and put them in a bowl of cold water with the lemon juice. Finely chop the onion, garlic and parsley and fry in the oil and half the butter.

Drain the artichokes well, cut them in half and remove the chokes. Slice them thinly and add them to the frying pan, stirring with a wooden spoon. Slice the stalks horizontally and add those too. After a few minutes pour in the wine and allow it to evaporate almost entirely. Bring the stock to the boil and pour it in. Stir well and turn the heat down to the minimum. Season with a pinch of thyme and cover the pan. Cook the artichokes until nearly all the liquid has been absorbed, then sprinkle with the sieved flour. Mix and pour in the boiling milk, stirring constantly. Simmer for a few minutes and add salt to taste. Preheat the oven to 180°C/350°F/gas 4.

Purée the artichoke mixture. Mix the Parmesan cheese and eggs into the purée, stirring vigorously.

Roll out the pastry to a thickness of 3 mm/⅛ inch, then line a buttered 34 x 20 cm/14 x 8 inch pie dish with low sides. Prick the pastry with a fork and sprinkle with a fine layer of breadcrumbs. Arrange the slices of cheese in the dish and then pour over the artichoke purée. Trim the pastry around the edges of the dish and roll out to make a cover for the pie, making sure it sticks to the pastry beneath. Prick the surface with a fork and bake in the lower part of the oven for about 35 minutes until it is cooked and golden brown. Serve piping hot.

Frittata della Fornarina

Omelette Baked in the Oven

1 small onion
olive oil
1 very large ripe tomato
1 bunch fresh basil
½ vegetable stock cube
4 eggs
salt and pepper
25 g/1 oz/¼ cup grated Parmesan cheese
butter

SERVES 4
PREP/COOKING: 50 MINS

Preheat the oven to 180°C/350°F/gas 4. Finely slice the onions and fry gently in 4 tablespoons of oil. Dice the tomato and add it to the onion with 2 basil leaves and the crumbled stock cube. Increase the heat and let the tomato dry out thoroughly. Remove from the heat and leave to cool. Discard the basil.

Beat the eggs in a bowl and season with a little salt and pepper. Add the grated Parmesan cheese and the cold tomato mixture.

Butter a 25 cm/10 inch round ovenproof dish. Cut out a circle of foil or greaseproof paper the same size as the dish, butter it and place it in the bottom of the dish, making sure that it sticks well. Pour in the egg mixture and cook in the oven for about 20 minutes.

As soon as the top of the omelette is golden brown, remove the dish from the oven and turn it out on to a plate, discarding the foil or paper. Slice, garnish with fresh basil leaves and serve.

'TORTA' LIGURE

Ligurian Pie

---

2 fresh artichokes
juice of 1/2 lemon
1 med. onion
1 garlic clove
a little parsley
about 75 g/3 oz/6 tbspoons butter
olive oil
100 ml/4 fl oz/1/2 cup vegetable stock
150 g/5 oz drained lettuce

1/2 mushroom-flavoured stock cube
flour
150 ml/5 fl oz/2/3 cup milk
2 eggs
50 g/2 oz/1/2 cup grated Parmesan cheese
350 g/12 oz frozen puff pastry, thawed
1 tbspoon breadcrumbs

SERVES 6–8
PREP/COOKING: 1 1/2 HRS

Trim the artichokes and remove leaves, placing them in cold water with the juice of half a lemon. Chop the onion and soften it, together with a garlic clove and a small bunch of parsley, in a knob of the butter and 2 tablespoons of oil.

Drain the artichokes, slice thinly and add to the mixture in the pan. Brown for a few minutes, pour over the stock and cook in a covered pan until they are tender and have absorbed all the liquid. Preheat the oven to 200°C/400°F/gas 6.

Chop the lettuce and sauté it in 25 g/1 oz/2 tablespoons of butter; sprinkle with the mushroom-flavoured cube and the flour. Stir, and gradually pour in the boiling milk. Leave to simmer for a few minutes, stir and pour into a bowl. Stir the artichokes, then add them to the lettuce mix. Add the beaten eggs, the Parmesan cheese and a little salt.

Line a buttered oval pie dish measuring about 30 x 20 cm/12 x 8 inches with the pastry, prick the base and sprinkle with about 1 tablespoon of breadcrumbs. Pour in the prepared mixture and cook in the oven for about 30 minutes. Serve hot.

CROSTINI MARINARI

Crostini with Clams

300 g/10 oz firm ripe tomatoes
salt and pepper
fresh basil
extra virgin olive oil

450 g/1 lb clams
2 garlic cloves
6 slices country bread

SERVES 6
PREP/COOKING: 40 MINS

Plunge the tomatoes into boiling water, skin them and dice very finely. Place in a bowl and season with a pinch each of salt and pepper, a handful of coarsely chopped basil leaves and a trickle of oil. Cover the bowl with cling film and leave the mixture to marinate in the fridge for about 30 minutes.

Preheat the oven to 220°C/425°F/gas 7. Meanwhile, wash the clams in several changes of water, then place in a frying pan with a tablespoon of hot oil flavoured with the garlic. When the clams have opened, remove them from the pan, shell them and set aside. Discard any that do not open.

Rub the bread with garlic and toast in the oven until lightly coloured. Place the tomatoes and clams on top. Arrange the crostini on a plate, trickle on a little oil, decorate as you wish, and serve immediately.

DESSERTS

The Italians are known for their scrumptious desserts. They can be as substanstial and elaborate as a pistachio and hazelnut charlotte, or as light and simple as seasonal fresh fruit. And finally, real Italian ice-cream, made from fresh fruit juices, eggs and cream, is a delight, so different from its manufactured equivalent. It's the perfect way to round off a delicious meal.

CHARLOTTE MERINGATA AL SORBETTO DI MANDARINO

Charlotte Meringue with Mandarin Sorbet

1 x 18 cm/7 inch sponge cake
75 ml/3 fl oz/1/3 cup Grand Marnier
300 g/10 oz strawberries
1/4 fresh pineapple, freshly diced
4 egg whites
salt
100 g/4 oz/1/2 cup caster sugar

FOR THE SORBET
150 ml/5 fl oz/2/3 cup mandarin juice, plus the peel from the squeezed fruit
100 g/4 oz/1/2 cup, plus 1 tbspoon caster sugar
1 egg white

SERVES 8
PREP/COOKING: 2 HRS

Steep the mandarin peel overnight in the juice with the sugar and 150 ml /5 fl oz/2/3 cup water. Next day, strain the infusion and churn in an ice-cream maker. As it begins to solidify, add one-third of an egg white beaten with the remaining sugar, and finish churning. Transfer to freezer.

Slice the cake lengthways into 1.5 cm/1/2 inch slices. Cut five or six of the longest into rectangles as long as the diameter of your mould; halve them into equal triangles and arrange them like rays in the mould, the points converging in the centre. Line the sides with some of the remaining slices, cutting off the excess. Brush the lining sponge with Grand Marnier diluted with a little water. Fill the mould with the strawberries, pineapple and sorbet, alternating the layers with the remaining cake. Chill in the freezer at least 4 hours.

Preheat the oven to 240°C/475°F/gas 9. Just before serving, beat the egg whites with a pinch of salt until very firm, adding the sugar little by little. Unmould the charlotte on to an ovenproof plate and cover it with this meringue, then bake in the hot oven for not more than 3–4 minutes.

COPPE DI ZABAIONE AL VINO BIANCO

Zabaglione Coupes with Sweet White Wine

FOR THE CHOCOLATE SPONGE
2 eggs
75 g/3 oz/6 tbspoons caster sugar
75 g/3 oz/¾ flour
cocoa powder
salt
butter and flour for the tin
75 ml/3 fl oz/⅓ cup Kirsch
200 g/7 oz cooking chocolate

100 ml/4 fl oz/½ cup double cream
fresh raspberries, for decoration

FOR THE ZABAGLIONE
1 whole egg, plus 8 yolks
100g/4 oz/½ cup sugar
200 ml/7 fl oz/ 1 cup dessert white wine
400 ml/14 fl oz/1¾ cup double cream, whipped

SERVES 8
PREP/COOKING: 2½ HRS

Preheat the oven to 180°C/350°F/gas 4. To make the chocolate sponge, beat the eggs and sugar together until they are light and fluffy. Carefully sprinkle on the sieved flour and cocoa (about 3 tablespoons) and beat until the mixture forms a smooth batter. Butter and flour a 20 cm/8 inch sandwich tin and pour in the batter. Bake in the oven for 25–35 minutes until cooked. Set aside to cool, then transfer to a piece of non-stick paper dusted with icing sugar. Brush the sponge with a mixture of Kirsch and cold water. Melt the chocolate over gentle heat with the cream, then spread this over the sponge. Using non-stick paper, roll up like a Swiss roll, starting from one of the longer sides.

Just before assembling the coupes, make the zabaglione: combine the whole egg, yolks, sugar and wine in a bowl, and stand it in a hot bain-marie over very moderate heat. Beat until foamy; leave to cool, then fold in the whipped cream. Divide between eight dishes. Slice the sponge into rounds and garnish the zabaglione with these. Top with fresh raspberries.

Pie di Fragole e Mele

Strawberry and Apple Pie

350 g/12 oz apples
40 g/1 1/2 oz/3 tbspoons butter
50 g/2 oz/1/4 cup caster sugar
3 tbspoons maraschino liqueur

350 g/12 oz strawberries
2 soft amaretti biscuits
6 soft sponge fingers
200 g/7 oz frozen puff pastry, thawed
beaten egg for glazing

SERVES 6
PREP/COOKING: 1 HR

Peel and core the apples and cut into small segments. In a large saucepan, heat the butter, put in the apples, sprinkle with sugar and brown over high heat. Cook for about 2 minutes, then moisten with the maraschino. Evaporate the liquid completely, and leave to cool.

Meanwhile, preheat the oven to 200°C/400°F/gas 6. Hull the strawberries, wash thoroughly and dry well. Cut into small segments and place in a round pie dish, together with the cold apples and the crumbled amaretti biscuits and sponge fingers.

Roll out the pastry and use it to cover the pie dish, making sure it adheres well to the edges. Cut off the excess and use the trimmings to make decorations. Arrange these on the pastry, glaze with the beaten egg and bake in the hot oven for about 30 minutes.

Place the pie dish on a serving plate and serve the pie straight from the dish.

PRUGNE NELLA RETE

Netted Plums

FOR THE SPONGE CAKE
a little flour
50 g/2 oz/4 tbspoons butter
3 eggs plus 1 egg yolk
250 g/8 oz/1 1/4 cups
   sugar
grated rind of 1 lemon
a little vanilla sugar
50 g/2 oz/1/2 cup
   cornflour
100 g/4 oz/1 cup flour

FOR THE TOPPING
10 large yellow plums
25 g/1 oz/2 tbspoons sugar
100 ml/4 fl oz/1/2 cup
   dry white wine
200 g/7 oz plum jam
200 ml/7 fl oz/scant 1 cup
   Amaretto liqueur

FOR THE CARAMEL
100 g/ 4 oz/1/2 cup sugar

SERVES 4
PREP/COOKING: 2 HRS

Preheat the oven to 350°F/180°C/gas 4. To make the sponge, grease and flour a 23 cm/9 inch dome-shaped cake tin. Melt 25 g/1 oz/2 tablespoons of butter and leave it to cool while beating together the whole eggs and yolk with the sugar, until the mixture is light and fluffy. Stir in the grated lemon rind, the vanilla sugar, cornflour and most of the sifted flour. Lastly, add the cool melted butter. Pour the mixture into the prepared cake tin and bake it in the oven for 35 minutes, or until a skewer inserted into the centre comes out clean. Cool on a wire rack.

While the sponge is baking, wash and dry the plums, cut them in half, remove the stones and place them in a pan in a single layer. Sprinkle with 25 g/1 oz/2 tablespoons of sugar, add the white wine and cook them over moderate heat with the lid on for 5 minutes. Take them out of the pan and drain them on kitchen towels. Add the plum jam and half the liqueur to the juice left in the pan. Stir over low heat until it becomes a thick syrup.

When the sponge is cool, cut it into three layers, moisten them with the remaining liqueur, spread them with the jam mixture (reserving 2 tablespoons) and reassemble the gateau on a serving plate. Spread the remaining jam on top and cover it with the cooked plum halves. Leave it in a cool place (not the refrigerator) while you prepare the caramel.

To make the caramel: place the sugar with 3 tablespoons of water over low heat, stirring gently at first until the sugar is completely dissolved. Cook until the sugar has completely caramelized. Dip a wooden spoon into the caramel and run it crisscross fashion over all the plums, like an irregular net. Serve immediately.

Banane 'Rosate' al Pistacchio

Bananas with Pistachios

4 ripe bananas	5 tablespoons red fruit or
25 g/1 oz/2 tbspoons sugar	rose hip jam
4 tbspoons rum	4–5 rose petals
25 g/1 oz/¼ cup pistachio nuts	

SERVES 4
PREP: 20 MINS

Peel the bananas and halve them lengthways. Arrange them on a large dish and sprinkle with the sugar and rum. Leave to stand in a cool place. Meanwhile, parboil the pistachios in salted water for a couple of minutes. Peel them while they are still hot and chop them finely. Put the jam into a bowl and stir until smooth. Place it in the centre of a serving dish and arrange the bananas around it. Pour the rum marinade over the bananas and top with the pistachios.

Garnish with 4–5 fresh rose petals (if available) and serve immediately.

Arance al Grand Marnier

Oranges in Grand Marnier

6 large ripe oranges, washed	6 sugar cubes 4 tbspoons Grand Marnier

SERVES 4
PREP/COOKING: 30 MINS + 30 MINS CHILLING

Pierce the washed oranges all over with a needle. Rub every side of a sugar cube over each orange. Place the sugar in a saucepan. Peel the oranges, remove all the pith and divide them into segments in a bowl. Squeeze any juice remaining in the peel over the sugar cubes.

Heat the sugar cubes gently until dissolved. When a light syrup has formed, remove the pan from the heat and pour in the Grand Marnier. Stir and allow to cool. Pour the liquid over the orange segments and refrigerate for 30 minutes before serving.

If you like, you can place the oranges in individual goblets and garnish to taste.

VENEZIANA CON PANNA E CASTAGNE

Venetian Cake with Cream and Chestnuts

1 kg/2 1/4 lb large round brioche, panettone or plain cake 350 g/12 oz peeled, boiled chestnuts 100 g/4 oz plain chocolate 50 g/2 oz walnuts	300 ml/1/2 pint/1 1/4 cups whipping cream 100 g/4 oz/1 cup icing sugar 150 ml/5 fl oz/2/3 cup rum 1 marron glacé

SERVES 10
PREP: 1 HR

Cut the cake into three equal layers. Purée the peeled, boiled chestnuts (or use a can of already puréed unsweetened chestnuts). Finely chop the chocolate and the walnuts. Whip the cream until stiff, sift in 75 g/3 oz/3/4 cup of the icing sugar, stirring with a top-to-bottom folding movement to avoid deflating the cream.

Place a layer of the cake on a serving plate, moisten it with half the rum, then spread it with half the whipped cream and half the chestnut purée, topped with half the chocolate and walnuts. Cover with the second layer of cake and fill in the same way. Cover with the top layer, place a small bowl in the centre and sprinkle the remaining icing sugar over the exposed surface of the cake. Remove the bowl and carefully place the candied chestnut in the centre of the cake.

Serve as soon as possible without refrigerating. If you prefer, the cake may be cut into more layers than indicated here in which case the filling ingredients should be divided equally among all the layers.

Pagoda di castagne

Chestnut Pagoda

250 g/8 oz chestnut purée	150 ml/5 fl oz/^{2}/$_3$ cup whipping cream
200 g/7 oz fresh Mascarpone cheese or cream cheese	1 sponge cake, about 23 cm/9 in
100 g/4 oz/1 cup icing sugar	100 ml/4 fl oz/1^1/$_2$ cup Cointreau
25 g/1 oz/^{1}/$_4$ cup cocoa powder	1 tbspoon chocolate threads
2 tbspoons brandy	1 tbspoon white chocolate chips
3 tbspoons Amaretto	

SERVES 8
PREP: 1 ^{1}/$_2$ HRS

Place the chestnut purée in a bowl and mix in the Mascarpone cheese, stirring with a wooden spoon until smooth. Sift over it 75 g/3 oz/^{3}/$_4$ cup of icing sugar and the cocoa powder, mix well, then add the brandy and Amaretto liqueur, making sure that each tablespoon is thoroughly absorbed before adding the next.

Whip the cream until firm, then fold in the rest of the sifted icing sugar, stirring with a wooden spoon from top to bottom rather than round and round. Spoon the cream into a piping bag with a small round nozzle, and keep in the refrigerator.

Place the sponge cake on a serving dish and moisten it with the Cointreau, then sieve on to it the mixture of chestnuts and Mascarpone cheese, arranging it in a small heap. Pipe the sweetened whipped cream around the edge, and sprinkle over the chocolate threads. Complete the decoration of the cake by placing the white chocolate chips on top of it and arranging the chocolate buttons evenly spread around it.

Keep the cake in the least cold part of the refrigerator until serving time

FANTASIA DI FRUTTA

Fruit Fantasy

---

3 firm, ripe mandarin oranges or clementines
2 kiwi fruits
1 small banana
3 red and 3 green maraschino cherries

1 tbspoon sugar
juice of $1/2$ lemon
2 tbspoons liqueur of your choice

SERVES 2
PREP: 30 MINS

Wash and dry the mandarins, then cut them in half crossways; use a grapefruit knife to loosen the flesh from the skin, without actually removing it. Peel the kiwi fruits and slice them thinly into 16–18 slices. Cut the same number of slices from the banana and finally cut both the red and green cherries in half.

Arrange the six half-mandarins in the centre of 2 small oval-shaped dishes and decorate with the cherries. Put the slices of kiwi fruit round the outside, topped with the banana slices, and leave to rest for a few minutes (do not place in the refrigerator).

Meanwhile put the sugar in a bowl, add the strained lemon juice and stir until the sugar is dissolved. Mix this cold syrup with the liqueur, stir again, pour over the fruit and serve immediately.

Crema all' Amaretto

Chocolate and Amaretto Cup

250 g/8 oz plain cooking chocolate
100 g/4 oz macaroons
4 egg yolks
100 g/4 oz/1½ cup sugar
75 g/3 oz/¾ cup flour
1 litre/1¾ pints/1 quart milk

1 sachet of vanilla sugar
50 g/2 oz butter, cut into small pieces
2–3 tbspoons Amaretto liqueur
50 g/2 oz flaked almonds

SERVES 6–8
PREP/COOKING: 50 MINS

Grate the chocolate and finely crush the macaroons. Whisk the egg yolks with the sugar until they form soft, whitish peaks. Fold in the sifted flour and 2 tablespoons of cold milk and stir until the mixture is smooth and free of lumps. Add the remaining milk and the vanilla sugar. Gently heat the mixture in a saucepan and bring it just to the boil, stirring constantly with a whisk. Cook for a few minutes, remove from the heat and stir in the butter, grated chocolate and crushed macaroons.

Pour the Amaretto liqueur into a serving bowl, making sure that the sides of the bowl are coated in the liqueur.

Pour in the prepared mixture and leave to cool. Top with the flaked almonds, cover with cling film and keep in the refrigerator until ready to serve.

Charlotte di Pistacchio e Nocciole

Pistachio and Hazelnut Charlotte

FOR THE SPONGE BASE
2 eggs
75 g/3 oz/6 tbspoons caster sugar
2 teaspoons vanilla essence
zest of 1/2 lemon
75 g/3 oz/3/4 cup flour

FOR THE FILLING
250 ml/8 fl oz/1 cup double cream
3 tbspoons gelatine
250 ml/8 fl oz/1 cup milk
3 egg yolks
2 teaspoons cornflour
100 g/4 oz pistachios, blanched and skinned
100 g/4 oz hazelnuts, toasted and skinned
70 g/2 1/2 oz/6 tbspoons caster sugar, plus 1 teaspoon
50 g/2 oz cooking chocolate

SERVES 12
PREP/COOKING: 1 3/4 HRS + CHILLING

Preheat the oven to 220°C/425°F/gas 7. Beat the eggs and sugar together until light and fluffy. Sift the flour with the vanilla and well-washed grated lemon zest and fold delicately into the egg mixture. Butter and flour a 23 cm/9 inch Swiss roll tin and line with greaseproof paper. Butter and flour the paper, pour in the sponge mixture and level the surface. Bake for about 10 minutes. Turn the sponge on to a tea-towel and set aside.

Grind the hazelnuts finely with 1 tablespoon sugar in a food processor to make a paste. Break the chocolate into pieces and place in a bowl with 50 ml/2 fl oz/1/4 cup unwhipped cream and the hazelnut paste. Set the bowl in a pan with two fingers of water and melt the chocolate over very low heat. Soften the gelatine in cold water. Heat the milk. Work the egg yolks with the sugar and cornflour. Add the hot milk, stir in the gelatine, then set over very low heat and heat, stirring continuously; do not let it boil. Divide the cream into two equal parts; add the chocolate mixture to one and the pistachios to the other. Blend the latter until smooth. Whip the remaining cream and fold two-thirds into the pistachio cream. Chill in the fridge for about 20 minutes.

To assemble the charlotte: line a loose-based round cake tin, 25 cm/10 inch diameter, 9 cm/3 1/2 inches deep, with some of the sponge base. Fold the remaining whipped cream into the chocolate cream. Take the pistachio cream out of the refrigerator (it should have begun to set) and pour it into the tin. Spread the chocolate cream on top. Cover with slices of sponge. Chill in the refrigerator for about 6 hours. Unmould and serve.

CROSTATA DI PRUGNE E MELE

Prune and Apple Tart

FOR THE PASTRY
200 g/7 oz butter
300 g/10 oz/2½ cups flour
1 egg
75 g/3 oz/6 tbspoons caster sugar
2 teaspoons of vanilla essence

FOR THE FILLING
250 g/8 oz stoned prunes
100 ml/4 fl oz/½ cup rum
800 g/1¾ lb apples
25 g/1 oz/2 tbspoons butter
juice of ½ lemon
caster and icing sugar
flaked almonds
1 egg, beaten

SERVES 10
PREP/COOKING: 2 HRS

Soak the prunes in the rum for about 1 hour. Work the butter and flour together, then make a well. Break the egg into the centre and add the sugar, vanilla and a pinch of salt. Mix, using your fingertips so as not to over-soften the butter (which would make the pastry lose its body). Roll the dough into a ball, wrap in cling film and refrigerate for 30 minutes,.

Preheat the oven to 190°C/375°F/gas 5. Peel and core the apples and dice finely. Place in a saucepan with the butter, lemon juice, 3 tablespoons caster sugar and a little cold water. Cover the pan and cook the apples over high heat for 7 minutes, then add the prunes and the rum. Cook until the fruit is dry and the apples are pulpy, then leave to cool.

On a lightly floured work surface, roll the dough into a circle 5 mm/¼ inch thick. Use it to line completely a greased 25 cm/10 inch tart tin, cutting off the excess dough. Pour the cooked fruit into the tart tin.

Re-roll the pastry trimmings, then, using a fluted cutter, cut into 1 cm/½ inch wide strips. Arrange these in a lattice pattern on the fruit and fill the spaces with flaked almonds (about 20). Brush the pastry with beaten egg and sift over a light veiling of icing sugar. Bake in the hot oven for about 40 minutes. Serve the tart at room temperature.

COUPELLE CON MOUSSE AL CIOCCOLATO

Little Pastry Cases with Chocolate Mousse

FOR THE PASTRY CASES
100 g/4 oz butter
4 egg whites
100 g/4 oz/1 cup
  icing sugar
100 g/4 oz/1 cup flour
2 teaspoons vanilla essence
 	
FOR THE MOUSSE
300 g/10 oz cooking
  chocolate
	50 ml/2 fl oz/1/4 cup rum
	250 ml/8 fl oz/1 cup
	  double cream
	
	FOR THE VANILLA SAUCE
	250 ml/8 fl oz/1 cup milk
	2 egg yolks
	75 g/3 oz caster sugar
	1 tbspoon flour
	2 teaspoons vanilla essence

SERVES 8
PREP/COOKING: 1 HR 40 MINS + CHILLING

First make the pastry cases (you can do this the day before if you keep them in a cool, dry place). Preheat the oven to 200°C/400°F/gas 6. Melt the butter without browning it, then cool. In a bowl, mix the unbeaten egg whites with the sugar, flour, vanilla and cooled melted butter to make a soft paste. Butter and flour a baking tray; on it place a tablespoon of the mixture, flattening it out with the back of a spoon to make a very thin disc 15–16 cm/6–6 1/2 inches diameter. Place the tray in the hot oven for about 4 minutes. Remove; the disc should be soft, pale in the centre and lightly browned at the edges. Lift it off the tray with a palette knife and mould it around the base of an upturned cup. Leave to cool, then unmould. Repeat the operation until all the paste is used up (you should end up with 8–10 pastry cases).

Break up the chocolate and place in a bowl with the rum. Stand the bowl in a pan with two fingers of tepid water, place over very low heat and melt the chocolate, stirring frequently and gently. Leave to cool. Whip the cream very stiffly. Fold it gently into the cooled chocolate.

Refrigerate for about 2 hours.

Finally, prepare the sauce: heat the milk and, meanwhile, mix the egg yolks with the sugar, vanilla and flour. Stir in the hot milk. Pour the mixture back into the pan and heat over very low heat, stirring continuously; on no account let it boil. Turn off the heat and leave the sauce to cool.

Just before serving, divide the mousse and vanilla sauce equally between the pastry cases.

CROSTATA ALL'ARANCIA CON PANNA MONTATA

Orange Tart with Whipped Cream

FOR THE CRUST
100 g/4 oz butter
300 g/10 oz/2½ cups flour
1 egg
100 g/4 oz/1½ cup icing sugar
1 teaspoon ground cinnamon

FOR THE FILLING
4 egg yolks
150 g/5 oz/¾ cup caster sugar
50 g/2 oz/1½ cup flour
grated zest of 1 orange
500 ml/18 fl oz/2¼ cups milk
2 tbspoons orange liqueur

TO DECORATE
4 oranges
200 ml/7 fl oz/scant 1 cup heavy cream
100 g/4 oz apricot jam

SERVES 6–8
PREP/COOKING: 1½ HRS

To prepare the crust: beat the butter into the flour, then place on a work surface and make a well. Break the egg into the centre and add the sugar and cinnamon. Knead fairly rapidly to avoid over-softening the butter, then wrap the dough in cling film and leave to rest in the refrigerator for about 30 minutes.

Meanwhile, make the filling: in a bowl, work the egg yolks with the sugar, flour and grated orange zest. Heat the milk and pour it on to the egg mixture in a thin stream, then pour the custard back into the pan and place on the heat. Stirring continuously to avoid lumps, simmer for 5 minutes, then remove from the heat, stir in the liqueur and leave to cool.

Preheat the oven to 190°C/375°F/gas 5. On a lightly floured surface, roll out the dough into a circle 3 mm/$^1/_8$ inch thick and use it to line a buttered and floured 25 cm/10 inch loose-bottomed flan tin. Fill with the orange-flavoured custard. Cut off the excess dough and pinch up the edges of the crust. Bake the tart in the hot oven for about 40 minutes.

While the tart is cooking, prepare the decoration: peel 3 oranges, removing all the pith, and cut into rounds. Whip the cream until very stiff. Make a glaze by boiling the jam for 3 minutes with one-third of a glass of water. Peel the remaining orange and cut the zest into very thin strips. Blanch for 2 minutes, then drain very carefully.

Remove the tart from the oven, unmould it on to a serving plate and leave to cool. Arrange the orange rounds on the custard, and brush them with the tepid apricot glaze. Put the cream in a piping bag with a fluted nozzle, and pipe it around the edge of the tart, then arrange the strands of orange zest on top.

Frutta mista glassata

Mixed Glazed Fruit

white grapes
strawberries
mandarin segments
dried apricots
tinned pineapple rings in syrup

FOR THE FONDANT
300 g/10 oz sugar lumps
25 g/1 oz glucose

FOR THE CARAMEL AND CRYSTALLISING
550 g/1 1/4 lb caster sugar

FOR THE CHOCOLATE GLAZE
150 g/5 oz cooking chocolate

SERVES 12
PREP/COOKING: 1 HR + COOLING

Hull, wash and thoroughly dry all the fresh fruit (use any you wish to use – those given above are suggestions only). Drain the pineapple rings and cut into segments. Prepare the fondant: over moderate heat, dissolve the sugar lumps with the glucose and 100 ml/4 fl oz/1/2 cup of water, and heat to 116°C/240.8°F on a sugar thermometer. Pour on to a marble slab and, working energetically with a spatula, knead until the fondant cools to a soft, translucent white mass. Dissolve it again in a bain-marie, then dip in about a third of strawberries, clusters of grapes, apricots and any other fruits, coating them well. Place the fruits on a wire rack and leave to dry in a cool place.

Make the caramel: dissolve 250 g/8 oz/1 1/4 cups caster sugar with 50 ml/2 fl oz/1/4 cup water, and boil to make a syrup at 160°C/320°F; dip in a further third of the grapes, mandarin segments and apricots, coating them completely. Arrange the caramelised fruit on a wire rack and leave to drain and dry in a cool place. (While you are caramelizing the fruit, tilt the pan, keeping the base away from the marble surface; the caramel will cool more slowly, allowing you to glaze more fruit. If the sugar does harden before you have finished, reheat it for a few moments.)

To make the chocolate coating: break up the chocolate and melt it in a bain-marie until it reaches 45°C/113°F. Immerse the bowl in cold water and, working the mixture with a wooden spoon, cool to 30–31°C/86–90°F, dip the remaining fruit into the chocolate; drain with a small slotted spoon and place the fruit on a wire rack to drain and dry.

Finally, crystallise the pineapple: drain it and boil for 25 minutes in a syrup made with 300 g/10 oz/1 1/2 cups sugar and 150 ml/5 fl oz/2/3 cup of water. Take out the pineapple, arrange on a wire rack, sprinkle with the remaining sugar and leave to dry in a cool place. (All the glazed fruit should be prepared a day in advance.)

To serve, arrange the fruit in little glass dishes.

Mousse d'arancia al cioccolato

Orange Mousse with Chocolate

600 g/1 1/4 lb fine cooking chocolate
350 ml/12 fl oz/1 1/2 cups milk
4 egg yolks
100 g/4 oz/1/2 cup sugar
25 g/1 oz/1/4 cup flour

75 ml/3 fl oz/1/3 cup Grand Marnier or other orange liqueur
zest of 3 oranges
300 ml/1/2 pint/1 1/4 cups double cream

SERVES 12
PREP/COOKING: 40 MINS + COOLING

Break up the chocolate and melt it in a bain-marie until it reaches 45°C/113°F on a sugar thermometer. Immerse the bowl in cold water and, working the chocolate with a wooden spoon, cool to 30–31°C/86–90°F. Pour some of the chocolate into glass dishes to coat them. Spread out the remaining chocolate very thinly on a marble surface and leave it to cool.

Prepare the custard: heat the milk. In a bowl, work the egg yolks with the sugar and flour. Pour in the milk in a thin stream, then place over very low heat and, stirring continuously to avoid lumps, simmer for about 3–4 minutes. Take off the heat and stir in the Grand Marnier and the carefully washed and grated orange zest. Leave to cool. Whip the cream until very stiff and fold it into the cooled custard.

Using a knife with a wide, sharp blade, scrape the chocolate off the marble to make flakes. Divide the cold custard between the chocolate-lined dishes, decorate with the chocolate flakes and serve immediately, or keep in the refrigerator.

Panettone farcito

Filled Panettone

10 x 10 kg/2 1/4 lb
  panettone
300 ml/1/2 pint/1 cup
  double cream
100 g/4 oz toasted flaked
  almonds
100 ml/4 fl oz/1/2 cup
  Cointreau or other orange
  liqueur
150 g/5 oz/3/4 cup
  caster sugar
icing sugar

FOR THE GREEN CREAM
1 tbspoon gelatine
50 g/2 oz shelled and
  peeled pistachios
50 g/2 oz/1/4 cup
  caster sugar + 1 tbspoon
250 ml/8 fl oz/1 cup milk
3 egg yolks
cornflour

FOR THE YELLOW CREAM
1 tbspoon gelatine
50 g/2 oz/1/4 cup caster
  sugar
2 teaspoons vanilla essence
250 ml/8 fl oz/1 cup milk
3 egg yolks
cornflour

SERVES 12
PREP/COOKING: 1 1/4 HRS + CHILLING

Cut the panettone into six 2.5 cm/1 inch thick rounds (you will only use five of these rounds, including the base and top).

Soften both amounts of gelatine. Make the green cream: chop the pistachios with a spoonful of sugar, put into the milk and heat. In a bowl, work the egg yolks with the 50 g/2 oz/1/4 cup sugar and a spoonful of cornflour. Whisk in the hot pistachio milk, then reheat the cream without boiling and stir in half the softened gelatine. Purée the cream in a blender and leave to cool. Make the yellow cream in the same way using the remaining gelatine and the vanilla, then leave to cool completely.

Whip the double cream until stiff and spread some of it on the edges of the panettone rounds, then sprinkle on the almonds. When the green and yellow creams start to set, fold half the whipped cream into each one and chill in the refrigerator for 1 hour.

Mix the Cointreau with 100 ml/4 fl oz/¼ cup water and use this to moisten the panettone rounds. Spread the green cream over two of them and the yellow cream over another two. Reassemble the panettone carefully, alternating the different coloured rounds and ending with a plain round of panettone.

Make a caramel by boiling the sugar with a little water until it has dissolved and completely caramelized. Take one strand at a time with two forks and stretch it over two wooden handles, until you have a pile of sugar strands. Arrange this on the top of the panettone, sprinkle with icing sugar and then serve.

SALSA AI PANETTONE

Panettone with Sauce

300 g/10 oz mixed berry fruits, such as strawberries, raspberries, blueberries
300 g/10 oz/1 1/2 cups caster sugar
50 ml/2 fl oz/1 1/4 cup Grand Marnier or other orange liqueur
1 x 1 kg/2 1/4 lb panettone

SERVES 12
PREP: 10 MINS, + MARINATING

Pick over the fruits and discard any that are bruised, then wash them thoroughly and drain well.

Marinate overnight in the sugar and liqueur. Just before serving, crush the fruits with a small whisk, leaving them in the marinade, and mix to obtain a thick sauce. Transfer to a bowl and bring to the table for your guests to help themselves. Slice the panettone into plain pieces (ie: as it comes in the box), or cut into 1.5 cm/3/4 inch slices and briefly toast in a very hot oven. Serve accompanied by the fruit sauce.

BAVARESE DI MELONE

Melon Bavarian Cream

20 g/¾ oz gelatine
1 perfectly ripe med. melon
75 g/3 oz/6 tbspoons
  granulated sugar
50 g/2 oz cleaned
  redcurrants

2 teaspoons vanilla essence
200 ml/7 fl oz/scant 1 cup
  whipping cream
50 g/2 oz strawberry jam

SERVES 8–10
PREP/COOKING: 1¼ HRS + AT LEAST 2 HRS CHILLING

Dissolve the gelatine in cold water. Wash and dry the melon, then halve it and remove the seeds. Remove the pulp with a spoon, without piercing the rind which will be used as a container. Place the pulp in a saucepan and add the sugar and the redcurrants.

Place the saucepan on the heat and, stirring occasionally with a wooden spoon, simmer gently until the mixture has the consistency of jam, making sure it does not stick to the bottom of the pan.

Remove from the heat, stir the mixture for a couple of minutes and pour it into a bowl; while it is still warm stir in the vanilla and the gelatine. Mix well to dissolve the gelatine, then let it cool. Whip the cream and fold it into the melon cream when it is cold but not yet firm, mixing with a motion from top to bottom rather than round and round (to prevent the cream from going flat). Pour the strawberry jam into a small bowl and stir vigorously with a spoon to make it smooth.

Spread a layer of the melon Bavarian cream in each half shell of the melon and pour over each layer some of the strawberry jam. Refrigerate for at least 2 hours so that the Bavarian cream will firm, then cut each half into 4–5 slices, using a very sharp knife; arrange them on a serving plate and serve.

'CESTINI' CON CREMA E RIBES

Redcurrant in Lemon Cream Baskets

5 large lemons, washed	1 tbspoon orange liqueur
2 small macaroons	8 bunches redcurrants
3 egg yolks	8 fresh mint leaves
100 g/4 oz/½ cup sugar	7 rolled wafers
25 g/1 oz/¼ cup flour	
300 ml/½ pint/1 ¼ cups milk	

SERVES 4
PREP/COOKING: 1 HR

Grate the rind of one lemon. Halve the other 4 lemons and squeeze them, reserving the juice. Scrape out the flesh and trim the bases so that they stand level.

Crumble the macaroons and divide them among the half-lemons. Add to the pan with the lemon rind, egg yolks, sugar, flour and 2 tablespoons of the milk, and beat to obtain a perfectly smooth mixture. Add the rest of the milk and, stirring continuously, bring to the boil. Remove from the heat and add the liqueur, then stand the pan in cold water and stir until the custard is completely cooled.

Wash the redcurrants and dry them on a cloth. Pick off the largest currants and arrange them over the macaroon crumbs in the lemon halves; fill up with the lemon cream, using a piping bag with a plain round nozzle. Garnish with redcurrants and a mint leaf and arrange on a flat dish, interspersed with the wafers. Serve immediately, before the cream can absorb any bitterness from the lemon pith.

If you do not wish to use lemon halves as containers, you could substitute individual pastry shells baked blind with dried beans to keep their shape. The baskets will also need to be served quickly, before the pastry loses its crispness.

PIRAMIDE DI BIGNE

Profiteroles in Spun Caramel

FOR THE PASTRY
100 g/4 oz butter, cut into pieces
150 g/5 oz/1 1/4 cups flour, sifted
4 eggs
a little butter

FOR THE CUSTARD
2 eggs + 2 egg yolks
150 g/5 oz/3/4 cup caster sugar
50 g/2 oz/1/4 cup flour
600 ml/1 pint/2 1/2 cups milk
2 teaspoons vanilla essence

FOR THE CARAMEL
150 g/5 oz/3/4 cup caster sugar

MAKES ABOUT 40 PROFITEROLES
PREP/COOKING: 2 HRS

Heat 150 ml/5 fl oz/2/3 cup of water, the butter and a pinch of salt in a saucepan. As soon as it boils, remove from the heat and pour in the flour. Mix and then cook over low heat, stirring, until it no longer sticks to the edges of the pan. Turn on to a working surface, spread out and leave to cool.

Preheat the oven to 190°C/375°F/gas 5. Return the mixture to the pan and mix in the eggs, one at a time. When the mixture is thick and smooth, spoon it into a piping bag. Pipe rosettes on to a buttered baking tray, making sure they are well separated – they will puff up and spread during cooking. Bake for 15 minutes. Before removing from the oven cut open 1 profiterole to check that it is cooked – it should be hollow and slightly crisp. Cool the profiteroles on a rack.

Meanwhile, beat the eggs, yolks and sugar until the mixture forms soft white ribbons. Sift in the flour and add the cold milk and vanilla essence. Heat gently and allow to thicken, stirring constantly. As soon as the mixture comes to the boil, plunge the pan into cold water to cool. Pipe the mixture into the profiteroles and arrange them on a serving plate.

Dissolve the sugar in 4 tablespoons of water over moderate heat. Let it boil until it has turned light brown, remove from the heat and stir to cool and thicken. When it begins to form threads, pour it over the profiteroles, holding the pan fairly high and moving it in circles so that the caramel falls in spun threads around the profiteroles. If it thickens too much, reheat it gently. Serve as soon as possible.

Torta 'Gianfranco'

Chocolate Gateau

a little butter and flour
3 eggs plus 2 egg yolks
250 g/8 oz/1 1/4 cups caster sugar
2 teaspoons of vanilla essence
300 g/10 oz plain cooking chocolate
100 g/4 oz/1 cup flour
50 g/2 oz/1 1/2 cup potato flour
3 tbspoons cocoa powder baking powder
150 ml/5 fl oz/2/3 cup milk
400 ml/3/4 pint/2 cups whipping cream
50 g/2 oz flaked almonds

SERVES 10
PREP/COOKING: 1 3/4 HRS

Butter a 25 cm/10 inch round cake tin and sprinkle with flour. Whisk the eggs briskly with 150 g/5 oz/3/4 cup of the sugar, a pinch of salt and the vanilla until they form soft peaks.

Preheat the oven to 180°C/350°F/gas 4. Melt 75 g/3 oz of the cooking chocolate over low heat and leave to cool. Mix the flour with the potato flour, cocoa and a heaped teaspoon of baking powder and sift into the egg mixture. Fold in the melted chocolate and pour the mixture into the prepared pan. Bake in the oven for about 30 minutes.

Meanwhile beat the egg yolks with the remaining flour, sugar and a pinch of salt. Gradually add the milk and bring to boil, stirring constantly. Remove the pan from the heat and leave to cool, stirring from time to time.

Cut 100 g/4 oz of the cooking chocolate into small pieces, melt it over low heat and add it to the mixture, stirring vigorously. Leave to cool.

Turn cake out on to a wire rack. Whisk the cream until stiff then fold it into the chocolate mixture. Cut the cake into three layers and sandwich together with two thirds of the mixture. Coat top and sides of cake with some of the mixture and sprinkle with the remainder of the cooking chocolate, grated. Pipe rosettes of chocolate mixture on the cake and decorate with flaked almonds. Refrigerate and serve within 4–5 hours.

Gelato al caffè

Coffee Ice Cream

50 g/2 oz/¾ cup coffee
1 tbspoon of vanilla essence
350 g/12 oz/1¾ granulated sugar

200 ml/7 fl oz/1¾ cups single cream
1 egg white

SERVES 6
PREP/COOKING: 30 MINS + FREEZING

In a small saucepan bring 350 ml/12 fl oz/1½ cups of water to the boil, pour in the coffee and, stirring constantly, simmer over very low heat until the foam has disappeared. Leave to infuse for about 15 minutes, so that the ground coffee sinks to the bottom of the saucepan; strain the liquid coffee into a bowl.

Add the vanilla and the sugar, stir until the sugar is dissolved then leave to cool. At this point mix in the cream and place in the refrigerator for at least 1 hour to cool completely.

Pour the mixture into an ice-cream machine or container, add the egg white whisked to a froth, with a pinch of salt, so that the ice-cream will be smooth and soft. Freeze until required.

GELATO ALLA VANIGLIA

Vanilla Ice Cream

600 ml/1 pint/2½ cups milk
150g/5 oz/¾ cup sugar

1 small vanilla pod/bean
5 egg yolks
1 egg white

SERVES 6
PREP/COOKING: 30 MINS + FREEZING

Heat most of the milk in a saucepan with the sugar, a pinch of salt and the vanilla pod until almost boiling. Remove from the heat and discard the pod. Meanwhile, beat the egg yolks then add, little by little, first the reserved cold milk, then the hot, stirring constantly. When the ingredients are well blended, pour the mixture back into the saucepan and heat for about 2 minutes, stirring.

Pour the mixture into a bowl and let it cool, stirring occasionally. Pour it into an ice-cream machine or container, straining it through a fine sieve. Halfway through the process add the egg white whisked to a froth with a pinch of salt so that the ice cream will be very smooth and soft.

Freeze until required.

GELATO AL PISTACCHIO

Pistachio Ice Cream

100 g/4 oz pistachio nuts
250 g/8 oz/1 1/4 sugar
600 ml/1 pint/2 1/2 cups milk

1 vanilla pod/bean
5 egg yolks

SERVES 6
PREP/COOKING: 30 MINS + FREEZING

Plunge the pistachio nuts into salted boiling water for 1 minute, then drain and shell them. Pound them in a mortar, adding a tablespoon of sugar from time to time, until they are reduced to powder.

Heat most of the milk with the remaining sugar and the vanilla pod and bring slowly to the boil, stirring occasionally with a wooden spoon. Remove from the heat and discard the pod.

Meanwhile, beat the egg yolks in a bowl with the powdered pistachio nuts, using a small whisk to obtain a smooth mixture. Add first the reserved cold milk, then the hot, stirring constantly. When the ingredients are well blended, pour the mixture back into the saucepan and heat for about 2 minutes, stirring. Pour the mixture into a bowl and let it cool, stirring occasionally. Pour into an ice-cream machine or container, straining it through a fine sieve.

Freeze until required.

Gelato all' amaretto

Amaretto Ice Cream

600 ml/1 pint/2½ cups milk
1 vanilla pod/bean
5 egg yolks

150 g/5 oz/¾ cup sugar
100 g/4 oz small macaroons
4 tbspoons Amaretto liqueur

SERVES 6
PREP/COOKING: 1½ HRS + FREEZING

Heat the milk in a saucepan with the vanilla pod and bring slowly to the boil; strain, remove from the heat and discard the pod. Leave to cool. Meanwhile, beat the egg yolks with a pinch of salt and the sugar until soft and frothy. Stir in the lukewarm milk, pouring it in a trickle, and whisk until well blended. Then pour the mixture back into the saucepan, place over very low heat and, stirring constantly, heat until the mixture is about to boil.

Remove from the heat and strain the liquid through a fine sieve, then leave to cool at room temperature, stirring occasionally. Add the finely crumbled macaroons and Amaretto liqueur. Place in the refrigerator for about 1 hour, then pour the mixture into an ice-cream machine or container. Freeze until required.

GELATO AL TORRONCINO

Torrone Ice Cream

150 g/5 oz assorted crystallised fruit
50 ml/2 fl oz/1 cup Maraschino liqueur
100 g/4 oz torrone (Italian nougat)

600 ml/1 pint/2½ cups fresh milk
1 vanilla pod/bean
200 g/7 oz/1 cup sugar
4 egg yolks

SERVES 6
PREP/COOKING: 1½ HRS + FREEZING

Coarsely chop the crystallised fruit, of different colours and flavours, place it in a small bowl and moisten it with the Maraschino. Pound the *torrone* to a powder.

In a saucepan heat most of the milk with the vanilla pod and the sugar. When the milk is hot and the sugar has dissolved, discard the pod.

Beat the egg yolks in a bowl adding first the reserved cold milk then the hot, pouring in a trickle and stirring constantly. When the ingredients are well mixed, pour back into the saucepan and heat for a couple of minutes, stirring, without bringing it to boil. Remove the saucepan from the heat and strain the mixture into a bowl. Let it cool, stirring occasionally, then leave it for at least 1 hour in the refrigerator.

Just before placing it in an ice-cream machine or container mix in the crystallised fruit and the *torrone*. Freeze until required.

Crostata di pesche all 'Amaretto

Peach and Macaroon Pie

a little butter and flour
100 g/4 oz/1 cup flour
50 g/2 oz/¼ cup sugar
grated rind of ½ lemon
1 egg yolk
50 g/2 oz/4 tbspoons butter
1 tbspoon dry vermouth
12 small macaroons
6 tbspoons peach jam
1 tbspoon apricot brandy
2 large yellow peaches
1 tbspoon Amaretto liqueur
redcurrants

SERVES 6–8
PREP/COOKING: 1 HR + COOLING

Preheat the oven to 190°C/375°F/gas 5. Butter and flour a round 23 cm/10 inch pie dish.

Sift the flour and add a pinch of salt, the sugar and the grated lemon rind. Make a well in the centre and add the egg yolk, the softened butter, cut into small pieces, and the vermouth. Knead rapidly into a smooth dough, then roll out and line the prepared dish with it; prick the bottom of the pastry with a fork. Crumble over 7 macaroons. Set aside 2 tablespoons of jam, place the rest in a bowl and stir in the apricot brandy. Spread evenly over the crumbs.

Peel, halve and stone the peaches, then cut them into equal slices and arrange them in a circle, slightly overlapping on the pastry; in the centre put the remaining macaroons and sprinkle them with the Amaretto liqueur. Bake for about 40 minutes.

Remove the pie from the oven and let it cool in the dish; then place it on a large round plate. Melt the remaining jam over low heat, strain it through a fine sieve and brush the peach slices and the macaroons with it. As soon as the glaze has cooled and is firm, garnish the pie with sprigs of redcurrants and serve.

DOLCE AL CUCCHIAIO

Zabaglione Trifle

FOR THE SPONGE CAKE
100 g/4 oz/1 cup flour
100 g/4 oz/1½ cup caster sugar
3 eggs
2 teaspoons of vanilla essence
salt
butter and flour for the tin

FOR THE ZABAGLIONE
50 g/2 oz/¼ cup caster sugar
50 ml/2 fl oz/¼ cup Marsala wine

3 egg yolks, plus 1 whole egg
salt

TO FINISH
3 Golden Delicious apples
1 tbspoon caster sugar
500 ml/18 fl oz/2¼ cups double cream
75 ml/3 fl oz/⅓ cup Maraschino
juice of 1 lemon
raspberries
butter for greasing

SERVES 10–12
PREP/COOKING: 2 HRS

Preheat the oven to 190°C/375°F/gas 5. Using the listed ingredients, make a sponge mixture: beat the eggs and sugar together until light and fluffy. Sift in the flour, vanilla and a pinch of salt and beat until the mixture makes a smooth batter. Butter and flour a 20 cm/8 inch cake tin and bake in the oven for about 35 minutes or until the cake springs back when lightly pressed with a finger. Turn out the cake and leave to cool on a wire rack. Increase the oven temperature to 240°C/475°F/gas 9.

Now prepare the zabaglione: combine all the ingredients with a pinch of salt in a stainless steel bowl. Stand the bowl in a bain-marie of tepid water, place over very low heat and whisk the eggs until risen, creamy and thick. Remove from the bain-marie and leave to cool. Core two of the apples, peel and slice thinly, then arrange on a greased baking tray. Sprinkle with the sugar, then cook in the hot oven for about 5 minutes. Whip the cream and fold about 200 ml/7 fl oz/1 cup into the prepared zabaglione. Dilute the maraschino with a little cold water. Cut the sponge cake into small slices, brush them with the maraschino, then arrange a few in the bottom of a bowl. Cover with half the zabaglione, and follow with alternate layers of apple, sponge cake, apple and zabaglione. Level the surface carefully.

Thinly slice the remaining apple, without peeling it. Dip the slices in lemon juice, then drain and arrange them around the edge of the trifle. Put the remaining whipped cream in a piping bag with a ridged nozzle and pipe decoratively on to the trifle. Finish the decoration with a couple of dozen raspberries, and keep in the refrigerator until you are ready to serve.

Composta di Albicocche

Fresh Apricot Compote

550 g/1 ¼ lb firm ripe apricots
100 g/4 oz apricot jam
1 tbspoon white rum
1 tbspoon apricot liqueur
grated rind of 1 lemon
1 lime for garnish
7 Maraschino cherries

SERVES 6
PREP: 15 MINS + 1 ½ HRS SOAKING

Remove the stalks from the apricots and wipe them with a damp cloth. Halve them, remove the stones, and slice them into a basin. Strain the jam, dilute it with the rum and liqueur and add the grated lemon rind. Mix well and pour over the apricots, stirring carefully. Cover the basin with cling film and leave in the least cold part of the refrigerator for at least 1 ½ hours, giving the mixture a gentle stir from time to time.

Distribute the apricots among six individual bowls. Garnish each one with five wafer-thin rings of lime and five slices of Maraschino cherry. Serve at once.

Zuccotto ricco

Rich Zuccotto

FOR THE SPONGE CAKE
3 egg yolks
150 g/5 oz/¾ cup caster sugar
salt
150 g/5 oz/1¼ cups white flour
2 teaspoons of vanilla essence
flour and butter for the tin

FOR THE FILLING AND TO FINISH
200 g/7 oz cooking chocolate
400 ml/14 fl oz/1¾ double cream
100 ml/4 fl oz/½ cup creme de cacao liqueur
langue de chat biscuits for serving

FOR THE PASTRY CREAM
4 egg yolks
150 g/5 oz/¾ cups caster sugar
50 g/2 oz/½ cup flour
500 ml/18 fl oz/2¼ cups milk
lemon zest

SERVES 12
PREP/COOKING: 2 HRS + CHILLING

Preheat the oven to 190°C/375°F/gas 5. Make the sponge cake (you can do this the day before). Beat the egg yolks with the sugar and a pinch of salt until the mixture forms a ribbon (when you lift the whisk, the mixture which falls from it does not sink back immediately into the mixture in the bowl, but remains lightly on the surface). Sift in the flour and vanilla from a height, folding them in carefully with a wooden spoon, stirring from bottom to top and vice-versa. Pour the mixture into a buttered and floured 23 cm/9 inch cake tin, and bake in the oven for about 35 minutes, or until a skewer inserted into the centre comes out clean. Remove from the oven, invert on to a wire rack and leave to cool.

Meanwhile, make the pastry cream: work the egg yolks with the sugar and flour. Heat the milk with a little lemon zest, then pour it into the egg mixture in a thin stream. Set over moderate heat and, stirring continuously, boil for about 5 minutes, then turn off the heat and leave to cool.

Melt 150 g/5 oz cooking chocolate and cool until it is tepid. Whip one-quarter of the double cream until very firm and mix it with the chocolate and the cooled pastry cream.

To assemble the zuccotto: cut the crusts off the sponge cake and slice it. Moisten with the liqueur diluted with 100 ml/4 fl oz/½ cup water. Use some of the slices to line a large, flat-bottomed bowl. Cut the rest into strips and fill the bowl with layers of chocolate cream and sponge strips. Chill in the refrigerator for at least 3 hours.

Unmould the zuccotto on to a serving plate. Whip the remaining cream, place in a piping bag with a ridged nozzle, and pipe it over the zuccotto. Melt the rest of the chocolate, place in an icing bag and decorate the zuccotto, finishing with a crown of *langues de chat* biscuits. Leave in the fridge until ready to serve: the decorated zuccotto will keep for about 6–8 hours.

COPPETTE DI CASTAGNE

Chestnut Cups

---

450 g/1 lb chestnuts, boiled and peeled
100 g/4 oz/1¼ cup caster sugar
4 tbspoons Cointreau
a little vanilla sugar
100 ml/4 fl oz/½ cup whipping cream
6 pistachio nuts

SERVES 4
PREP/COOKING: ABOUT 30 MINS + COOLING

Place the chestnuts in a bowl that just holds them. Heat the sugar with 3 tablespoons of water, letting it dissolve gradually then come to the boil. Remove from the heat, add the Cointreau and vanilla sugar, stir and pour this mixture over the chestnuts. Cover the bowl with cling film and leave it to cool completely, during which time the chestnuts will absorb much of the syrup.

Divide the chestnuts between four individual cups. Whip the cream until firm and, using a piping bag, decorate each cup with a ring of cream rosettes. Blanch the pistachio nuts for a few seconds in slightly salted boiling water, remove the skins and dry them on kitchen towels. Chop them finely and sprinkle them on the cream. Serve immediately, since the chestnuts are at their best straight after cooling.

Pesche ai Pinoli

Peaches with Pine Nuts

4 equal-sized yellow peaches, perfectly ripe
butter
1 clove
5 cm/2 inch piece lemon rind
2 tbspoons granulated sugar
6 tbspoons brandy
8 tbspoons pine nuts

SERVES 4
PREP/COOKING: 45 MINS

Remove the stems from the peaches, then wash and dry them; cut them in half with a small sharp knife and remove the stones.

Melt a large knob of butter in a saucepan, then arrange the eight peach halves on the bottom of the pan, cut side down. Fry very gently for a few moments with the pan uncovered, then add the clove and the piece of lemon rind. Sprinkle the fruit with the sugar and moisten with the brandy. Move the pan slightly to make sure the peaches aren't stuck to the bottom, then lower the heat to the minimum, cover, and cook the peaches for about 20 minutes until they are poached and glazed.

Place the peaches, cut side upwards, on a serving dish and in the hollow of each place a spoonful of pine nuts. Reduce the cooking liquid slightly, then strain it directly on to the fruit.

Serve immediately while still hot – though peaches prepared in this way are also excellent lukewarm.

Cestini all'uva

Baskets of Grapes

2 egg whites
75 g/3 oz/6 tbspoons sugar
75 g/3 oz/³/₄ cup flour
75 g/3 oz/6 tbspoons butter

450 g/1 lb vanilla ice cream
275 ml/9 fl oz/about 1 cup whipping cream
a large bunch of black grapes

SERVES 6
PREP/COOKING: 45 MINS

Preheat the oven to 220°C/425°F/gas 7. Beat the egg whites in a bowl until stiff then gradually whisk in the sugar and keep beating for 2–3 minutes. Add 2 tablespoons of flour and 4 tablespoons of melted butter, stirring to form a smooth batter.

Grease and flour a baking tray. Pour about 3 tablespoons of the batter separately on to it, keeping them well apart. Spread the mixture on the tray with the back of a spoon into three thin omelettes about 13 cm 5 inches in diameter. Bake for 6–7 minutes until golden at the edges. Remove them from the oven and, working quickly with a fish slice, transfer each on to an upturned glass.

While soft, press them against the glass bottom to shape into baskets. Repeat with the remaining mixture. Set aside, still on the glasses, to firm up.

When cool and firm, put in a scoop of ice cream in the centre of each basket. Decorate with whipped cream and garnish all around with the washed and dried grapes. Serve at once.

FICHI SPEZIATI CON RIBES E GELATO

Figs with Redcurrants and Ice Cream

1 kg/2¼ lb fresh figs, not overripe	a few whole cloves
100 g/4 oz/½ cup sugar	6 tbspoons brandy
50 g/2 oz/½ cup raisins	rind of 1 lemon
ground cinnamon	12 thin slices fruit cake or loaf
ground ginger	redcurrants

SERVES 6
PREP/COOKING: 40 MINS + 1 HR MARINATING

Using a small, sharp knife, peel the figs. Cut each one into four or six according to size and place in a stainless steel saucepan. Add the sugar, raisins, a large pinch of cinnamon, a pinch of ginger and a few cloves. Pour over 2 tablespoons of the brandy. Cut a 7 cm/3 inch piece of lemon rind into needle-fine strips and add to the other ingredients. Cover the mixture and leave in a cool place for about 1 hour.

Cook the figs over low heat for about 15 minutes from the moment the liquid begins to simmer. Keep the pan uncovered and stir gently from time to time. Immerse the saucepan in cold water to cool quickly.

Arrange the fruit cake in a glass salad bowl and pour over the remaining brandy. Spread the fig mixture on top and cover. Keep in the refrigerator until it is time to serve. Then sprinkle some stemmed, washed redcurrants on top and decorate with scoops of ice cream.

Torta 'festa della mamma

Mother's Day Cake

butter
100 g/4 oz/1 cup flour
3 eggs plus 4 egg yolks
300 g/10 oz/1 1/2 cups caster sugar
2 teaspoons vanilla essence
50 g/2 oz/1/2 cup potato flour

1 tablespoon gelatine
150 ml/5 fl oz/2/3 cup Marsala wine
100 ml/4 fl oz/1/2 cup Amaretto liqueur
100 ml/4 fl oz/1/2 cup whipping cream
5 large ripe strawberries

SERVES 10–12
PREP/COOKING: 1 1/4 HRS + AT LEAST 2 HRS CHILLING

Preheat the oven to 180°C/350°F/gas 4. Butter and flour a round, hinged cake tin about 25 cm/10 inches in diameter. Beat three of the eggs with 150 g/5 oz/3/4 cup of the sugar, half the vanilla essence and a pinch of salt until frothy. Add the remaining flour and the potato flour sieved together through a fine sieve. Fold them in very gently with an up-and-down movement rather than a circular one using a wooden spoon. Pour the batter into the cake tin and bake in the oven for about 35 minutes, or until a skewer inserted into the centre comes out clean. Turn the cake out on to a rack to cool.

Meanwhile, soften the gelatine in a little cold water. In a copper bowl beat the 4 egg yolks together with the remaining sugar and vanilla sugar. When the mixture is frothy add the Marsala, making sure that each tablespoon is thoroughly absorbed before adding the next. Then add 3 tablespoons of the Amaretto liqueur, pouring it in a trickle and stirring all the time. Place the copper bowl over a pan of barely simmering water and, still stirring, heat the zabaglione cream until it is very hot. At this point remove it from the heat and fold in the gelatine. Mix thoroughly until the gelatine has dissolved, then pour the zabaglione cream into a bowl and let it cool.

Cut the cake into three layers of equal thickness and place the lowest one back in the tin used to bake it, lined with greaseproof paper. Sprinkle the cake with a third of the remaining Amaretto liqueur and spread over it a third of the warm zabaglione cream. Repeat the same procedure with the second and third layers of cake. Refrigerate the cake for at least 2 hours, when the zabaglione cream will have set.

Beat the cream until stiff and put it in a piping bag. Wipe the strawberries and hull four of them, then cut them in half lengthways. Slide the blade of a small knife between the side of the mould and the cake, then open the hinge and detach the side of the mould. Slide the cake on to a serving dish by removing first the bottom of the mould and then the greaseproof paper. Garnish the top with the whipped cream and the strawberries. Serve immediately.

TURBANTE ROSA FRAGOLA

Strawberry Mousse

2 tbspoons gelatine
a little almond oil
250 g/8 oz just-ripe strawberries
100 g/4 oz/1/2 cup sugar
400 ml/3/4 pint/1 3/4 cups whipping cream

4 tbspoons Cointreau
2 tbspoons desiccated coconut
10 equal-sized strawberries, with their stalks, for garnish
fresh mint leaves for garnish

SERVES 8–10
PREP/COOKING: 1 HR + OVERNIGHT CHILLING

Soak the gelatine in cold water. Lightly oil a 1 litre/1 3/4 pint/1 quart pudding basin with the almond oil. Hull the strawberries and wash them rapidly under cold running water. Lay them out to dry on a double layer of kitchen towels. When they are completely dry, process them in a blender with the sugar and pour the purée into a bowl.

Whip the cream until it is stiff then gently fold it into the strawberry purée, mixing in with a wooden spoon with an up-and-down movement to prevent the cream from deflating. Heat the Cointreau in a small saucepan until it begins to simmer. Remove from the heat and stir in the gelatine until it has dissolved. Add the desiccated coconut to the strawberry mixture, then slowly pour in the Cointreau and gelatine in a trickle. Mix constantly with an up-and-down folding movement.

Pour into the basin, bang it gently, cover with cling film and refrigerate overnight. Turn the mousse out on to a serving dish and garnish with the strawberries and the mint leaves. Serve at once.

Crostata 'Sera di Maggio'

May Evening Pie

> 150 g/5 oz/1 1/4 cups flour
> 150 g/5 oz/3/4 cup
>   granulated sugar
> grated rind of 1/2 lemon
> 75 g/3 oz/6 tbspoons butter
> 1 small egg
> 15 g/1/2 oz/2 tbspoons
>   gelatine
>
> 550 g/1 1/4 lb ripe
>   strawberries
> 100 ml/4 fl oz/1/2 cup
>   Cointreau
> 150 ml/5 fl oz/2/3 cup
>   whipping cream
> a few mint leaves for
>   garnish

SERVES 8
PREP/COOKING: 1 HR + 3–4 HRS CHILLING

Mix the flour, 50 g/2 oz/1/4 cup of sugar, the grated lemon rind and a pinch of salt together and make a well in the centre. Cut the softened butter into small pieces and place in the well with the egg; mix quickly to a smooth dough. Roll it into a ball, wrap it in greaseproof paper or cling film and let it rest in the refrigerator for about 30 minutes.

Meanwhile preheat the oven to 180°C/350°F/gas 4. Butter and flour a round pie dish 23 cm/9 inches in diameter. Roll out enough dough to line the dish and prick it with a fork; cover it with a sheet of foil and place a few dried beans on top. Bake the pastry for about 30 minutes. Remove the beans and foil and let the pastry shell cool inside the dish.

Dissolve the gelatine in a little cold water. Remove the stems from 450 g/1 lb of the strawberries, wash them in very cold water, drain them, then cut them into small pieces. Place them in a liquidiser together with the remaining sugar and liquidise them first at low speed then at high speed for a couple of minutes. Heat the Cointreau in a saucepan; remove it from the heat and, while still hot, fold in the gelatine, stirring it until it is completely dissolved; add the strawberries and stir the mixture for a further 30 seconds.

Turn out the pastry shell on to a serving dish and pour over the strawberry mixture, distributing it evenly. Keep the tart in the refrigerator for

3–4 hours or, even better, overnight, to set the filling.

A short time before serving, beat the whipping cream until stiff, put it in a piping bag, and decorate to taste, finishing off with the remaining strawberries, washed but not stemmed, and a few mint leaves. Serve immediately.

CREMA SFORMATA CON MANDORLE E UVETTA

Pudding with Almonds and Raisins

---

75 g/3 oz/¾ cup raisins
150 ml/5 fl oz/⅔ cup dry white wine
100 g/4 oz almonds
2 eggs
150 g/5 oz/¾ cup caster sugar
2 slices white bread, crumbled

300 ml/½ pint/1 ¼ cups single cream
300 ml/½ pint/1 ¼ cups milk
ground nutmeg
1 teaspoon ground cinnamon
butter

SERVES 6
PREP/COOKING: 1 ½ HRS

Preheat the oven to 180°C/350°F/gas 4. Soak the raisins in the white wine. Parboil the almonds in a little water for a few minutes, drain and peel them. Toast them in the oven for 3–4 minutes. Chop finely in a liquidiser.

Reduce the oven temperature to 150°C/300°F/gas 2. Beat the eggs, add the sugar and whisk to form a ribbon. Mix in the chopped almonds, the crumbled bread and the drained raisins. Add the cream and milk and flavour with a pinch of ground nutmeg and the cinnamon.

Butter a 25 cm/10 inch ovenproof pie dish and pour in the mixture. Cook in the preheated oven for at least 1 hour. The cake is ready when the centre springs back when pressed with a finger. Cool in the dish and then turn on to a plate. This dish may be served with whipped cream piped on the top or served separately.

CREMA DI RICOTTA, FRITTA

Fried Ricotta Slices

100 g/4 oz ricotta cheese
75 g/3 oz/6 tbspoons sugar
100 g/4 oz/1 cup flour
5 eggs
200 ml/7 fl oz/1 cup single cream
300 ml/$^{1}/_{2}$ pint/1 $^{1}/_{4}$ cups milk
oil
a little semolina

SERVES 4–6
PREP/COOKING: 40 MINS

Sieve and mash the ricotta and mix it with the sugar, a little salt and the sifted flour. Stir in the eggs, one at a time, to form a smooth, creamy paste. Whisk in the cream and milk.

Heat the mixture in a small saucepan, stirring constantly with a whisk, and allow it to thicken. Remove from the heat as soon as it starts to boil.

Grease a baking tin with plenty of oil and pour in the mixture, spreading it to a thickness of about 1 cm/$^{1}/_{2}$ inch. Leave to cool and set then cut it into diamond shapes. Coat the diamonds in the semolina.

Heat plenty of oil in a large frying pan and fry the diamonds a few at a time, turning them carefully so that they brown on all sides. Drain on kitchen towels and arrange on a plate. Serve warm or cold.

Crostata di Mascarpone all'uva e mela

Grape and Apple Cheesecake

FOR THE CRUST
100 g/4 oz/1 cup flour
50 g/2 oz/1 cup caster sugar
100 g/4 oz butter
2 egg yolks
grated rind of 1 lemon
a little butter and flour

FOR THE FILLING
200 g/7 oz Mascarpone cheese

50 g/2 oz/1 cup icing sugar
2 egg yolks
2 tbspoons brandy

FOR THE TOPPING
20 small macaroons
a large bunch green grapes
1 apple
5 tbspoons caster sugar
5 mint leaves

SERVES 8
PREP/COOKING: 1½ HRS

To make the crust: put the sifted flour, sugar and a pinch of salt together in a bowl and add the butter, cut into small cubes. Rub it in with your fingers until the mixture resembles coarse breadcrumbs. Add the egg yolks and lemon rind. Roll the dough into a ball, wrap it in cling film and leave it in the refrigerator for 30 minutes.

Meanwhile preheat the oven to 190°C/375°F/gas 5. Grease and flour a round 25 cm/10 inch pie dish with a smooth bottom and fluted sides.

Roll out the pastry and line the pan, pricking the bottom with a fork. Bake in the oven for about 20 minutes or until well cooked and golden. Leave to cool in the tin.

Now prepare the filling: beat the cheese and sugar together, incorporating the egg yolks one at a time. Add the brandy.

Crumble the macaroons finely. When the pie shell is cold, take it out of the pie dish and set it on a plate. Sprinkle the macaroons over the bottom and pour in the filling. Wash and dry the grapes and arrange them on top together with thin slices of apple.

Dissolve the sugar in 1 tablespoon of water over low heat. When it is a thick syrup, brush it, still hot, over the fruit. Decorate the centre of the cake with the mint leaves and keep it in a cool place or the least cold part of the refrigerator until required.

Serve the grape and apple cheesecake within a couple of hours.

CAPRICCIO SETTEMBRINO

September Fruit Salad

2 apples
juice of 1 lemon
50 g/2 oz/¼ cup sugar
1 peach

350 g/12 oz red plums
250 g/8 oz green grapes
3 tbspoons Cointreau

SERVES 4
PREP: 30 MINS + 1 HR CHILLING

Peel and core the apples, cut into quarters and then dice. As they are ready, put them into a bowl containing the strained lemon juice. Add the sugar, then mix carefully with a wooden spoon.

Remove the stalks from the peach and the plums and wipe with a damp cloth. Cut in half and remove the stones, then dice and add to the apples in the bowl. Wipe the grapes with a damp cloth and remove stalks and pips if necessary. Cut the larger grapes in half. Add to the rest of the fruit. Mix well and pour over the Cointreau.

Cover with cling film and refrigerate for at least 1 hour. Mix carefully before serving.

Torta di Ricotta alla Panna

Ricotta Pie with Sultanas

350 g/12 oz frozen short
   crust pastry, thawed
a little flour
a little butter
50 g/2 oz/1½ cup sultanas
100 g/4 oz candied peel

350 g/12 oz full-cream
   ricotta cheese
3 eggs
100 g/4 oz/1½ cup sugar
grated rind of 1 lemon
a little icing sugar

SERVES 8
PREP/COOKING: 1 HR + THAWING

Roll out the pastry on a lightly floured board and use it to line a buttered, floured 23 cm/9 inch pie dish. Cut off the excess dough and shape into a ring with which to thicken the sides of the pie; then prick the base with a fork.

Preheat the oven to 180°C/350°F/gas 4. Wash and dry the sultanas; cut the candied peel into small cubes. Sieve the ricotta into a bowl and mix in, one at a time, the yolks of the three eggs, then the sugar, the grated rind of the lemon, the diced candied peel and the sultanas, stirring vigorously. Beat the egg whites with a pinch of salt until they are quite stiff and fold them into the mixture.

Pour the mixture into the pastry shell and tap the dish to remove air bubbles in the mixture. Bake for about 45 minutes. Finally, turn out and leave it to cool. Before serving, sprinkle with icing sugar.

Torta Meringata

Meringue Gateau

FOR THE MERINGUE
a little oil
3 egg whites
250 g/8 oz/2 cups
  icing sugar
a little vanilla sugar

FOR THE ÉCLAIRS
butter
50 g/2 oz/1/2 cup flour
1 egg

FOR THE CUSTARD
3 eggs
100 g/4 oz/1/2 cup sugar

a little vanilla sugar
50 g/2 oz/1/2 cup flour
600 ml/1 pint/2 1/2 cups
  milk
1 tbspoon cocoa powder
1 tbspoon Grand Marnier
1 tbspoon Maraschino
  liqueur
100 ml/4 fl oz/1/2 cup
  whipping cream

SERVES 10
PREP/COOKING: 4 HRS

To prepare the meringue: lightly grease a 28 cm/1 inch circle of greaseproof paper with a little oil and place it on a small baking tray. Preheat the oven to 130°C/225°F/gas 1. Whisk the egg whites with a pinch of salt and sieve in 200 g/7 oz of icing sugar and the vanilla sugar, a little at a time, beating briskly until the mixture is well risen and firm. Using a piping bag with a round nozzle, cover the circle of greaseproof paper by piping two overlapping spirals. Sprinkle the remaining icing sugar on top and bake for a couple of hours; then turn off the oven and leave an hour before taking it out to cool.

To prepare the éclairs: preheat the oven to 190°C/375°F/gas 5 and butter and flour a small baking tray. Bring 4 tablespoons of water to the boil in a saucepan with 25 g/1 oz/2 tbspoons of diced butter and a pinch of salt.

As soon as the butter is completely melted, remove from the heat and sieve in the flour, beating briskly with a wooden spoon. Return the pan to the heat and continue to cook, stirring continuously, until the mixture begins to sizzle and come away from the sides of the pan. Turn it on to a plate and spread it out to cool.

Return it to the pan and beat in the egg, making sure the mixture is completely smooth. Using a piping bag with a round nozzle, pipe at least 30 finger shapes on the prepared baking tray, spaced apart to allow them to spread. Bake for 15 minutes then turn them out to cool on a wire rack.

To prepare the custard: beat the eggs, the sugar, vanilla sugar, flour and a pinch of salt together in a saucepan. When smooth, gradually add the milk. Bring to the boil, stirring all the time. Remove from the heat and divide into two, adding the cocoa powder and Grand Marnier to one half and the Maraschino to the other. Let them cool, stirring frequently, then put them into two separate piping bags with round nozzles.

To assemble the gateau: whip the cream and pipe it into the eclairs, then sprinkle them with a little icing sugar. Just before serving, set the meringue base on a large plate, make a ring round the edge with the yellow custard and set the eclairs on it. Cover the rest of the meringue with alternate stripes of the two custards and serve.

Mele golose

Stuffed Baked Apples

25 g/1 oz almonds, blanched
25 g/1 oz hazelnuts, blanched
25 g/1 oz peanuts, blanched
25 g/1 oz walnuts, blanched
25 g/1 oz plain chocolate, broken into pieces
10 apples, equal in size and not too ripe
butter
1 small cinnamon stick
3 cloves
spiral of lemon rind, 7.5 cm/3 in long

150 ml/5 fl oz/$^2/_3$ cup sweet white wine
150 g/5 oz/$^3/_4$ cup caster sugar
4 egg yolks
25 g/1 oz/4 tbspoons cornflour
a little vanilla sugar
600 ml/1 pint/$2^1/_2$ cups milk
4 tbspoons Calvados or brandy
25 g/1 oz pistachio nuts
150 ml/5 fl oz/$^2/_3$ whipping cream

SERVES 10
PREP/COOKING: $1^1/_2$ HRS + CHILLING

Preheat the oven to 190°C/375°F/gas 5. Put the almonds, hazelnuts, peanuts, walnuts, and chocolate into a liquidiser and process at maximum speed for a few seconds until the ingredients are all ground to a paste. Put the mixture in a bowl.

Peel the apples and, using an apple corer, cut into the base, stopping when you reach the stalk: you should hollow out the core just up to the stalk end, leaving it closed at the top. Remove the apple flesh from the cores, chop it and add to the liquidised nuts in the bowl, and mix together well.

Stuff each apple with the mixture, pressing it in with a teaspoon. Butter an ovenproof dish which is just the right size to hold the apples in one layer and arrange them in it. Break up the cinnamon stick and put this in the dish, along with the cloves and the lemon rind. Pour in the wine and sprinkle over 50 g/2 oz/¼ cup of sugar. Bake in the oven for about 45 minutes, basting from time to time with the juices.

Remove the cooked apples from the oven and set them aside while you prepare the custard. Beat the egg yolks in a saucepan with the remaining sugar, cornflour, vanilla sugar and a pinch of salt. Then pour in the milk in a slow trickle, mixing constantly with a small whisk. Bring to the boil, remove from the heat and add the Calvados. Arrange the cooked apples on a serving dish and pour the custard over them at once.

Blanch the pistachio nuts in boiling salted water, chop them and sprinkle them over the custard-covered apples. Whip the cream until it is stiff and put in a piping bag. Decorate the apples with swirls around the outside and one in the centre. Keep in a very cool place or in the least cold part of the refrigerator until you are ready to serve.

CHARLOTTE DI PANETTONE
Panettone Charlotte

> about 450 g/1 lb apples
> about 650 g/1 ½ lb pears
> 100 g/4 oz butter
> 100 g/4 oz/½ cup sugar
> 150 ml/5 fl oz/⅔ cup
>   dry white wine
>
> 350 g/12 oz panettone
>   which has become a little
>   hard
> 2 eggs
> 150 ml/5 fl oz/⅔ cup milk
> 100 ml/4 fl oz/½ cup double
>   cream

SERVES 8
PREP/COOKING: 2½ HRS+COOLING AND CHILLING

Preheat the oven to 180°C/350°F/gas 4. Peel, core and quarter the apples and pears. Heat two frying pans with half the butter in each. When the butter is hot, put the apples in one frying pan and the pears in the other. Sprinkle each with 1 tablespoon of sugar and pour half the wine into each. Cook over low heat until the fruit is cooked but still firm.

Meanwhile liberally butter a 1.5 litre/3 pint/1½ quart pudding basin, then cut two foil strips, about 5 cm/2 inches wide and long enough to place crossways inside the basin with about 2 cm/¾ inch at the ends to hang over the rim. Butter these too.

Cut the panettone into thin slices. Place a layer of panettone on the bottom of the basin and press to make stick. Then place half the apples on top. Cover with another layer of panettone and then a layer of pears. Continue alternating the panettone, apples and pears in this way, finishing with a layer of panettone. Press down lightly so there are no spaces left.

Beat the eggs with the remaining sugar and dilute with the milk and cream. Pour the mixture over the panettone and prick with a skewer to help the liquid penetrate. Leave the charlotte to rest for about 15 minutes, then bake for about 1½ hours. Remove from oven and leave to cool.

Turn it out on to a serving dish with the help of the strips of foil (which should then be discarded). Refrigerate for a couple of hours before serving.

Panettone farcito al mandarino

Panettone filled with Mandarin Orange Custard

about 2 tbspoons gelatine
4 eggs, separated
100 g/4 oz/½ cup sugar
1 mandarin orange
50 g/2 oz/½ cup flour
300 ml/½ pint/1 ¼ cups milk
100 ml/4 fl oz/½ cup mandarin orange juice
1 panettone
4 tablespoons Cointreau liqueur
400 ml/¾ pint/1 ¾ cups whipping cream

SERVES 10–12
PREP/COOKING: 1 HR + 6–8 HRS CHILLING

Dissolve the gelatine in cold water. Whisk together the egg yolks and the sugar in a saucepan until pale and frothy. Grate the mandarin orange rind and add this, then sift in the flour. Mix again, then dilute with the milk and mandarin juice, adding them in a trickle. Bring slowly to the boil, stirring constantly with a wooden spoon. Remove from the heat and dissolve the gelatine in the mixture. Leave to cool, stirring gently from time to time in order to prevent a skin forming.

Meanwhile, turn the panettone upside down and, using a sharp-pointed knife, cut out a circle from the base, about 2 cm/¾ inch from the edge. Set the circle aside. Hollow out the inside of the panettone, always keeping about 2 cm/¾ inch from the edge. Make a large cavity and pour in the Cointreau. Whip the cream and fold it into the cold mandarin-flavoured custard. Use an up-and-down movement, not a circular one, to prevent the cream from going flat. Pour the mixture into the panettone and replace the circle in the base to restore its original form. Place it upside-down in a bowl which is just the right size to hold the panettone and cover with cling film.

Refrigerate for 6-8 hours or, better still, overnight. Turn out on to a serving dish and serve. Cut with a sharp, serrated knife to avoid crumbling it.